Jambula Tree

Jambula Tree

A selection of works
from the Caine Prize
for African Writing

First published in 2008 by
New Internationalist™ Publications Ltd
Oxford OX4 1BW, UK
www.newint.org
New Internationalist is a registered trade mark.

First published in 2008 in southern Africa by
Jacana Media (Pty) Ltd
10 Orange Street
Sunnyside
Auckland Park 2092
South Africa
+2711 628 3200
www.jacana.co.za

Cover illustration: Grizelda Holderness.

Printed on recycled paper by T J International Limited, Cornwall, UK, who hold environmental accreditation ISO 14001.

British Library Cataloguing-in-Publication Data.
A catalogue record for this book is available from the British Library.

Library of Congress Cataloguing-in-Publication Data.
A catalogue for this book is available from the Library of Congress.

New Internationalist ISBN: 978-1-904456-73-5
Jacana Media ISBN: 978-1-77009-574-8

Contents

Introduction

This year for the first time our annual Caine Prize anthology contains not only the stories shortlisted for the previous year's Prize, and the stories written at this year's workshop, but also the stories shortlisted for this year's Prize.

This year's shortlist includes *Mallam Sile*, by the Ghanaian writer, Mohammed Naseehu Ali, from his collection *The Prophet of Zongo Street*, published by Amistad, an imprint of Harper Collins, New York, 2005; and *Cemetery of Life*, by Uzor Maxim Uzoatu (Nigeria) published in Wasafiri No 52, Autumn 2007; as well as three stories published in *African Pens* by Spearhead, an imprint of New Africa Books, Cape Town, 2007: *For Honour* by Stanley Onjezani Kenani, of Malawi; *Poison* by Henrietta Rose-Innes (South Africa); and *The Day of the Surgical Colloquium* by Gill Schierhout, also from South Africa.

Ugandan writer Monica Arac de Nyeko's ground-breaking story *Jambula Tree* won the 2007 Prize from a strong shortlist, including Uwem Akpan's heart-rending *My Parents' Bedroom*, which appeared in the *New Yorker* in June 2006, *Jimmy Carter's Eyes* by E C Osondu, also from Nigeria, which appeared in AGNI Fiction Online in 2006, *Bad Places* by Henrietta Rose-Innes from the South African *New Contrast* magazine and Nigerian Ada Udechukwu's *Night Bus*, published in the *Atlantic Monthly*, August 2006.

Monica Arac was the first Caine Prize winner to benefit from the new arrangement generously made by Georgetown University whereby Caine Prize winners are invited to spend a month's residence there as guests of the Department of English Literature.

Monica Arac, Henrietta Rose-Innes and Ada Udechukwu were able to attend the 2008 workshop, which had to be moved from Kenya, because of the uncertain situation there, to Monkey Valley, at Noordhoek, near Cape Town, which had been the venue for our first two workshops, in 2003 and 2004. The 2008 workshop's twelve participants came from seven different countries, Botswana, Kenya, Nigeria, Sierra Leone, Uganda, Zambia and South Africa. This was the widest spread of any single workshop so far, and the total number of African countries represented at all our workshops is now fourteen.

The 2008 workshop was made possible thanks to an extremely generous donation from Miles Morland. As in the past, Kenya Airways provided flight tickets for four participants. We are very grateful to them, and to the Prize's principal funders, the Ernest Oppenheimer Memorial Trust, for their continuing support.

Next year will see the tenth anniversary of the Caine Prize, and we plan to mark the occasion with a special anthology of all the ten winning stories to date, alongside stories by the three African winners of the Booker Prize (out of which the Caine Prize was born), Nadine Gordimer, Ben Okri and J M Coetzee.

Nick Elam
Administrator of the Caine Prize

Caine Prize Stories 2007:
Winner and Shortlist

Jambula Tree
(Winner)

Monica Arac de Nyeko

I HEARD OF YOUR return home from Mama Atim our next door neighbour. You remember her, don't you? We used to talk about her on our way to school, hand in hand, jumping, skipping, or playing run-and-catch-me. That woman's mouth worked at words like ants on a cob of maize. Ai! Everyone knows her quack-quack-quack-mouth. But people are still left wordless by just how much she can shoot at and wreck things with her machine-gun mouth. We nicknamed her Lecturer. The woman speaks with the certainty of a lecturer at her podium claiming an uncontested mastery of her subject. I bet you are wondering how she got to know of your return. I could attempt a few guesses. Either way, it would not matter. I would be breaking a promise. I hate that. We made that promise never to mind her or be moved by her. We said that after that night. The one night no one could make us forget. You left without saying goodbye after that. You had to, I reasoned. Perhaps it was good for both of us. Maybe things could die down that way. Things never did die down. Our names became forever associated with the forbidden. Shame.

Anyango – Sanyu.
My mother has gotten over that night. It took a while, but she did. Maybe it is time for your mother to do the same. She should start to hold her head high and scatter dust at the women who laugh after her when she passes by their houses. Nakawa Housing Estates has never changed. Mr Wangolo our SST teacher once said those houses were just planned slums with people with broken dreams and unplanned families for neighbours. Nakawa is still over one thousand families on an acre of land they call an estate. Most of the women don't work. Like Mama Atim they sit and talk, talk, talk and wait for their husbands to bring home a kilo of offal. Those are the kind of women we did not want to become. They bleached their

9

skins with Mekako skin lightening soap till they became tender and pale like a sun-scorched baby. They took over their children's *dool* and *kwepena* catfights till the local councillor had to be called for arbitration. Then they did not talk to each for a year. Nakawa's women laugh at each other for wearing the cheapest sandals on sale by the hawkers. Sanyu, those women know every love charm by heart and every juju man's shrine because they need them to conjure up their husbands' love and penises from drinking places with smoking pipes filled with dried hen's throat artery. These women know that an even number is a bad sign as they watch the cowry shells and coffee beans fall onto cowhide when consulting the spirits about their husbands' fidelity. That's what we fought against when we walked to school each day. Me and you hand in hand, towards school, running away from Nakawa Housing Estates' drifting tide which threatened to engulf us and turn us into noisy, gossiping and frightening housewives.

You said it yourself, we could be anything. Anything coming from your mouth was seasoned and alive. You said it to me, as we sat on a mango tree branch. We were not allowed to climb trees, but we did, and there, inside the green branches, you said – we can be anything. You asked us to pause for a moment to make a wish. I was a nurse in a white dress. I did not frighten children with big injections. You wished for nothing. You just made a wish that you would not become what your father wanted you to be – an engineer, making building plans, for his mansion, for his office, for his railway village. The one he dreamt about when he went to bed at night.

Sanyu, after all these years, I still imagine shame trailing after me tagged onto the hem of my skirt. Other times, I see it, floating into your dreams across the desert and water to remind you, of what lines we crossed. The things we should not have done when the brightness of Mama Atim's torch shone upon us – naked. How did she know exactly when to flash the light? Perhaps asking that question is a futile quest for answers. I won't get any! Perhaps it is as simple as accepting that the woman knows everything. I swear if you slept with a crocodile under the ocean, she would know. She is the only one who knows first-hand whose husband is sleeping with whose daughter at the estates inside those one-bedroomed houses. She knows whose son was caught inside the fences at Lugogo Show Grounds; the fancy trade fair centre just across Jinja Road, the main road which meanders its way underneath the estates. Mama Atim knows who is soon dying from gonorrhoea, who got it from someone, who got it from so-and-so who in turn got it from the soldiers who used to guard Lugogo Show Grounds, two years ago. You remember those soldiers, don't you? The way they sat in the sun with their green uniforms and guns hanging carelessly at their shoulders. With them the AK47 looked almost harmless – an object that was meant to be held close to the body – black ornament. They whistled after young girls in tight mini skirts that held onto their bums. At night, they drank Nile Lager, tonto, Mobuku and sung *harambe*, *soukous* or *chaka-chaka* songs.

Eh moto nawaka mama
Eh moto nawaka
I newaka tororo
Nawaka moto
Nawaka moto
Nawaka moto

Eh fire, burns mama
Eh fire, burns
It is burning in Tororo
It is burning
It is burning
It is burning

Mama Atim never did pass anywhere near where they had camped in their green tents. She twisted her mouth when she talked about them. What were soldiers doing guarding Lugogo? She asked. Was it a frontline? Mama Atim was terrified of soldiers. We never did find out why they instilled such fear in her. Either way it did not matter. Her fear became a secret weapon we used as we imagined ourselves being like goddesses dictating her fate. In our goddess-hands, we turned her into an effigy and had soldiers pelt her with stones. We imagined that pelting stones from a soldier was just enough to scare her into susuing in her XXL mothers' union panties. The ones she got a tailor to hem for her, from left-over materials from her children's nappies. How we wished those materials were green, so that she would see soldiers and stones in between her thighs every time she wore her green soldier colour, stone pelting colour and AK-47 colour. We got used to the sight of green soldiers perched in our football fields. This was the new order. Soldiers doing policemen's work! No questions, Uganda *yetu*, *hakuna matata*. How strange it was, freedom in forbidden colours. Deep green – the colour of the morning when the dew dries on leaves to announce the arrival of shame and dirt. And everything suddenly seems so uncovered, so exposed, so naked.

Anyanyo – Sanyu.
Mama Atim tells me you have chosen to come back home, to Nakawa Housing Estates. She says you refuse to live in those areas on the bigger hills and terraced

roads in Kololo. You are coming to us and to Nakawa Housing Estates, and to our many houses lined one after another on a small hill overlooking the market and Jinja Road, the football field and Lugogo Show Grounds. Sanyu, you have chosen to come here to children running on the red earth, in the morning shouting and yelling as they play *kwepena* and *dool* – familiar and stocked with memory and history. You return to dirt roads filled with thick brown mud on a rainy day, pools of water in every pothole and the sweet fresh smell of rain on hard soil. Sanyu, you have come back to find Mama Atim.

Mama Atim still waits for her husband to bring the food she is to cook each night. We used to say, after having nine sons and one daughter she should try to take care of them. Why doesn't she try to find a job in the industrial area like many other women around the housing estates? Throw her hips and two large buttocks around and play at entrepreneurship. Why doesn't she borrow a little *entandikwa* from the micro-finance unions so she can buy at least a bale of second-hand clothes at Owino market where she can retail them at Nakawa market? Second-hand clothes are in vogue, for sure. The Tommy Hilfiger and Versace labels are the in 'thing' for the young boys and girls who like to hang around the estates at night. Second-hand clothes never stay on the clothes hangers too long, like water during a drought, they sell quickly.

Mummy used to say those second-hand clothes were stripped off corpses in London. That is why they had slogans written on them such as – 'You went to London and all you brought me was this lousy T-shirt!' When Mummy talked of London, we listened with our mouths open. She had travelled there not once, not twice, but three times to visit her sister. Each time she came back with her suitcase filled up with stories. When her sister died, Mummy's trips stopped like that bright sparkle in her eye and the Queen Elizabeth stories, which she lost the urge to retell again and again. By that time we were grown. You were long gone to a different place, a different time and to a new memory. By then, we had grown into two big girls with four large breasts and buttocks like pumpkins and we knew that the stories were not true. Mummy had been to Tanzania – just a boat trip away on Lake Victoria, not London. No Queen Elizabeth.

Mama Atim says you are tired of London. You cannot bear it anymore. London is cold. London is a monster which gives no jobs. London is no cosy exile for the banished. London is no refuge for the immoral. Mama Atim says this word immoral to me – slowly and emphatically in *Japadhola*, so it can sink into my head. She wants me to hear the word in every breath, sniff it in every scent so it can haunt me like that day I first touched you. Like the day you first touched me. Mine was a cold unsure hand placed over your right breast. Yours was a cold scared hand, which held my waist and pressed it closer to you, under the jambula

12

tree in front of her house. Mama Atim says you are returning on the wings of a metallic bird – Kenya Airways. You will land in the hot Kampala heat which bites at the skin like it has a quarrel with everyone. Your mother does not talk to me or my mother. Mama Atim cooks her kilo of offal which she talks about for one week until the next time she cooks the next kilo again, bending over her charcoal stove, her large and long breasts watching over her saucepan like cow udders in space. When someone passes by, she stops cooking. You can hear her whisper. Perhaps that's the source of her gonorrhoea and Lugogo Show Ground stories. Mama Atim commands the world to her kitchen like her nine sons and one daughter. None of them have amounted to anything. The way their mother talks about me and you, Sanyu, after all these years, you would think her sons are priests. You would think at least one of them got a diploma and a low-paying job at a government ministry. You would think one of them could at least bring home a respectable wife. But *wapi!* Their wives are like used bicycles, ridden and exhausted by the entire estate manhood. They say the monkey which is behind should not laugh at the other monkey's tail. Mama Atim laughs with her teeth out and on display like cowries. She laughs loudest and forgets that she, of all people, has no right to urinate at or lecture the entire estate on the gospel according to St Morality.

Sometimes I wonder how much you have changed. How have you have grown? You were much taller than I. Your eyes looked stern; created an air about you – one that made kids stop for a while, unsure if they should trample all over you or take time to see for sure if your eyes would validate their preconceived fears. After they had finally studied, analyzed, added, multiplied and subtracted you, they knew you were for real. When the bigger kids tried to bully me, you stood tall and dared them to lay a finger on me. Just a finger, you said grinding your teeth like they were aluminium. They knew you did not mince words and that your anger was worse than a teacher's bamboo whipping. Your anger and rage coiled itself like a python around anyone who dared, anyone who challenged. And that's how you fought, with your teeth and hands but mostly with your feet. You coiled them around Juma when he knocked my tooth out for refusing to let him have his way on the water tap when he tried to cheat me out of my turn.

I wore my deep dark green uniform. At lunch times the lines could be long and boys always jumped the queue. Juma got me just as I put my water container to get some drinking water after lunch. He pushed me away. He was strong, Sanyu. One push like that and I fell down. When I got up, I left my tooth on the ground and rose up with only blood on the green; deep green, the colour of the morning when the dew dries off leaves.

You were standing at a distance. You were not watching. But it did not take you too long to know what was going on. You pushed your way through the crowd and before the teachers could hear the commotion going on, you had your legs coiled around Juma. I don't know how you do it, Sanyu. He could not move.

Juma, passed out? Hahahahahahaha!

I know a lot of pupils who would be pleased with that. Finally his big boy muscles had been crushed, to sand, to earth and to paste. The thought of that tasted sweet and salty like grasshoppers seasoned with onion and *kamulari* – red, red-hot pepper.

Mr Wangolo came with his hand-on-the-knee-limp and a big bamboo cane. It was yellow and must have been freshly broken off from the mother bamboos just outside the school that morning. He pulled and threatened you with indefinite expulsion before you let big sand-earth-paste Juma go. Both you and Juma got off with a two-week suspension. It was explicitly stated in the school rules that no one should fight. You had broken the rules. But that was the lesser of the rules that you broke. That I broke. That we broke.

Much later, at home, your mother was so angry. On our way home, you had said we should not say how the fight started. We should just say he hit you and you hit him back. Your house was two blocks from ours and the school was the nearest primary school to the estate. Most of the kids in the neighbourhood studied at Nakawa Katale Primary School all right, but everyone knew we were great friends. When your mother came and knocked upon our door, my mother had just put the onions on the charcoal stove to fry the goat's meat. Mummy bought goat's meat when she had just got her salary. The end of the month was always goat's meat and maybe some rice if she was in a good mood. Mummy's food smelt good. When she cooked, she joked about it. Mummy said if Papa had any sense in his head, he would not have left her with three kids to raise on her own to settle for that slut he called a wife. Mummy said Papa's new wife could not cook and that she was young enough to be his daughter. They had to do a caesarean on her when she gave birth to her first son. What did he expect? That those wasp hips could let a baby's head pass through them?

When she talked of Papa, she had that voice. Not a 'hate voice' and not a 'like voice', but the kind of voice she would use to open the door for him and tell him welcome back, even after all these years when he never sent us a single cent to buy food, books, soap or Christmas clothes. My Papa is not like your Papa, Sanyu. Your Papa works at the Ministry of Transport. He manages the Uganda railways, which is why he wants you to engineer a railway village for him. You say he has gotten so intoxicated with the railway that every time he talks of it, he rubs his palms together like he is thinking of the best ever memory in his life. Your father has a lot of money. Most of the teachers knew him at school. The kids had heard about him. Perhaps that is why your stern and blank expression was interpreted with slight overtones. They viewed you with a mixture of fear and awe; a rich man's child. Sometimes Mummy spoke about your family with slight ridicule. She said no one with money lived in Nakawa Housing Estates of all places. If your family had so much money, why did you not go to live in Muyenga, Kololo and Kansanga with your Mercedes-Benz lot? But you had new shoes every term. You had two new green uniforms every term. Sanyu, your name was never called out aloud by teachers, like the rest of us whose parents had not paid school tuition on time and we had to be sent back home with circulars.

Dear Parent,

This is to remind you that unless this term's school fees are paid out in full, your daughter/son……….. will not be allowed to sit for end of term exams….

Blah blah blah…

Mummy always got those letters and bit her lip as if she just heard that her house had burnt down. That's when she started staring at the ceiling with her eyes transfixed on one particular spot on the brown tiles. On such days, she went searching through her old maroon suitcase. It was from another time. It was the kind that was not sold in shops anymore. It had lost its glitter and I wished she never brought it out to dry in the sun. It would be less embarrassing if she brought out the other ones she used for her Tanzania trips. At least those ones looked like the ones your mother brought out to dry in the sun when she did her weekly house cleaning. That suitcase had all Mummy's letters – the ones Papa had written her when, as she said, her breasts were firm like green mangoes. Against a kerosene lamp, she read aloud the letters, reliving every moment, every word and every promise.

I will never leave you.
You are mine forever.
Stars are for the sky, you are for me.
Hello my sweet supernatural colours of the rainbow.
You are the only bee on my flower.
If loving you is a crime I am the biggest criminal in the world.

Mummy read them out aloud and laughed as she read the words on each piece of stained paper. She had stored them in their original Air Mail envelopes with the green and blue decorations. Sometimes papa had written to her in aerogramme. Those were opened with the keenest skill to keep them neat and almost new. He was a prolific letter-writer, my papa with a neat handwriting. I know this because often times I opened her case of memories. I never did get as far as opening any letter to read; it would have been trespassing. It did not feel right, even if Mummy had never scolded me for reading her 'To Josephine Athieno Best' letters.

I hated to see her like that. She was now a copy-typist at Ramja Securities. Her salary was not much, but she managed to survive on it, somehow, somehow. There were people who spoke of her beauty as if she did not deserve being husbandless. They said with some pity, 'Oh, and she has a long ringed neck, her eyes are large and sad. The woman has a voice, soft, kind and patient. How could the man leave her?' Mummy might have been sad sometimes, but she did not deserve any pity. She lived her life like her own finger nails and temperament: so calm, so sober and level-headed, except of course when it came to reading those Papa letters by the lantern lamp.

I told you about all this, Sanyu. How I wished she could be always happy, like your mother who went to the market and came back with two large boys carrying her load because she had shopped too much for your papa, for you, for your happy family. I did not tell you, but sometimes I stalked her as she made her way to buy things from the noisy market. She never saw me. There were simply too many people. From a distance, she pointed at things, fruit ripe like they had been waiting to be bought by her all along. Your mother went from market stall to market stall, flashing her white Colgate smile and her dimpled cheeks. Sometimes I wished I were like you; with a mother who bought happiness from the market. She looked like someone who summoned joy at her feet and it fell in salutation, humbly, like the *kabaka* subjects who lay prostrate before him. When I went to your house to do homework, I watched her cook. Her hand stirred groundnut soup. I must admit, Mummy told me never to eat at other people's homes. It would make us appear poor and me rather greedy. I often left your home when the food was just about ready. Your mother said, in her summon-joy-voice: 'Supper is ready. Please eat.' But I, feigning time consciousness always said, 'I have to run home, Mummy will be worried.' At such times, your father sat in the bedroom. He never came out from that room. Every day, like a ritual, he came home straight from work.

'A perfect husband,' Mummy said more times than I can count.

'I hate him,' you said more times than I could count. It was not what he didn't do, you said. It was what he did. Those touches, his touches you said. And you could not tell your mother. She would not believe you. She never did. Like that time she came home after the day you taught Juma a good lesson for messing around with me. She spoke to my mother in her voice which sounded like breaking china.

'She is not telling me everything. How can the boy beat her over nothing? At the school tap? These two must know. That is why I am here. To get to the bottom of this! Right now!'

She said this again and again, and Mummy called me from the kitchen where I had escaped just when I saw her knock on our back door holding your hands in hers and pulling you behind her like a goat!

'Anyango, Anyangooooo,' Mummy called out.

I came out, avoiding your eyes. Standing with her hands held in front of me with the same kind of embarrassment and fear that overwhelmed me each time I heard my name called by a teacher for school fees default.

They talked for hours. I was terrified, which was why I almost told the truth. You started very quickly and repeated the story we had on our way home. Your mother asked, 'What was Anyango going to say again?' I repeated what you had just said, and your mother said, 'I know they are both lying. I will get to the bottom of this at school in two weeks' time when I report back with her.' And she did. You got a flogging that left you unable to sit down on your bum for a week.

When you left our house that day, they talked in low voices. They had sent us outside to be bitten by mosquitoes for a bit. When they called us back in, they said nothing. Your mother held your hand again, goat style. If Juma had seen you being pulled like that, he would have had a laugh one hundred times the size of your trodden-upon confidence. You never looked back. You avoided looking at me for a while after that.

Mummy had a list of 'don'ts' after that for me too. They were many.

Don't walk back home with Sanyu after school.
Don't pass by their home each morning to pick her up.
Don't sit next to her in class.
Don't borrow her text books. I will buy you your own.
Don't even talk to her.
Don't, don't, don't do anymore Sanyu.

It was like that, but not for long. After we started to talk again and look each other in the eyes, our parents seemed not to notice, which is why our secondary schools applications went largely unnoticed. If they complained that we had applied to the same schools and in the same order, we did not hear about them.

1 St Mary's College Namagunga
2 Nabisunsa Girls' School
3 City High School
4 Modern High School

You got admitted to your first choice. I got my third choice. It was during the holidays that we got a chance to see each other again. I told you about my school.

That I hated the orange skirts, white shirts, white socks and black boy's Bata shoes. They made us look like flowers on display. The boys wore white trousers, white shorts, white socks, and black shoes. At break time, we trooped like a bunch of moving orange and white flowers to the school canteens, to the drama room, and to the football field.

You said you loved your school. Sister Cephas, your Irish headmistress, wanted to turn you all into Black English girls. The girls there were the prettiest ever and were allowed to keep their hair long and held back in puffs, not one inch only like at my school.

We were seated under the jambula tree. It had grown so tall. The tree had been there for ages with its unreachable fruit. They said it was there even before the estate houses were constructed. In April the tree carried small purple jambula fruit which tasted both sweet and tang and turned our tongues purple. Every April morning when the fruit started to fall, the ground became a blanket of purple.

When you came back during that holiday, your cheeks were bulging like you had hidden oranges inside them. Your eyes had grown small and sat like two short slits on your face. And your breasts, the two things you had watched and persuaded to grow during all your years at Nakawa Katale Primary School, were like two large jambulas on your chest. And that feeling that I had, the one that you had, that we had – never said, never spoken – swelled up inside us like fresh mandazies. I listened to your voice rise and fall. I envied you. I hated you. I could not wait for the next holidays when I could see you again. When I could dare place my itchy hand onto your two jambulas.

That time would be a night, two holidays later. You were not shocked. Not repelled. It did not occur to either of us, to you or me, that these were boundaries we should not cross nor should think of crossing. Your jambulas and mine. Two plus two jambulas equals four jambulas – even numbers should stand for luck. Was this luck pulling us together? You pulled me to yourself and we rolled on the brown earth that stuck to our hair in all its redness and dustiness. There in front of Mama Atim's house. She shone a torch at us. She had been watching, steadily like a dog waiting for a bone it knew it would get; it was just a matter of time.

Sanyu, I went for confession the next day, right after Mass. I made the sign of the cross and smelt the fresh burning incense in St Jude's church. I had this sense of floating on air, confused, weak, and exhausted. I told the priest, 'Forgive me Father for I have sinned. It has been two months since my last confession.' And there in my head, two plus two jambulas equals four jambulas…

I was not sorry. But I was sorry when your father with all his money from the railways got you a passport and sent you on the wing of a bird; hello London, here comes Sanyu.

Mama Atim says your plane will land tomorrow. Sanyu, I don't know what you expect to find here, but you will find my Mummy; you'll find that every word she types on her typewriter draws and digs deeper the wrinkles on her face. You will find the Housing Estates. Nothing has changed. The women sit in front of their houses and wait for their husbands to bring them offal. Mama Atim's sons eat her food and bring girls to sleep in her bed. Your mother walks with a stooped back. She has lost the zeal she had for her happiness-buying shopping trips. Your papa returns home every day as soon as he is done with work. My Mummy says, 'That is a good husband.'

I come home every weekend to see Mummy. She has stopped looking inside her maroon case. But I do; I added the letter you wrote me from London. The only one I ever did get from you, five years after you left. You wrote:

A.

I miss you.

S.

Sanyu, I am a nurse at Mengo Hospital. I have a small room by the hospital, decorated with two chairs, a table from Katwe, a black and white television and two paintings of two big jambula trees which I got a downtown artist to do for me. These trees have purple leaves. I tell you, they smile.

I do mostly night shifts. I like them, I often see clearer at night. In the night you lift yourself up in my eyes each time, again and again. Sanyu, you rise like the sun and stand tall like the jambula tree in front of Mama Atim's house.

Monica Arac de Nyeko is a Ugandan writer of fiction. She studied at Makerere University and the University of Groningen.

My Parents' Bedroom

Uwem Akpan

I'M NINE YEARS AND seven months old. I'm at home playing peekaboo in my room with my little brother, Jean. It's Saturday evening and the sun has fallen behind the hills. There's silence outside our bungalow, but from time to time the evening wind carries a shout to us. Our parents have kept us indoors since yesterday.

Maman comes into the room and turns off the light before we see her. Jean cries in the darkness, but once she starts kissing him he begins to giggle. He reaches up to be held, but she's in a hurry.

'Don't turn on any lights tonight,' she whispers to me.

I nod. '*Yego*, Maman.'

'Come with your brother.' I carry Jean and follow her. 'And don't open the door for anybody. Your papa is not home, I'm not home, nobody is home. Do you hear me, Monique, huh?'

'*Yego*, Maman.'

'Swallow all your questions now, bright daughter. When your papa and uncle return, they'll explain things to you.'

Maman leads us through the corridor and into her room, where she lights a candle that she has taken from our family altar, in the parlor. She starts to undress, tossing her clothes on the floor. She tells us that she's going out for the night and that she's already late. She's panting, as if she'd been running; her body is shining with sweat. She slips into the beautiful black evening dress that Papa likes and combs out her soft hair. I help her with the zipper at the back of her dress. She paints her lips a deep red and presses them together. The sequins on her dress glitter in the candlelight as if her heart were on fire.

My mother is a very beautiful Tutsi woman. She has high cheekbones, a narrow nose, a sweet mouth, slim fingers, big eyes, and a lean frame. Her skin is so light that you can see the blue veins on the back of her hands, as you can on the hands of Le Père Mertens, our parish priest, who's from Belgium. I look like Maman, and

21

when I grow up I'll be as tall as she is. This is why Papa and all his Hutu people call me Shenge, which means 'my little one' in Kinyarwanda.

Papa looks like most Hutus, very black. He has a round face, a wide nose, and brown eyes. His lips are as full as a banana. He is a jolly, jolly man who can make you laugh till you cry. Jean looks like him.

'But, Maman, you told me that only bad women go out at night.'

'Monique, no questions tonight, I told you.'

She stops and stares at me. As I'm about to open my mouth, she shouts, 'Quiet! Go, sit with your brother!'

Maman never shouts at me. She's strange today. Tears shine in her eyes. I pick up a bottle of Amour Bruxelles, the perfume Papa gives her because he loves her. Everybody in the neighborhood knows her by its sweet smell. When I put the bottle in her hands, she shivers, as if her mind has just returned to her. Instead of spraying it on herself, she puts it on Jean. He's excited, sniffing his hands and clothes. I beg Maman to put some on me, but she refuses.

'When they ask you,' she says sternly, without looking at me, 'Say you're one of them, OK?'

'Who?'

'Anybody. You have to learn to take care of Jean, Monique. You just have to, huh?'

'I will, Maman.'

'Promise?'

'Promise.'

Maman heads for the parlor, and Jean trails after. He's whimpering to be held. I carry the candle. We sit down on our big sofa, and Maman blows the candle out. Our parlor is never totally dark, because of the crucifix in the corner, which glows yellow-green. All-translucent, as Papa likes to say. Jean toddles to the altar, as usual. He places his hands on the crucifix, as if playing with a toy. The glow enters into his fingers, making them green, and he turns to us and laughs. In quick strides, I bring him back. I don't want him to pull down the crucifix, which leans against the wall, or the vase of bougainvillea beside it. It's part of my duty to tend to the altar. I love the crucifix; all my relatives do. Except Tonton Nzeyimana – the Wizard.

The Wizard is Papa's father's brother. He is a pagan and he is very powerful. If he doesn't like you, unless you're a strong Catholic, he can put his spell on you, until you become useless. The color of his skin is milk with a little coffee. He never married because he says he hates his skin and doesn't want to pass it on. Sometimes he paints himself with charcoal until the rain comes to wash away his blackness. I don't know where he got his color from. My parents say it's a complicated story about intermarriage. He's so old that he walks with a stick. His lips are long and droopy, because he uses them to blow bad luck and disease into people. He likes to frighten children with his ugly face. Whenever I see the Wizard, I run away. Papa, his own nephew, doesn't want him in our house, but Maman tolerates the Wizard. 'No matter, he's our relative,' she says. Tonton André, Papa's only brother, hates him even more. They don't even greet each other on the road.

Though I'm a girl, Papa says that the crucifix will be mine when he dies, because I'm the firstborn of the family. I will carry it till I give it to my child. Some people laugh at Papa for saying that it'll come to me, a girl. Others shrug and agree with Papa, because he went to university and works in a government ministry. Sometimes when Tonton André and his wife, Tantine Annette, visit us, they praise Papa for this decision. Tantine Annette is pregnant, and I know that they would do the same if God gave them a girl first.

Without his ID, you'd never know that Tonton André is Papa's brother. He's a cross between Papa and Maman – as tall as Maman but not quite as dark as Papa. He's got a tiny beard.

Tantine Annette is Maman's best friend. Though she's Tutsi like Maman, she's as dark as Papa. Sometimes on the road, the police ask for her ID, to be sure of her roots. These days, my parents tease her that she'll give birth to six babies, because her pregnant stomach is very big. Each time she becomes pregnant, she miscarries, and everybody knows that it's the Wizard's spell. But the couple have been strong in their faith. Sometimes they kiss in public, like Belgians do on TV, and our people don't like this very much. But they don't care. Tonton André takes her to a good hospital in Kigali for checkups, and Papa and our other relatives contribute money to help them, because both of them are only poor primary-school teachers. The Wizard offered to give his money, too, but we don't allow him to. If he gave even one franc, his bad money would swallow all the good contributions, like the sickly, hungry cows in Pharaoh's dream.

Maman stands up suddenly. 'Monique, remember to lock the door behind me! Your papa will soon be back.' I hear her going into the kitchen. She opens the back door and stops for a moment. Then the door slams. She's gone.

I light the candle again and go into the kitchen and lock the door. We eat rice and fish and return to our room. I dress Jean in his flannel pajamas and sing him to sleep. I change into my nightie, and lie down beside him.

In a dream, I hear Tonton André's voice. He sounds as anxious as he did yesterday afternoon, when he came to call Papa away. 'Shenge, Shenge, you must open the door for me!' Tonton André shouts.

'Wait, I'm coming,' I try to tell him, but in my dream I have no voice, and my legs have melted like butter in the sun. There's a lot of commotion, and gunshots that sound like bombs.

'Come to the front door, quick!' he shouts again.

I wake up. Tonton André is actually yelling outside our house.

I go into the parlor and turn on the fluorescent lights. My eyes hurt. People are banging on our front door. I see the blades of machetes and axes stabbing through the door, making holes in the plywood. Two windows are smashed, and rifle butts and *udufuni* are poking in. I don't know what's going on. The attackers can't get in through the windows with their guns and small hoes, because they're covered with metal bars. Afraid, I squat on the floor, with my hands covering my head, till the people outside stop and pull back.

I hear Tonton André's voice again, but this time it's calm and deep, as usual, and everything is quiet outside.

'Poor, sweet thing, don't be afraid,' he says, now laughing confidently like Jean. 'They're gone. Your papa is here with me.'

I pick my way through the broken glass and open the door. But Tonton André comes in with a group. Men and women, all armed.

'Where's Maman?' he asks me.

'Maman went out.'

He looks like a madman. His hair is rough, as if he had not combed it for a year. His green shirt is unbuttoned and he's without shoes.

'*Yagiye hehe?*' someone from the mob asks, disappointed. 'Where's she gone?'

'She didn't say,' I answer.

'Have you seen your Papa this evening?' Tonton André asks.

'*Oya.*'

'No? I'll kill you,' he says, his face swollen with seriousness.

I scan the mob. 'You told me Papa was with you… Papa! Papa!'

'The coward has escaped,' someone in the crowd says.

'*Nta butungane burimo!*' others shout. 'Unfair!'

They look victorious, like football champions. I know some of them. Our church usher, Monsieur Paschal, is humming and chanting and wears a bandanna. Mademoiselle Angeline, my teacher's daughter, is dancing to the chants, as if to reggae beats. She gives a thumbs-up to Monsieur François, who is the preacher at the nearby Adventist church.

Some of them brandish their IDs, as if they were conducting a census. Others are now searching our home. Sniffing around like dogs, they've traced Maman's Amour Bruxelles to Jean and are bothering him so he begins to cry. I run to our room and carry him back to the parlor. I can hear them all over the place, overturning beds and breaking down closets.

Suddenly, I see the Wizard by the altar. He turns and winks at me. Then he swings his stick at the crucifix, once, twice, and Christ's body breaks from the cross, crashing to the floor. Limbless, it rolls to my feet. Only bits of its hands and legs are still hanging on the cross, hollow and jagged. The cross has fallen off the altar, too. The Wizard smiles at me, enjoying my frustration. When he's distracted for a moment, I grab Jesus' broken body and hide it under Jean's pajama top. I sit down on the sofa and put Jean on my lap. The Wizard now searches excitedly for the body of Jesus. He is like an overgrown kid looking for his toy.

He turns to me. 'Shenge, do you have it?'

I look away. 'No.'

'Look at me, girl.'

'I don't have it.'

I hold on tighter to Jean.

The Wizard switches off the lights. Jean bursts into laughter, because now his stomach glows like Jesus. The Wizard turns the lights on again and comes toward us, smiling a bad smile. Jean is not afraid of the old man. When the Wizard reaches for Jesus, Jean fights him off, bending almost double to protect his treasure. The Wizard is laughing, but Jean bites the man's fingers with his eight teeth. I wish he had iron teeth and could bite off the Wizard's whole hand, because it's not funny. But the old man teases us, dangling his tongue and making stupid faces. When he laughs, you can see his gums and all the pits left by his fallen teeth. Now, wheezing from too much laughter, he snatches Christ's body from Jean and puts it in his pagan pocket.

Tonton André is bitter and restless. Since I told him that my parents have gone out, he hasn't spoken to me. I'm angry at him, too, because he lied to get in and now the Wizard has destroyed my crucifix and stolen Christ's body.

When I hear noises in my parents' room, I run in there with Jean, because my parents never allow visitors in their bedroom. There are two men rummaging through their closet. One man is bald and wearing stained yellow trousers, the bottoms rolled up – no shirt, no shoes. He has a few strands of hair on his chest, and his belly is huge and firm. The other man is young, secondary school age. His hair and beard are very neat, as if he were coming from the barber. He's bug-eyed and tall and is wearing jean overalls, a T-shirt, and dirty blue tennis shoes.

The big-bellied man looks at the younger man mischievously and asks me to hug him. Before I can say anything, he wriggles out of his yellow trousers and reaches for me. But I avoid his hands and slip under the bed with Jean. He pulls me out by my ankles. Pressing me down on the floor, the naked man grabs my two wrists with his left hand. He pushes up my nightie with the right and tears my underpants. I shout at the top of my voice. I call out to Tonton André, who is pacing in the corridor. He doesn't come. I keep screaming. I'm twisting and holding my knees together. Then I snap at the naked man with my teeth. He hits my face, this way and that, until my saliva is salted with blood. I spit in his face. Twice. He bangs my head on the floor, pinning my neck down, punching my left thigh.

'*Oya!* No! Shenge is one of us!' the Wizard tells him, rushing into the room.

'Ah... leave this little thing... to me,' the naked man says slowly. His short pee is pouring on my thighs and my nightie, warm and thick like baby food. I can't breathe, because he has collapsed on me with his whole weight, like a dead man. When he finally gets up, hiding his nakedness with his trousers, the Wizard bends down, peering at me, and breathes a sigh of relief.

'Shenge, can you hear me?' the Wizard says.

'Ummh.'

'I say, you're all right!'

'All right.'

'Bad days, girl, bad days. Be strong.' He turns to my attacker and growls, 'You're lucky you didn't open her womb. I would've strangled you myself!'

'Jean,' I whisper. 'Where's my brother?'

The overalls man finds him under the bed, curled up like a python, and drags him out. Jean lays his big head on my chest. An ache beats in my head as if the man were still banging it on the floor. My eyes show me many men in yellow trousers and overalls, many Wizards. The floor is rising and falling. I try to keep my eyes open but can't. Jean keeps feeling my busted mouth.

Someone lifts me and Jean up and takes us back to the parlor. Tonton André is sitting between two men, who are consoling him. He's got his head in his hands, and the Wizard is standing behind him, patting his shoulder gently.

As soon as Tonton André sees us, he springs to his feet. But they pull him down and scold him and tell him to get ahold of himself. He's not listening, though.

'My bastard brother and his wife are not home?' he says very slowly, as if he were coming out of a deep sleep. 'He owes me this one. And I'm killing these children if I don't see him.'

'My nephew,' the Wizard says, thudding his stick once on the floor. 'Don't worry. He must pay, too. Nobody can escape our wrath this time. Nobody.'

'*Koko, ni impamo tuzabigira,*' people start murmuring in agreement.

I don't know what Papa could owe his younger brother. Papa is richer than he is. Whatever it is, I'm sure that he'll repay him tomorrow.

The crowd calms down. People stand in groups and carry out their conversations, like women at the market. I get the impression that there are more people outside. Only Monsieur François is impatient, telling the others to hurry up so that they can go elsewhere, that the government didn't buy them machetes and guns to be idle.

After a while, the Wizard leaves Tonton André and comes over to us. 'Young girl,' he says, 'you say you don't know where your parents are?'

'I don't know,' I say.

'When they return, tell them all the roads are blocked. No escape. And you, clever girl,' the old man says, tapping me on the chest, 'if you want to live, don't leave this house for anything. Ghosts are all over our land. Bad ghosts.' He whisks his cane and tosses his head as if he were commanding the ghosts into existence. And then he goes out, in the flow of the crowd.

I lock up as soon as everyone has left. The flowers are crushed, the altar cloth trampled upon. Pieces of glass are everywhere. The drawers from the writing desk are hanging out, and the bookshelf has fallen over. The TV is now facing the wall, and a cold wind ruffles the window blinds. I find the cross, and put it back on the altar.

I want to sleep, but fear follows me into my room. My fingers are shivering. My head feels heavy and swollen. There's a pebble in my left thigh where the naked man hit me. My mouth is still bleeding, staining the front of my nightie. I shouldn't have tricked the Wizard. What are the ghosts he summoned going to do to us? He has put his spell on Tonton André, too. Jean is covered in goose bumps. I'm too afraid to tidy up our room. We huddle in one corner, on the mattress, which has been tossed onto the floor. I start to pray.

I wake to the sound of my parents and other people arguing in the parlor. There's a lot of noise. It's not yet dawn, and my whole body is sore. One side of my upper lip is swollen as if I had a toffee between it and my gum. I don't see Jean.

I limp into the parlor but see only my parents and Jean. Maybe I was dreaming the other voices. My parents stop talking as soon as they see me. Maman is seated on the sofa like a statue of Marie Mère des Douleurs, looking down. Papa stands near the altar, holding Jean and scooping hot spoonfuls of oatmeal into his mouth. Jean's eyes are dull and watery, as if he hadn't slept for days. Shaking his head, he shrieks and pushes the food away. 'Eat up, kid, eat up,' Papa says impatiently. 'You'll need the energy.'

My family isn't preparing for Mass this Sunday morning. The parlor lights are off, the furniture still scattered from last night. The doors and windows are closed, as they have been since Friday, and the dinner table is now pushed up against the front door. Our home feels haunted, as if the ghosts from the Wizard's stick were still inside.

I hurry toward my father. 'Good morning, Papa!'

'Sh-h-h… yeah, good morning,' he whispers. He puts Jean down on the floor and squats and holds my two hands. 'No noise. Don't be afraid. I won't let anyone touch you again, OK?'

'*Yego*, Papa.'

I want to hug him, but he blocks me with his hands. 'Don't turn on any lights, and don't bother Maman now.'

'The Wizard said that ghosts are –'

'No ghosts here… Listen, no Mass today. Le Père Mertens went on home leave last week.' He's not looking at me but peering out through the window.

I hear a sneeze from the kitchen, stifled like a sick cat's. I search my parents' faces, but they're blank. A sudden fear enters my body. Maybe I'm still dreaming, maybe not. I push closer to Papa and ask him, 'Tonton André is now friends with the Wizard?'

'Don't mention André in my house anymore.'

'He brought a man to tear my underpants.'

'I say leave me alone!'

He goes to the window and holds on to the iron bars so that his hands are steady, but his body is trembling. His eyes are blinking fast and his face is tightened. When Papa gets quiet like this, he's ready to pounce on anyone. I go to the sofa and sit down silently. When I slide over to Maman, she pushes me away with one hand. I resist, bending like a tree in the wind, then returning to my position. Nothing interests Maman today, not even Jean, her favorite child. She doesn't say any sweet thing to him or even touch him today. She acts dumb, bewitched, like a goat that the neighborhood children have fed sorghum beer.

From the window, Papa turns and looks at me as if I'm no longer his sweet Shenge. When he sees Jean sleeping on the carpet by Maman's feet, he puts the blame on me: 'Stubborn girl, have you no eyes to see that your brother needs a bed? Put him in the bedroom and stop disturbing my life.'

But I circle the parlor, like an ant whose hole has been blocked. I am scared to go to my room, because of the ghosts. Papa grabs my wrist and drags me into my room. He turns on the light. Our toys litter the floor. He puts the mattress back on the bed and rearranges the room. But it's still messy. Papa is cursing the toys, destroying the special treats that he and Maman bought for us when they visited America. He kicks the teddy bear against the wall and stamps on Tweety and Mickey Mouse. Papa's hands are very dirty, the gutters around his nails swollen with black mud. When he sees me looking at him, he says, 'What are you staring at?'

'I'm sorry, Papa.'

'I told you not to turn on the lights. Who turned on this light?' I turn off the light. 'Go get your stupid brother and put him to bed. You must love him.'

'*Yego*, Papa.'

I go to the parlor and hope that Maman will intervene. She doesn't, so I bring Jean back to the bed.

'And stay here, girl,' Papa says. He goes back to the parlor, slamming the door.

When I was younger, I used to ride into the hills on Papa's wide shoulders. We were always visiting Maman's family's place, in the next valley. Papa told me that when he first met Maman she was my age, and they played together in these hills. They went to the same primary school and university.

In the hills, you can see the clouds moving away, like incense smoke in a church. Our country is full of winds, and in the hills they blow at your eyes until tears stain your cheeks. They suck through the valleys, like hungry cows. The birds rise and tumble and swing, their voices mixing with the winds. When Papa laughs his jolly-jolly laugh, the winds carry his voice, too. From the top of the hills, you can see that the earth is red. You can see stands of banana and plantain trees, their middle leaves rolled up, like yellow-green swords slicing the wind. You can see fields of coffee, with farmers wading through them, piggybacking their baskets. When you climb the hills in the dry season, your feet are powdered with dust. When it rains, the red earth runs like blood under a green skin. There are tendrils everywhere, and insects come out of the soil.

I walk tall and proud in our neighborhood. The bullies all know that Papa would attack anyone who messes with me. Even when he is drunk on banana beer, my tears sober him. Sometimes he even goes after Maman, for making his girl sad. He scolds his relatives when they say that it's risky that I look so much like Maman. Papa likes to tell me that he wanted to go against his people and wed Maman in our church when I was born, even though she hadn't given him a son yet. Maman wouldn't hear of it, he says. She wanted to give him a male child before they had the sacrament of matrimony. Papa tells me everything.

Maman's love for me is different. Sometimes she looks at me and becomes sad. She never likes going out in public with me, as she does with Jean. She is always tense, as if a lion will leap out and eat us.

'Maman, I'll always be beautiful!' I told her one day, as Papa was driving us back from a lakeside picnic. Maman was in the passenger's seat, Jean on her lap. I was behind.

'You could be beautiful in other ways, Monique,' she said.

'Leave the poor girl alone,' Papa told her.

'I don't understand,' I said.

'You will when you grow up,' she said.

This time when I wake up, rays of yellow morning are leaking in through the holes in the door and the torn blinds. They riddle the gloom, and I can see dust particles dancing within them. Our neighborhood is quiet. When I go into the parlor, Papa is moving from window to window to ensure that the blinds leave no space for outsiders to peep in. Maman is standing at the table, straining her eyes as she examines two framed photographs.

One is from my parents' traditional wedding. It's ten years old. I was in Maman's belly then. All the women are elegantly dressed, the *imyitero* draping over them like Le Père Mertens's short vestment. Married women who have given birth to sons wear *urugoli* crowns. Maman got hers only last year, when Jean was born. There are some cows tethered in the background. They were part of the dowry Papa offered for Maman. But no matter what I try to focus on, my eyes go to Tonton André's smiley face. I cover it with my hand, but Maman pushes my fingers off. I look at the other picture instead, which was taken last year, after my parents' church wedding. Papa, Maman, and I are in front. I'm the flower girl, my hands gloved and a flower basket hanging down from my neck with white ribbons. Maman holds baby Jean close to her heart, like a wedding bouquet.

'Maman, Jean is lonely in the bedroom,' I say.

'I hope he sleeps the whole day,' she says, without looking at me.

'Won't ghosts steal him?'

'He'll get used to them. Go get yourself some food, Monique.'

'*Oya*, Maman, I don't want to eat.'

'Then go and shower.'

'Alone? I don't want to shower.'

She touches my nightie. 'You need to shower.'

'Maman, when wizards pee...'

'Don't tell me now.' She looks at Papa. 'She needs a shower.'

Hearing this, I raise my nightie to show Maman my swollen thigh, but she slaps it down, saying, 'You'll get a new pair of underpants. Your face will be beautiful again.'

I return my attention to the pictures. I scratch at Tonton André's face with my nails to erase him from our family. But the glass saves him.

Maman isn't looking at the photos anymore; her eyes are closed, as if in prayer. I pick up a brass letter opener and begin to scratch the glass over my Tonton's face. The sound distracts Papa from the window and he gives me a bad look. I stop.

'Why did you come down – come *back*?' he says to Maman, searching my face to see whether I've understood the question.

I haven't.

He turns back to Maman. 'Woman, why? Return to where you were last night. Please. Leave.'

'Whatever you do,' she says, 'do not let my daughter know.'

'She should!' he says, then recoils from the force in his own voice.

My parents are hiding something from me. Maman is very stubborn about it. Their sentences enter my ears as randomly as a toss of the dice on our Ludo board. Papa looks guilty, like a child who can't keep a secret.

'I can't bear it,' he says. 'I can't.'

'If Monique knew where I was last night,' Maman argues, 'your family would've forced it out of her and shed blood.'

As they talk, invisible people are breathing everywhere – at least twenty ghosts are in the air around us. When Maman speaks, the ghosts let out groans of agreement, but my parents don't seem to hear them.

Papa shakes his head. 'I mean, you should never have come back. I could have convinced them…'

'We needed to be with the children.'

I don't understand why Maman is saying she wants to be with me when she won't even look my way. I see dirty water dripping down the white wall beside me. It is coming from the ceiling. At first, it comes down in two thin lines. Then the lines widen and swell into one. Then two more lines come down, in spurts, like little spiders gliding down on threads from a branch of the mango tree in our yard. I touch the liquid with the tip of my finger. Blood.

'Ghost! Ghost!' I scream, diving toward Papa.

'It's not blood,' he says.

'You are lying! It's blood! It's blood!'

Papa tries to get between me and the wall, but I get in front of him and hug him. I cling to his body, climbing upward until my hands are around his neck and my legs wrapped around his waist. He tries to muffle my shouts with his hands, but I wriggle and twist till he bows under my weight, and we nearly topple over. He staggers and regains his balance, then he releases his breath, and his stiff body softens. He puts his arms around me and carries me to the sofa. He holds my face to his heart, hiding me from the blood. I stop shouting. Maman is grinding her teeth, and there is a stubborn look on her face –maybe the Wizard has fixed her, too.

My body continues to tremble, no matter how hard Papa holds me. I tell him about last night, and he consoles me, telling me not to cry. Tears fill his eyes, too, then pour down onto me, warm and fast. I've never seen him cry before. Now he can't stop, like me. He's telling me he will always love me, putting my head on his shoulder, stroking my braided hair. Once again, I'm Papa's Shenge.

'They're good ghosts,' he sobs, kissing my forehead. 'Good people who died.'

'Papa, I tricked the Wizard.'

'Don't think of last night.'

He gives me a piggyback ride to the bathroom. He takes off my nightie and tosses it into the dustbin, then turns on the taps to run the bath. In the walls, the pipes whistle and sigh, but today it feels as if I were hearing the blood flowing through the strange veins of ghosts. The heat of the bath sends mist through the room, and Papa moves within it, still sobbing and wiping his tears with the sleeve of his shirt.

When he cleans my face, his hands smell like raw eggs. I reach out and switch on the light; his dirty hands seem to shock him. He washes them in the sink. We're sweating in the heat and the steam. But when I try to pull back the window blinds, he stops me. In the mirror, my mouth looks as if I'd been dropped on it. I can't brush my teeth. With warm water and iodine from the closet, he cleanses my lip.

He leaves me to wash myself, tells me that I should not be afraid; he'll be right outside the door. After the bath, he goes with me to my room, and I dress in a pair of jeans and a pink T-shirt.

Back in the parlor, we sit together, away from the blood wall, my head on his shoulder. I'm hungry. He offers to make me food, but I say no, because I can't move my mouth to eat.

'Look, we cannot run away from this,' Maman says.

Papa shrugs. 'But I cannot do it. How do I do it?'

They're talking about secret things again.

'You can,' she says. 'Yesterday you did it to Annette.'

'I should never have gone to André's place yesterday. Big mistake.'

'We owe André our co-operation. He's a madman now.'

Papa goes to the window, and looks out. 'I think we should run to those UN soldiers by the street corner.'

'*Ndabyanze!* No way! If your brother doesn't get what he wants when he returns, he will hurt all of us.'

'The soldiers are our only hope.'

'They? Hopeless.'

'No.'

'My husband, whatever you decide, let our children live, OK?'

'Maman, are we going to die?' I ask.

'No, no, my dear,' Maman says. 'You're not going to die. *Uzabaho.* You will live.'

Outside, the mid-morning sun is now very bright, and, though the blinds are still drawn, I can see my parents' clothes clearly now. Papa's light-brown jeans are covered with dark stains. Maman is very dirty, her dress covered with dust

32

and dirt, as if she'd been wrestling on the ground all night. She smells of sweat. I knew that it was a bad idea for her to go out last night; she never goes out at night. She tells me that there are many bad women who do, because Rwanda is getting poorer and poorer.

'Maman, Maman!' Jean shrieks suddenly. He must be having a nightmare. She shakes her head guiltily but doesn't go to him, as if she'd lost her right to be our mother. I go with Papa into our bedroom, and Jean climbs all over him, but wails for Maman. A muffled sneeze breaks the silence again. A ghost is gasping for air, as if it were being stifled. We hold on to Papa, who has brought holy water into the bedroom with him.

'It's OK, it's OK,' Papa says, looking around and sprinkling the holy water, as if he has come to console the ghosts, not us. Together we listen to the ghosts' raspy breathing. The breaths come further and further apart. They stop. Papa and the other ghosts start to sigh, as if the ailing one had died a second death. There are tears in Papa's eyes, and his mouth is moving without words. He is commanding ghosts, like the Wizard, but without a stick.

Someone begins to pound on our front door. Papa quickly hands Jean to me. 'Don't open the door!' he hisses to Maman in the parlor, then turns to me. 'And don't take your brother out there!' He stays with us, but his mind is in the parlor, where we can hear Maman pushing aside the table, opening the front door, and whispering to people. We hear chairs and tables being moved. Then there's a grating sound. On the roof, I can hear big birds flapping their wings for takeoff. Then quiet. The people must have left, and Maman is alone again in the parlor.

Somebody wails in a house down the road. Jean begins to cry. I pat him on the back and sing for him in a whisper. He's licking his lips, because he wants food. Papa takes us into the parlor and offers Jean the remains of the oatmeal. He chews the cold chunks hungrily. 'Young man, I told you to eat the whole thing in the morning,' Papa says. 'You children are a burden to us!' He gives me bread slices and milk from the fridge. I soak the slices and swallow them without chewing.

A mob is chanting in the distance; it sounds like it's making its way toward our house. Papa goes to the window. Another voice begins to wail. A third voice, a fourth, a fifth, a child's – it sounds like my friend Hélène. Before I can say anything, Papa says, 'Shenge, forget about that Twa girl.'

Hélène and I sit next to each other at school. She's the brightest in our class, and during recreation we jump rope together in the schoolyard. She's petite and hairy, with a flat forehead like a monkey. Most of the Twa people are like that. They're few in our country. My parents say that they're peaceful and that when the world talks about our country they're never mentioned.

Hélène is an orphan, because the Wizard fixed her parents last year.

33

Mademoiselle Angeline said that he cursed them with AIDS by throwing his *gris-gris* over their roof. Now Papa is paying Hélène's school fees. We're also in the same catechism class and Papa has promised to throw a joint party for our first Holy Communion. Last year, Hélène took the first prize in community service in our class – organized by Le Père Mertens. I came in second. We fetched the most buckets of water for old people in the neighborhood. He said if you're Hutu you should fetch for the Tutsis or the Twa. If you're Tutsi, you do it for the Hutus or the Twa. If you're Twa, you serve the other two. Being both Tutsi and Hutu, I fetched for everybody with my small bucket.

'We can't take her in,' Papa says, and shrugs. 'And how does this crisis concern the Twa?'

Suddenly, Maman yanks the table away from the door again and unlocks it. But she doesn't open the door, just leans on it. More choked cries crack the day like a whip. There are gunshots in the distance. Papa approaches Maman, his hands shaking. He locks the door and takes her back to her seat. He pushes the table back against the door.

Maman stands up suddenly and pulls out the biggest roll of money I've ever seen from inside her dress. The notes are squeezed and damp, as if she had been holding on to them all night. 'This should help for a while,' she says, offering the roll to Papa. 'I hope the banks will reopen soon.' He doesn't touch the money. 'For our children, then,' she says, placing the money on the table.

I tell Papa, 'We must give the money to Tonton André to pay him back.'

'*Ego imana y'Urwanda!*' Maman swears, cutting me off. 'My daughter, shut up. Do you want to die?'

Her lips quake as if she has malaria. Papa pulls his ID from his back pocket and considers the details with disgust. He gets Maman's card out of his pocket, too. Joining the two together, he tears them into large pieces, then into tiny pieces, like confetti. He puts the scraps on the table and goes back to his security post at the window. Then he comes back and gathers them up, but he can't repair the damage. He puts the pieces into his pocket.

Evening is falling. Maman walks stiffly across the room and kneels by the altar. Papa speaks to her, but she doesn't reply. He touches her and she begins to sob.

'By this, your Shenge's crucifix,' Maman says, getting up, 'promise me you won't betray the people who've run to us for safety.'

He nods. 'I promise… *ndakwijeje.*'

Slowly, Maman removes the gold ring from her finger and holds it out for Papa.

'Sell this and take care of yourself and the children.'

Papa backs away, his eyes closed. When he opens them, they're clouded, like a rainy day. Maman comes over to me and places the money on my palms and puts the ring on top of it.

'Don't go away, Maman. Papa loves you.'

'I know, Monique, I know.'

'Is it because you went out last night?'

'No, no, I did not go out last night!' she says. I leave everything on the altar, kneel in front of Papa, and beg him with all my love to forgive her though she's lying. He turns away. I go back to the sofa. 'Your papa is a good man,' Maman says, hugging me.

I push Jean against her, but she avoids his eyes. I think of Le Père Mertens. I plead with Maman to wait for him to return from Belgium to reconcile them. 'If you confess to Le Père Mertens,' I say, 'Jesus shall forgive you.'

There's a light knock on the door. Maman sits up, pushing Jean off like a scorpion. Someone is crying softly outside our door. Maman walks past Papa to push aside the table and open the door. It's Hélène. She's sprawled on our doorstep. Maman quickly carries her inside, and Papa locks the door.

Hélène is soaked in blood and has been crawling through the dust. Her right foot is dangling on strings, like a shoe tied to the clothesline by its lace. Papa binds her foot with a towel, but the blood soaks through. I hold her hand, which is cold and sticky.

'You'll be OK, Hélène,' I tell her. She faints.

'No, St Jude Thadée, no!' Maman exclaims, gathering Hélène's limp body in a hug. 'Monique, your friend will be fine.'

I can hear a mob coming, but my parents are more interested in Hélène. Papa climbs onto a chair, then onto the table. He opens the hatch of the parlor ceiling and asks Maman to relay Hélène to him.

'Remember, we've too many up there,' Maman says. 'When I came down, you had five in there… and I put two more in just hours ago. The ceiling will collapse.'

They take Hélène into our room, and Maman pulls open the hatch. A cloud of fine dust explodes into the room from the ceiling. They shove Hélène's body in.

Now I understand – they are hiding people in our ceiling. Maman was in the ceiling last night. She tricked me. Nobody is telling me the truth today. Tomorrow I must remind them that lying is a sin.

As the mob closes in on the house, chanting, the ceiling people begin to pray. I recognize their voices as those of our Tutsi neighbors and fellow-parishioners. They're silent as Papa opens the front door to the crowd, which is bigger than last night and pushes into our home like floodwater. These people look tired, yet they sing on like drunks. Their weapons and hands and shoes and clothes are covered with blood, their palms slimy. Our house smells suddenly like an abattoir. I see the man who attacked me; his yellow trousers are now reddish brown. He stares at me; I hold on to Papa, who is hanging his head.

Maman runs into her bedroom. Four men are restraining Tonton André, who still wants to kill us all. I run to Maman and sit with her on the bed. Soon, the mob enters the room, too, bringing Papa. They give Papa a big machete. He begins to tremble, his eyes blinking. A man tears me away from Maman and pushes me toward Jean, who's in the corner. Papa is standing before Maman, his fingers on the knife's handle.

'My people,' he mumbles, 'let another do it. Please.'

'No, you do it, traitor!' Tonton André shouts, struggling with those holding him. 'You were with us when I killed Annette yesterday. My pregnant wife. You can't keep yours. Where did you disappear to when we came last night? You love your family more than I loved mine? Yes?'

'If we kill your wife for you,' the Wizard says, 'we must kill you. And your children, too.' He thuds his stick. 'Otherwise, after cleansing our land of Tutsi nuisance, your children will come after us. We must remain one. Nothing shall dilute our blood. Not God. Not marriage.'

Tonton André shouts, 'Shenge, how many Tutsis has Papa hidden–'

'My husband, be a man,' Maman interrupts, looking down.

'Shenge, answer!' someone yells. The crowd of Hutus murmur and become impatient. '*Wowe, subiza.*'

'My husband, you promised me.'

Papa lands the machete on Maman's head. Her voice chokes and she falls off the bed and onto her back on the wooden floor. It's like a dream. The knife tumbles out of Papa's hand. His eyes are closed, his face calm, though he's shaking.

Maman straightens out on the floor as if she were yawning. Her feet kick, and her chest rises and locks as if she were holding her breath. There's blood everywhere – on everybody around her. It flows into Maman's eyes. She looks at us through the blood. She sees Papa become a wizard, sees his people telling him bad things. The blood overflows her eyelids, and Maman is weeping red tears. My bladder softens and pee flows down my legs toward the blood. The blood overpowers it, bathing my feet. Papa opens his eyes slowly. His breaths are long and slow. He bends down and closes Maman's eyes with shaky hands.

'If you let any Tutsi live,' they tell him, 'you're dead.' And then they begin to leave, some patting him on the back. Tonton André is calm now, stroking his goatee. He tugs at Papa's sleeve. Papa covers Maman with a white bedspread and then goes off with the mob, without looking at me or Jean. Maman's ring and money disappear with them.

I cry with the ceiling people until my voice cracks and my tongue dries up. No one can ever call me Shenge again. I want to sit with Maman forever, and I want to run away at the same time. Sometimes I think she's sleeping and hugging Hélène under the bedspread and the blood is Hélène's. I don't want to wake them up. My mind is no longer mine; it's doing things on its own. It begins to run backward, and I see the blood flowing back into Maman. I see her rising suddenly, as suddenly as she fell. I see Papa's knife lifting from her hair. She's saying, 'Me promised you.'

'Yes, Maman,' I say. 'You promised me!'

Jean is startled by my shout. He stamps around in the blood, as if he were playing in mud.

I begin to think of Maman as one of the people in the ceiling. It's not safe for her to come down yet. She's lying up there quietly, holding on to the rafters, just as she must have been last night when the man in the yellow trousers attacked me. She's waiting for the right time to cry with me. I think that Tonton André is hiding Tantine Annette in his ceiling and fooling everyone into believing that he killed her. I see her lying, face up, on a wooden beam, with her mountain belly, the way I lie on the lowest branch of our mango tree and try to count the fruit. Soon, Tonton André will bring her down gently. She'll give birth, and my uncle will cover her mouth with Belgian kisses.

Jean yanks the cloth off Maman and tries to wake her. He straightens her finger, but it bends back slowly, as if she were teasing him. He sticks his fingers into Maman's hair and kneads it, the blood thick like red shampoo. As the ceiling people weep, he wipes his hands on her clothes and walks outside, giggling.

I wander from room to room, listening for her voice among the ceiling voices. When there's silence, her presence fills my heart.

'Forgive us, Monique,' Madame Thérèse says from the parlor ceiling.

'We'll always support you and Jean,' her husband stammers from above my room. 'Your parents are good people, Monique. We'll pay your school fees. You're ours now.'

'Get this dead body off me,' Grandmaman de Martin groans from the corridor. 'It's dead, it's dead!'

'Just be patient,' someone close to her says. 'We'll send the dead down carefully before they fall through.'

Some praise God for the way my parents' marriage has saved them. Grandmaman de Martin becomes hysterical, forcing everyone else to rearrange themselves in the ceiling in the hallway. I identify each voice, but Maman's voice isn't there. Why hasn't she said something to me? Why doesn't she order me to go and shower?

All the things that Maman used to tell me come at me at once, and yet separately – in play, in anger, in fear. There is a command, a lullaby, the sound of her kiss on my cheek. Perhaps she is still trying to protect me from what is to come. She's capable of doing that, I know, just as she stopped Papa from telling me that he was going to smash her head.

'I'm waiting for Maman,' I tell the ceiling people.

'She's gone, Monique.'

'No, no, I know now. She's up there.'

'*Yagiye hehe?* Where?'

'Stop lying! Tell my mother to talk to me.'

The parlor ceiling is now creaking and sagging in the middle, and Madame Thérèse starts to laugh like a drunk. 'You're right, Monique. We're just kidding. Smart girl, yes, your maman is here but she will come down only if you go outside to get Jean. She's had a long day.'

'*Yego*, Madame,' I say, 'wake her up.'

'She's hearing you,' Monsieur Pierre Nsabimana says suddenly from the kitchen. He hasn't said anything all this while. His voice calms me, and I move toward it, my eyes fixed on the ceiling. Someone begins the Catena in a harsh, rapid whisper. It's not Maman. She always takes her time to say her prayer.

'Do you want your Maman to fall with the ceiling on you?' Monsieur Pierre says.

'No.'

'Then, girl, leave the house, and don't come back!'

The ceiling above the altar begins to tear apart from the wall and people scurry away from that end, like giant lizards. I pick up the broken crucifix and hurry outside.

There are corpses everywhere. Their clothes are dancing in the wind. Where blood has soaked the earth, the grass doesn't move. Vultures are poking the dead with their long beaks; Jean is driving them away, stamping his feet and swirling his arms. His hands are stained, because he's been trying to raise the dead. He's not laughing anymore. His eyes are wide open, and there's a frown on his babyish forehead.

Then he wanders toward the UN soldiers at the corner, their rifles shiny in the twilight. They're walking away from him, as if they were a mirage. The vultures are following Jean. I scream at them, but they continue to taunt him, like stubborn mosquitoes. Jean doesn't hear. He sits on the ground, kicking his legs and crying because the soldiers won't wait for him. I squat before my brother, begging him to climb on my back. He does and keeps quiet.

We limp on into the chilly night, ascending the stony road into the hills. The blood has dried into our clothes like starch. There's a smaller mob coming toward us. Monsieur Henri is among them. He's carrying a huge torch, and the flame is eating the night in large, windy gulps. These are our people on Maman's side, and they're all in military clothes. Like another football fan club, they're chanting about how they're going to kill Papa's people. Some of them have guns. If Papa couldn't spare Maman's life, would my mother's relatives spare mine? Or my brother's?

I slip into the bush, with Jean on my back, one hand holding the crucifix, the other shielding my eyes from the tall grass and the branches, my feet cold and bracing for thorns. Jean presses hard against me, his face digging into my back. 'Maman says do not be afraid,' I tell him. Then we lie down on the crucifix to hide its brightness. We want to live; we don't want to die. I must be strong.

After the mob runs past us, I return to the road and look back. They drag Maman out by the legs and set fire to the house. By the time their fellow-Tutsis in the ceiling begin to shout, the fire is unstoppable. They run on. They run after Papa's people. We walk forward. Everywhere is dark, and the wind spreads black clouds like blankets across the sky. My brother is toying with the glow of the crucifix, babbling like mad.

Uwem Akpan is a Jesuit priest from the Diocese of Ikot Ekpene in Nigeria. He has degrees from Creighton University, Nebraska, and Gonzaga University, Washington. After completing his MFA at the University of Michigan last year, the university retained him as the Career-in-the-Making Fellow in its Institute for the Humanities. The first of his short stories were serialized in the Nigerian *Guardian*. He has also published poems, articles and short stories in *Review for Religious, Hekima Review, Company, Jesuit & Friends, Kwani?*, and the *New Yorker*. His collection of short stories was published in May 2008.

Jimmy Carter's Eyes

E C Osondu

WHEN SHE WAS THREE the girl accidentally upturned the boiling pan with which her mother was frying bean cakes on herself. The hot oil left two thick lumps of scar tissue across her eyes, blinding her. Her mother had told everyone who came to sympathize with her that she believed that a nurse had said they'd cut off the scar tissue in the hospital and the girl would be able to see again. Actually, she had not been told this by a real nurse but by a doll-baby nurse. This was the name given to auxiliary nurses in the general hospital where she had stayed with the child for three months, watching the eyes covered by gauze and gentian violet.

No one blamed her for what happened to the child. No one in the village spent all their days watching their children. A woman had thousands of chores – fetching water and firewood, washing clothes, cooking for the family – and looking after the children somehow fitted itself around these activities. She had left the child by the boiling oil and had run inside to fetch her salt container. She needed to sprinkle a pinch of salt into the boiling oil to know if it was time to dunk the ground beans into it. By the time she ran back out, the little girl had grabbed the boiling pan of oil. She had screamed and a crowd had gathered quickly. As is traditional in the village when such things happen, many took a look at the child and ran back to their homes to bring different medications, some useful but most useless. One came with an expired bottle of gentian violet, another came with a smelly black bottle filled with the fat from the boa constrictor killed five years back. One came with a lump of wet cassava which she said would cool the skin and leave no scars. All these were dumped on the girl's face. Someone screamed for the Midwife. The Mid ran the village dispensary. She did more than deliver babies: she wrote prescriptions, sold drugs, and gave injections. Mid took a look at the child and ordered that she be taken to the General Hospital in the local government headquarters which was a good ten miles away. A commercial motorcycle taxi was called, and the woman, holding the child close to her, rode

41

away to the hospital. The crowd gathered around the fire which had grown cold and began to talk about the incident.

'It is always money, money, money for the young women nowadays. In my time this would not have happened.'

'It was not her fault. She has to take care of herself and the baby. You know her husband simply woke up one morning and walked away.'

'I have seen worse burns in my time. She is young and the skin will heal very nicely. You'll be shocked when you see the same child many years hence. There will be no single blemish on her skin.'

'My boa oil can heal anything. They need not have taken her to the hospital – just a drop of the oil every morning and she would heal perfectly.'

'Oh the oil from the boa constrictor that was killed years back, I remember it was so big people thought it was a log of wood that had fallen across the road. From the black marks on its back you can tell it had lived for close to forty years.'

'I have a bottle of the oil myself. I simply forgot to bring it.'

'I wonder why Mid told her to take the child to the General Hospital. With the different medications we have applied even if the skin was burnt by the fires of purgatory she should heal.'

'You know she is the eyes and ears of the government among us here. Her job is more than giving babies with running stomach salt and sugar solution to drink. They sent her here to speak as the voice of the government. If you disobey her you could get into trouble.'

'You know since she got here the tax collectors now know the best days to come, they now come on days when everyone is at home. Who do you think tells them?'

People in the crowd looked at each other as if they had spoken too much and began to disperse. Towards evening, the driver of the motorcycle taxi came to tell the woman's neighbors that she had asked that they bring a few of her clothes to the hospital. She also told them to search under her sleeping mat and bring all the money there to the hospital.

The people in the village gathered and drew up a roster of people who would take food to her in the hospital. Some volunteered to go and pass a night with her in the hospital but were told not to bother by the woman. The hospitals were overcrowded and families of patients slept in the open verandah of the hospital. Those who had gone to the hospital said the place stank of carbolic acid and death. They said that because of frequent power outages, the ice melted from the bodies of the corpses in the mortuary and the corpses stank like decomposed frozen mackerel. They said the doctors and nurses had their own private clinics and preferred that patients came to consult them there rather than in the General Hospital. They said the child's eyes were covered with gauze and that she could not swallow and had to be fed through a straw.

The woman and her daughter stayed in the hospital for a long time. Longer than people stayed in the hospital when they went to have their hernias removed. No one followed the roster anymore; the villagers became busy with the planting of their crops. Another woman began to fry akara by the roadside and people began to buy from her. Occasionally people spoke of the woman and her daughter and then looked away embarrassedly.

One day the woman returned with the little girl who had by now grown a bit. Two thick layers of scar tissue now covered the girl's eyes. She was blind, which was rather odd. A blind little girl was unheard of. In the village, people became blind when they grew old. They said everyone chooses the part of his body that would age more than the other parts. Some chose their ears and became deaf as they grew old. Others chose to age in their teeth and lost all of them.

The girl's mother smiled and did not say much. She did not complain that she had been abandoned in the hospital. She soon went back to her business of frying akara by the side of the road. There was no animosity between her and the other woman who had also started frying akara. She said the sky was wide enough for birds to fly without their wings touching each other.

The child sat by her mother and would sometimes pass salt and other items to her. The mother would leave her to go into the house and people would come and buy akara and the girl would collect their money and give them the correct change. This was very strange because the girl had not been to school and even if she had she was blind, so how could she distinguish between one currency note and another?

One day a little girl went missing in the village. Sometimes children would go missing but they would normally be found within a few hours. This was different. No one had seen the girl. When a child went missing, the mother of the child would tie her headscarf tightly around her waist and go around the village crying and asking 'Who has seen my child?' It was generally believed that by the time she lost her voice, the missing child would be found. By the second day the child was still missing. The mother had lost her voice but the child was not yet found. When the mother walked past the woman frying bean cakes, crying and screaming, 'Who has seen my child?' the blind girl spoke for the first time.

'I know who stole the missing girl.'

'Be quiet and don't get us both into trouble.'

'I saw him give the girl a piece of candy; he tied her mouth with a rag, and threw her into a jute bag and rode away on his motorcycle.'

The woman had never heard the child say that many words. Whenever the child chose to speak, she spoke in a whisper. Many people assumed she never spoke at all.

The mother called out to the woman. She said out loud what the child had said. The villagers gathered. There was only one man they knew who rode a motorcycle and had a jute bag: the man who bought cocoa beans from the villagers. They sent some young men after him. They caught him with the child two towns away. He had cut a hole in the bag through which he fed the girl. He had kidnapped the child for juju money-making rituals. It was rumored that little virgin girls could be charmed and made to vomit money through juju. He cried and said the devil made him do it.

The parents of the kidnapped girl brought a gift for the blind girl and her mother. There was no attempt to explain how the girl arrived at the knowledge she had. Some people said she must have heard something. They said her blindness had sharpened her ears. Her mother suspected something but said nothing.

One day the girl said softly to the mother, 'Father is never coming back.'

'Why do you say that? I am not sure you remember your father, you were so tiny when he left.'

'He ran away with the Catechist's wife's younger sister.'

'How do you know that?' the woman asked, puzzled and frightened.

'They were traveling to Mokwa. He was going to start a new life with her, the car in which they were traveling broke down on the way; all the passengers came down while the driver opened the bonnet to find out what was wrong. He was crossing to the other side of the road to ease piss, and a car coming from the other side knocked him down.'

'Oh my child how do you know these things?' the woman asked.

'They buried him by the roadside, his grave is overgrown with weeds, he's never coming back.'

The woman was quiet for a while. Everything about the story sounded true. She began to cry quietly to herself.

All things eventually come to light. People in the village sensed the girl's true powers and began to come to her for answers.

'Will there be plenty of rain this year so I can plant cassava instead of yams?'

'My black sheep did not come home with the rest of my sheep last night. Where could it be?'

'My son who lives in the city has not come home for five years. Is he dead or in prison?'

'My son who died three years ago: was his death a natural death or did my husband's other wife poison him while I was out of the house?'

'Is the price of cocoa going to rise or fall this year?'

'My husband has been sick for years now; do you think he will recover?'

The girl answered all their questions in a whisper, she answered honestly.

Her answers sometimes caused trouble, tore families apart. Her mother would sometimes speak to her by way of signs to be quiet but she spoke up all the time. The answers flowed out of her mouth like a gentle stream. She said what she had to say and was quiet.

Prosperity began to come to the village because of her. People planted the right crops at the right time and got very rich harvests. Evil was rare. People stopped stealing because they knew she would find them out. More farmers bought motorcycles. Life had never been better.

The mother stopped frying akara. She made a comfortable living from the gifts the girl received. She was happy for once in all her life. She always felt the girl's eyes on her and sometimes shivered slightly when she felt the girl was looking at her. The girl's voice did not change, her breasts were small. The mother was happy when she began to bleed in tiny drops every month. 'Thank goodness she is a woman,' she said to herself.

People said different things about the source of her power but no one denied it.

'Her power is from the river goddess. When she speaks it is the river goddess speaking.'

'It is the Holy Virgin that gives people such gifts, that is why she is called the voice of the dumb and the eyes of the sightless.'

'She is not Catholic, not even Christian – she does not mention the name of God.'

'God who took away her eyes gave her the gift of sight, and now she sees more than those of us with two eyes.'

People said all sorts of things but still came to her for answers. On occasion the mother would say the girl was tired and needed to rest, but the girl would come out of her room and provide answers to whomever needed them. People reminded the mother that she could now afford to take the child to the Baptist Missionary Hospital in the big city. The mother acted as if she did not hear them. She did not think it was wise to tamper with the will of God, she told those who were bold enough to ask her. Besides, if the girl thought it was such a good thing she would have said so. Quite a few agreed with the mother; after all, those of them with two eyes did not see as much as she did.

At about this time, the former American President Jimmy Carter launched his River Blindness Eradication Program. The program sent doctors and nurses to villages to distribute drugs for the prevention of river blindness. They did eye examinations and distributed glasses which the villagers referred to as Anya Jimmy Carter – Jimmy Carter's Eyes. The frames of the glasses were second-hand, gifts and donations from affluent Americans. This time around though, it was going to be slightly different; they were coming with eye surgeons to help remove

45

cataracts. The bearer of this piece of news was the Midwife. She told the villagers that she had made it happen, that the village was not originally in the plan for the cataract surgery; she had lobbied for them to be included.

People were excited about this piece of good news. One of the old men in the village said the former President was kind because he had been a groundnut farmer before he became a President.

They had already been to the nearby village and had sent a notice to the chiefs that they were coming. The Midwife said they would be moving from house to house.

At first everyone looked forward to the visit until the woman mentioned that this would be an opportunity for her daughter to have the scar tissue covering her eyes removed. It was free and the girl was bleeding, she was now a woman and needed to get married. She had only said this to a few people. It soon got round the village that the girl was going to undergo surgery. There was anger, there were complaints, there was resentment and then people began to complain aloud.

'This program is not for people like her, it is for people losing their eyes to river blindness.'

'She lost her eyes due to her mother's carelessness. Her mother should bear the cost of her surgery in a proper hospital.'

'What guarantee is there that she will see again? Even if the skin is lifted, I hear the eyeballs are dead and blank. Please, no one should make the poor child suffer for nothing.'

'They say her mother wants a husband for the girl, I know many men that will gladly marry her the way she is, she is a bag of wealth.'

'It is the mother that needs a husband. Why did she never remarry after her husband ran away, as we all know the husband is dead, the girl said it herself.'

'The girl belongs to the entire village now, not to her mother alone. She ceased being the mother's property as soon as she received her gift.'

'You are right you know – if the gift was for her alone she would have stopped at telling her mother about her father's disappearance.'

'You are right, she sees things for everyone, she was sent to prosper the village.'

'Why are the Americans sending the eye doctors to us? Do they mean to tell us they have cured all the blind people in America?'

'The Elders should meet and tell the woman what to do just in case she does not know.'

Word got to the ears of the Elders, and they being people who acted in the interest of the inhabitants of the village, decided to prevail on the mother of the girl to do the right thing. They made their points – they told her that her daughter's gift was for the good of all, that if it was for her mother alone she would have been seeing things for the mother alone. They spoke to the woman for a very long time. The woman told them that the girl was already bleeding and was a woman. She wanted her to marry and have children. Midwife came along with the Elders. She explained the difference between a cataract and the girl's condition. It was very possible that the girl would not recover her sight after the surgery, this might traumatize the girl and she may even lose the gift of speech which would be a double tragedy. They talked to the woman for a long time. The Elders told her that they would gladly marry the girl off to any of their sons. She cried, and then she nodded and agreed with them.

On the day the American eye doctors came, the woman and her daughter locked their doors and remained inside till they left. Some people got new glasses; some had surgery. Everyone was happy. The girl and her mother were referred to as heroes who had put the interest of the town above their own interest.

When the planting season began, people came to the girl with their questions but alas she had no answers. The stream had dried up.

'It was not our fault. We should not blame ourselves for it,' one of the villagers said.

'Whatever has a beginning must have an end; even the deepest ocean has a bottom. She was bound to stop seeing things one day anyway.'

'It is the white man's strong juju that did it, or don't you know that white people are powerful?'

'The blind girl and her mother should consider themselves lucky; if it were in some other village they would have stoned them to death for possessing witchery powers.'

And so life returned to normal in the village and everybody's conscience was at peace. Occasionally when a sheep went missing, the owner would be heard to bite his fingers and mutter, 'if only that blind girl still had her powers.'

Epapaphras Chukwuenweniwe Osondu was born in Nigeria. He worked as an advertising copywriter for many years before moving to New York to attend Syracuse University to study Creative Writing. He holds an MFA for Creative Writing and is a fellow at the university. He has won The Nirelle Galson Prize for Fiction and his story *A Letter From Home* was adjudged as one of the 'Top Ten Stories on the Internet in 2006'. EC now lives in New York with his wife and three children.

Bad Places

Henrietta Rose-Innes

WAKING, SHE WAS FOR a moment surprised by the bright blue hand that lay before her face. The fingers flexed, startled – her own hand then. Elly sat up squinting against the odd, prismatic light. Beside her, Michael lay on his back, Nadia with her head on his belly, fingers lightly spread on the cobalt skin. The pigment on their bodies had bled a little into the sand, creating a delicate corona around all three.

This long, empty beach was not one she recognised. They had arrived in darkness, and she remembered only a deserted parking lot, stumbling, a roaring tunnel. The tide was far out now across a stretch of grey sand that shone like wet cement. Behind them, an unbroken line of dune. By the height of the sun, she guessed it must be early morning; but already so hot. Putting a hand to her face, Elly was surprised by an insect flutter – the silver eyelashes, she'd forgotten. She tugged them off and dropped them into the sand. And the sparkly light switched at once to a more terrestrial glare.

The surf receded before her as she stood and went to wash her arms and face; the body paint was itching. Her skin goosebumped in the icy water, but remained stubbornly blue, dusted with tiny silver points of glitter.

Elly was a small girl, spare and freckled; when she looked down over her flat chest she could count the ribs. The skin was tight across her concave stomach, empty since yesterday lunchtime. Blue skin, silver bikini top, sequined mini, and a silver pouch where she kept her car keys and money, strapped where another girl's belly would be. Her head ached a little, and the muscles in her jaw. I'm twenty-nine, she thought dully.

Their footprints wavered unevenly down the beach from the parking-lot, erased where they dipped below the tide line, reappearing, three sets. Her own feet were tiny next to Michael's, with his long toes; Nadia's were also long, but slender and slightly pigeon-toed. Elly placed her feet over the narrower prints, feeling in her knees the exact differences between the girls' strides. She often played this game on the beach, letting her feet briefly take her into another body: some footprints slowed you down, some made you skip or shuffle or straighten your back.

But now she was impatient. She scuffed sulkily at Nadia's tracks with her kid's feet. It was too hot; time to go.

'Nadia.'

They slept on, deep in their coupled slumber.

'Guys. I'm going to wait in the car.'

She turned. And trod in her own footprints up the beach: toes in heel, heel on toes. The milled trail wandered a little, skewing drunkenly to and fro, up towards the tar, where she could see the mica glint of her car windscreen.

Abruptly, a line of clear tracks cut across, straight up from the water: something that had breached during the night and struck out for the dunes. Large feet, larger than Michael's, heavy and purposeful. Elly hesitated.

Turning away from the sea, she slipped her right foot into the stranger's print. It was smooth-soled and deep, a sandy slipper. The soles were crisply defined, the big toes crooked a little inwards. She stood awkwardly for a moment, twisted at the hips. The left foot seemed impossibly far away: a huge stride, for Elly almost a leap. Her hips cracked when she tried it. Tiring, to inhabit this body; it required a strong, long-legged man. He grew before her. Standing up suddenly and emphatically in his footprints: tall, broad-shouldered, handsome perhaps, walking away. She followed, concentrating on the tricky, loping stride.

The heat felt like dense liquid sinking into her scalp, and the sand underfoot was growing hotter, too. She walked without thought – five minutes, ten, until colour and detail bleached from her vision. The prints became less distinct, finally lost in the dry, looser sand. When she raised her eyes she found herself brought far up and away from the beach, right on the dune crest. She could see the three clear insect tracks of their night journey, and the stranger's trail cutting across, straight as a ruled line to where she stood. The bodies of her friends were distant, slight and motionless.

From here she looked down onto the other, secret side of the dune. Beyond was the steep wall of a higher dune, the dip between narrow and intimate, like the cleft between a sleeper's arm and body. At the bottom, the smooth geometry of the slopes was disturbed by an irregular collection of boulders, some low grey-green shrubs. It looked quiet down there in the shade. She took two steps down, her feet pushing miniature crescent sandslides down the slope.

Hitching up the silver skirt, Elly squatted to pee. As her head dropped below the lip of the dune, the noise of the surf was abruptly stilled. Her ears were numb and ringing still from the long night, the bass, the voices. But slowly she felt the silence infiltrate her, like some cool fluid, saturating, insulating. She could hear the tiniest sounds now: a faint insect rasping; the trickle of urine rearranging grains of quartz; the squeak of the dry sand under her toes; the scratch of a twig against the sequins. A tiny, flame-red mite, the size of a grain of salt, crawled up over her toe, carefully negotiated one hair, two, and trekked out across the blue toenail. Beyond these tiny sounds, nothing; just this miniature toiling, the heat rising off the sand. The soles of her feet were burning now.

The stream of urine was absorbed immediately into a neat little sinkhole, and stopped. She turned a little on her heels, eyes slitted, to peer down into the dune hollow. A soft ticking sound, as if tiny grains of sand were cracking open in the heat, like seeds. Elly had slept only a few hours on the beach; her eyes moved sleepily over the texture of sand, stone, leaves, the gaps and cracks of shade between them, random and harmonious.

Except. There: something dully silver, draped incongruously against the rock. A human thing. Placed by hands, constrained by knots.

Elly stood with quick instinct, wary, pulling down her skirt as the landscape's camouflage fell away. The stones slid into a different focus, revealing their arrangement and their function: not ten metres away stood a house, with walls, a roof, a door. There, where one smooth fawn rock leant against another, she saw now the chink between them was stacked with putty-coloured flints. A roof of rusty corrugated iron was wedged at an angle between the boulders, creating a kind of portico; a silvery curtain hung across the gap below. Around this entrance, the sand was trampled flat and two neat lines of stones marked a pathway.

Shame made Elly scuff sand over her traces. She should go now. But her eyes were so tired; they wanted only to rest in the blue shade between the rocks down there, shade that would be as cool as fresh water. A prickle of new sunburn seemed to push her forward, a soft-palmed red hand on the back of her neck. The loose sand crumbled of its own accord beneath her feet, conspiring in her descent, delivering her, step by sliding step, down towards that shadowed lintel.

She touched the edge of the silver curtain – a sack for fertilizer or cement. The material was dusty, stiff but yielding. Perhaps no one had moved it for months, years. It parted with a rustle.

Her eyes were too sun-bleached to make out the detail, but there was silence in there, the neutral air of an empty house. A kind of antechamber with a low, rocky roof. As she knelt, the shade fell over her face, sensuous, irresistible: like lowering her face into a shallow bowl of cool water. She could feel the tightness of the sunburn softening as she was drawn in by the skin of her cheeks, around the eyes. She let the sacking fall closed behind her: a soft shutter falling behind her corneas, a deep quenching blink.

Sight returned slowly. In the grey filtered light, Elly breathed in experimentally. The place smelt inorganic; no fug of habitation, except perhaps by heatless creatures of frugal respiration: sand-lice, insects, crabs. No scuttles. No sighs. The floor under her knees was cool – cardboard, the slightly damp, spongy texture was not unpleasant. She crawled a little further, into a larger space. The roof was higher here. As her pupils expanded, soft shapes separated in the dimness. Smooth round objects, blue and grey, nothing straight or sharp. Walls and floor smoothed into each other, the angles softened by sand silted into the corners, by the creased and fraying folds of cardboard.

White shells placed in a line against the base of the boulder-wall. A shelf of silvery driftwood carrying a chipped china cow. A plastic tea-tray with a picture of a peacock on it, carefully propped against the uneven wall. Tins that had once held beans and pilchards, their metal lips beaten smooth, in ordered rows. The stub of a candle on a flat stone, a ghost of black smoke streaking the rock wall behind it. Stone table, stone stools. Beyond, the far reaches of the cave were concealed in dimness, a tattered green nylon fishing net draped across one corner. Nursery whispers: Hansel and Gretel, Goldilocks. Elly let her breath out softly.

Against the wall to the right was a shallow hollow dug into the sand, lined with the mauve dimpled cardboard used to pad fruit boxes. It looked inviting. Elly swivelled on her heels and eased back into the pit, legs stretched out straight. Too big for her, a giant's easy-chair – comfy though. Elly felt her neck relax, then her back; she let go of the weight of her head. Her eyelids were fluttering, flicking closed uncontrollably like the weighted lids of antique dolls.

Here and there, the walls and floor were marked with flecks of light where the sun poked its fingers through. They looked like the ghost spots cast by a mirror-ball. Or like the little moons that fell through the leaves of big green trees, oak and plane and mulberry...

Oak trees are best for playing houses, or big pines with lumpy roots, or inside the hedge. Down at the bottom of the school, where it's wild. Me and Nadia play there before class, also at lunch, also after. The oak's ours. We took it when the standard fives got too old for housey-housey and went away. We fought for it.

There's battles and tea parties. We sweep the sandy floor and arrange our best things: plates and knives and forks and tea-sets.

Sometimes, our house shows us it still has a tree life: fungus on the twig cutlery, or a stone chair rolling over to show a dead lizard, or a black poison centipede coming out from under a pine-needle pillow...

The beast came thundering towards her on a standing wave of a million legs, waving its huge sandy pincers, roaring. She knocked her head back against the wall in fright and came quickly awake. Lurching forward onto her hands and knees on the cardboard floor with a choked gasp, she listened. Something's here.

Only when the sound came again – another snort, shorter and guttural, a whistle, then that groaning roar – did she recognise the snoring. A man.

He was hidden in the dark corner of the irregularly-shaped room, behind the green net. At first, her eyes took in only the ragged honeycomb of the nylon; then they slid beyond it, through the hand-sized gaps to the shapes beyond.

Huge, charcoaled soles, and gigantic toes pointing slightly inwards. She saw now why the footprints had been so deep and defined: his feet were shod with calluses as tough as hooves. Leaning forward silently, she found the long narrow legs, disappearing at the knees into the folds of a dark coat; fists clenched against his thighs. And at the far end, jammed against the rocky confines, a face turned away, exposing a sinewy neck. The cords of the throat seemed to strain against each ferocious snore, stressed by the passage of air. Asleep, but not at ease. The sound of his struggle filled the cavern.

Again, for Elly the world seemed to shift, refocus, correct. The colours dirtied, darkened, flattened. The roof was suddenly too low, the air thicker. She had made a mistake, passed somehow into another country: this was not the land of acorn-cup teacups and leafy beds. As if regaining a lost sense of smell, Elly was penetrated by the sour, familiar stench of unwashed bodies, of days-old drinker's sweat.

Stealthily, she reversed, in a slow-panic scuttle like a crab's. But halfway across the space a star of light on the far wall caught her eye like a silver hook. The sun was reflecting off something lying on a ledge in the wall, just above the sleeping giant's chest. A little alien figurine, chrome, with glittery black almond-shaped eyes in its big head. It took her four or five motionless seconds to understand what it was doing here, this detached piece of herself. My keyring. The keys to her car.

He's a bergie, Elly calmed herself. She crawled closer, pushing past the shreds of green webbing. Knelt at the man's side, she kept her breaths small and unobtrusive: crab breaths, sand-flea breaths. She was so close now she not only smelled him, but felt his odour as a warmth on her face. The big man groaned, sighed, gave a phlegmy rumble; but did not wake. The alien, eye-level, stared back at her with the hostage's piteous stunned gaze. It looked impossibly bright and clean: a child's thing.

The roof was too low for her to stand, but kneeling, she could barely reach across his great bowed chest. She had to balance on the balls of her feet and lean forward, bracing herself with her left hand against the rock. She arched over him, sucking in her stomach, reaching for her keys with her right. The bare skin of her belly was only millimetres from his clothing. The substance of the overcoat was unidentifiable, matted and with a slight dull oily shine, like the hide of an old, scarred animal.

She didn't see him wake; only felt the huge hand closing over her right arm, above the elbow. The grip was unlike any human's she had yet experienced: no give in it at all, as if her arm were instantly set into a stone cuff; she could not move without being bruised against its rigidity. In a stiff movement from the waist, the man sat up, crumpling her back onto her folded legs. She was helpless, a lizard in his fist. His face was close to hers now, with his tigerish methylated breath.

She saw him intensely. A worn, weary face, although she realised with surprise – from the smoothness of his neck and forehead – that he was not an old man. A gull-feather was stuck skewly into his matted beard. His skin was a muddy tea brown, rubbed on the ridges and prominences with a mineral grey like pencil lead. Impossible to tell what colour that skin had been originally, to imagine it clean, soft, a baby's cheeks. The pupils of his eyes were gigantic, rimmed by a narrow ring of milky blue. But he was not blind. He was watching her.

'Sorry,' she said.

He raised his free hand, and with a thumb so worn and hard it might have been encased in plaster, he rubbed her eyelid, her cheek. He scowled at the smear of silver and blue sparkles that came off on his skin.

'It's...' she swallowed. 'It's a costume. Dressing up.'

He didn't understand. He shook her, left and right, as if to gently dislodge some sense from her mouth. She pointed crookedly with her chin at the keys on the cave wall.

'My keys. I just want my keys. Then I'll go.'

His grip had not shifted or slackened. He held her a little raised from the ground, so that she could not rest her weight fully on her feet; her legs started to ache beneath her. But he was patient. They held the pose for a minute, two; long enough for the sun to move its precise indicating needle away from the keys, and into her right eye. She dipped her face.

He opened his hand, letting her fall painfully onto her folded legs. Elly rolled on her side, watching him. His eyes rested mildly on her lap. From a distance, clearly, she watched his fingers creep forward, touch her silver skirt. She did not breathe. It was the cloth he was interested in: his tannin-brown nail fingered it slowly, sleepily, the sun scattering in little silver moons off the fabric.

'My keys. Please.'

Suddenly he hit her full in the face, an open-hand slap with a palm like a piece of wood. Her whole head rang.

'This is my place.' A husky voice, unused. 'Mine.'

Elly nodded stupidly. Nobody had ever hit her like that.

He became animated, businesslike. He clicked his fingers, a startlingly loud noise, like branches snapping. All impatience now.

'Cigarettes. Cigarettes. Come.'

Quickly obedient, she zipped open her pouch, pulled out a crumpled packet of Stuyvesants and handed it to him. He checked how many were left, then nodded towards the purse.

'And that. Come come come.'

She did what he said, handed over the whole purse, money, credit cards, whatever. He put it into an inside pocket of his coat without checking.

'Ja. Now *voetsek*.'

Elly was plummeting helplessly younger, three years old now, huge childish tears coming.

'My keys...'

'*Voetsek!*' – raising a hand.

She stumbled backwards, scrambled somehow back through the dim wormhole cave, through that dry rustling aperture, out into the white-out sun, panting, safe for a second.

He followed from his hole, coat flapping, roaring, flinging sand like a great sand-lion. It stung – he was hurling sand with raging intent, as if each handful were a half-brick. Then there really were stones coming at her; he seemed to be ripping up the very substance of his home. She was brought to her knees by a pebble to the check, struggled up again. Something hard and shiny cut her lip and fell into the sand. Stinging, she picked up the keys and ran, blindly, uphill, headlong.

Out into the dune field she ran, away from the sea, into a wasteland: broken glass and bottlenecks and human shit, flies gathering around bloody things in the bushes. Elly was surely lost now, lost for good.

But in truth it is only ten or twenty minutes before she stumbles over a dune, clutching the keys so hard they hurt her palm. And sees the parking lot below. Maybe more, because the sun is set at its full and furious height, and she is quite incandescent with sunburn, sizzling with cuts on her feet, her face, her arms. Maybe an hour or two.

Or perhaps much longer. Because standing there she knows she is changed, quite changed. And who are these children, turning their blue-streaked faces towards her now with cries of sharp relief, their costumes torn and spoiled?

As she descends from the dune and heads towards the others waiting at the car, it seems to them too that Elly is altered – taller maybe, more substantial; and walking with the long deliberate stride of some much larger being.

Henrietta Rose-Innes was born in 1971 and lives in Cape Town. She is the author of two novels, *Shark's Egg* (2000) and *The Rock Alphabet* (2004), both published by Kwela Books, and was the compiler of an anthology of South African writing, *Nice Times! A Book of South African Pleasures and Delights* (Double Storey, 2006). Her short stories and essays have appeared in a variety of publications in South Africa and elsewhere. A translated anthology of short pieces will be published in Germany in 2008, and *The Rock Alphabet* has been published in Romanian translation. She was the winner of the 2007 Southern African PEN short story award.

Night Bus

Ada Udechukwu

'OH, MAKE UNA FORM line!' The security officer's voice rose and silenced the conversations around him. He waved the barrel of his automatic in a wide arc over the people congregated around the night bus to Lagos.

Passengers scrambled to form a line. The officer strolled past and prodded the cartons, suitcases, and bags that stood alongside their owners. Satisfied with his inspection, he returned to the head of the line, saluted no one in particular, and mounted the bus steps. He leaned against the door, pinched snuff into his nostrils, and surveyed the passengers below him. From time to time he inhaled deeply, let loose a violent sneeze, hacked up phlegm, spat, and wiped his mouth with the back of his hand.

The conductor began ticketing passengers. Whenever he cleared a traveler for boarding, the officer left his post. He examined hand luggage first. He conducted a body search on male passengers by running his hands along their clothing, feeling pockets, and occasionally ordering their contents displayed. Women were treated to a metal detector waved back and forth over their clothing.

Uloma held her ticket out to the conductor. He motioned toward the open luggage compartments at the side of the bus. She shook her head, tightening her grip on the duffel strap.

Visibly annoyed, the conductor pointed to the bag and said, 'Sista, you no fit take am inside.'

Uloma smiled. 'Oga, no vex. E go fit for inside. I dey carry dis bag before.'

'Na oga security go decide.' The conductor tilted his head in the direction of the security officer, who now stood at the bottom of the steps, poised to intervene.

Uloma gazed at the conductor. With palms clasped in front of her, she pleaded, 'Oga, biko. Tell am breakable dey for bag.'

'You ladies. Na so-so trouble you dey cause me,' the conductor muttered. He jerked a thumb at the officer and asked, 'You wan make I talk to am?'

Uloma nodded.

The conductor left to confer with the officer. They spoke for several minutes. Twice the officer pointed to the luggage bins beneath the bus, packed with bags as large as Uloma's, and to the duffel she carried.

'I don tell am,' the conductor said, in a voice loud enough for all to hear. A moment later he leaned over to the officer and whispered in his ear.

Impatient murmurs rose from the waiting passengers.

Uloma looked behind her. She saw no sign of Monye, even though they'd agreed to meet at the station by three o'clock. She rocked on her heels, an arm cradled under the duffel to relieve her shoulder of its weight. Although everything appeared to be working out as he had said it would, Monye's lateness unnerved her.

Minutes passed. The duffel strap cut into her shoulder. She raised it and shifted it to the other side. Beneath her clothes and other personal items, several thousand dollars for the secondhand Mercedes that Monye planned to buy from a dealer in Cotonou lay under the duffel's false bottom. The exchange rate had been good that week – 140 naira to the dollar. The naira that Monye had carried to the exchange bureau had been reduced to the compact packets of dollars now hidden in the duffel. He'd explained about the money the night before, when he fixed the bag. Tomorrow morning, while Uloma bought bales of used clothing for resale back at her stall in the Aba market, he'd negotiate for the car. Together they'd drive the car across the border from neighboring Benin and return to Nigeria, where he would sell the car for a good profit.

The officer and the conductor burst into laughter. Uloma looked at them. The officer winked at her, pointed to his chest, and waved with both hands. Uloma waved, and stretched her lips into a forced smile.

Within seconds the officer dismissed the conductor and sauntered over to Uloma. His bowlegged waddle heightened the ridiculous effect of tight trousers tucked into boots in imitation of a commando uniform. He stood before her, his fly only partially zipped, revealing aquamarine nylon underpants. She cursed Monye for putting her in a situation where she needed to ask a favor of this oaf. The day before, Monye's request that she make sure the duffel stayed with her had seemed simple enough; now the prospect of debasing herself sickened her.

The officer grinned, took hold of Uloma's arm, and led her around the bus. She needed all of her willpower not to tell him to get his hands off her.

'Fine woman, why you no fit put your bag for under? I tink say you know na extra we dey charge for overweight.' The officer's sly smile amplified the lie he told.

Uloma wrinkled her nose at the fermenting mixture of beer and kola nuts on his breath. A window opened above them, and she gazed up at the passengers staring down in anticipation of the drama to follow. Beads of sweat trickled from her armpits. She hugged her duffel to her.

'Wetin dey for bag? E be like you wan hide sonting. Oya, drop am, make I see what you carry.' The officer pointed to the space between his feet.

Uloma put the duffel down. The officer knelt and rummaged among her things. He pulled aside layers of folded clothes and dug deep into the bag. When he encountered something that interested him – a toilet bag, a packet of sanitary pads, a makeup kit – he held it up and queried her about it. He ignored the novels and magazines at the bottom of the bag, squeezed something, and pulled it out.

'Wetin dey for here?' The officer held up a black plastic bag.

'Oga, biko.' Uloma extended her hands.

The officer swung the bag and laughed when Uloma groped for it. He tossed the bag into the air, caught it, untied the double knot at its neck, and peered inside. A pungent odor escaped, and the officer grimaced at the bloodstained panties.

Uloma covered her mouth and smiled into her palm, glad that she had heeded Monye's advice about packing the underwear.

The officer hastily stuffed the bag back into the duffel and stood up. 'Sista, n'only because I like you. So, find kola, make I chop.' He motioned to his mouth. His eyes ran the length of Uloma's body and came to a stop at her breasts.

She handed him a folded bill. He checked its denomination and slipped it into his pocket. Uloma reached for the duffel. The officer's hand brushed over her breast. He flashed a smile at her, and the dull red of his tongue filled the gap between his front teeth, pulsing like a live animal. She flushed, fighting an urge to strike him.

'Make we go,' the officer said, and turned on his heel.

The two of them rounded the front of the bus. Sighs came from the waiting passengers. A wave of grumbles rolled from the back of the line, and people stepped out to eye Uloma. She bowed her head.

The officer returned to his perch on the steps. He waved Uloma over to the conductor and signaled the man to resume ticketing. Loud protests filled the air. Several people called out, 'Ye-ye woman,' 'Ashawo,' 'E be say like you don give am de ting.' Uloma blushed at the abuse, her face hot.

The conductor ignored her when she held out her ticket. One after another he cleared passengers for boarding. Soon a plump middle-aged woman in an expensive brocade wrappa stepped forward. A stiff headtie sat on her head, its towering crown secured with a large knot whose two loose ends spread out like wings behind her. The conductor grinned and greeted the woman effusively. Oblivious of the waiting passengers, the two of them enquired about the health of family members and conversed about mutual acquaintances.

Uloma glanced behind her. Monye still hadn't arrived. She couldn't understand his delay. This trip had been his idea. Weeks before, when he had suggested she accompany him, she had protested about making another journey so soon after her regular monthly trip to buy stock for her used-clothing business – she hadn't yet sold three-quarters of the goods she'd bought on her previous trip. But Monye had persuaded her that it was a good opportunity to beat the Christmas rush. He'd also assured her that after his deal with the car, the traditional marriage ceremony she longed for was next on his agenda.

The conductor turned to Uloma. 'Sista, you don settle am?' he asked with a smirk on his face.

She nodded.

'Oya, now, bring my own.'

Uloma held out her ticket. The conductor sighed and shook his head. He rubbed one palm over the other.

Uloma placed a twenty-naira note under her ticket and handed it back.

On her way into the bus she squeezed past the officer. He pinched her arm. But when she looked back, he made a show of adjusting his cap. She paused beside the driver's seat and surveyed the bus. Behind her the officer accosted a passenger.

'My broda, wey you dey go?' the officer asked.

'That lady you pass now-now, nko,' a man retorted.

Uloma looked over her shoulder.

The officer glanced at her and snickered. 'I don check am behind.'

Both men laughed.

Uloma turned away. She walked down the aisle, stopped halfway at a pair of vacant seats, and took the one by the window. Perched on the seat beside her, the duffel looked normal, no different from the way it had looked before Monye created the false bottom. She located the seam, pulled at a loose thread, and pressed it down again, appalled that she had doubted Monye. She understood why so many dollars were needed: the car dealerships in Benin insisted on being paid in foreign currency. Monye had told her what he'd done with the bag – how much cash he'd hidden, and exactly how he'd packed it. For once he'd trusted her with the details of his business, explaining the technicalities of registering and licensing, and also the process of 'settling' people in the motor-licensing office. When she asked why he couldn't carry the money on him, as she carried hers, he said that if anyone knew he had all those dollars, he'd be forced to pay double the bribes he anticipated.

Yet something continued to bother her about his insistence that she hold the money for him. Inexplicably, her thoughts wandered to old gossip from her university days. On campus, Monye had stood out, with his good looks, sports car, and expensive lifestyle. Rumors – none of them good – abounded about the source of his seemingly endless supply of cash. But the rumors did not hurt his reputation with women. He'd asked her out once, and she'd accepted, surprised that he'd notice someone like her.

Uloma stowed the duffel under the seat in front of her and glanced at her watch; in another hour the bus would leave the station. She debated whether to move to the aisle seat. The window offered a view of the roadside, but if she were next to the aisle, she'd be able to see anything coming toward the bus. She made a hasty sign of the cross to protect herself from any trouble. Unzipping the duffel, she retrieved a bag containing a jar of groundnuts and a packet of biscuits, and she placed it on the seat beside her. She zipped up the duffel and placed it back on the floor, between her feet.

Although this was the sixth time she had traveled on the night bus to Lagos, the journey still frightened her. Recently, after a spate of hijackings and robberies, all the major transporters had started moving in convoys, with an armed guard on each bus. She knew that when they got to Onitsha, their final stop in the east, they'd be joined by five more buses, and from then on until they reached Lagos, buses would be behind and in front of them. That meant that there would be at least six armed guards. But this did not alleviate her fears.

The long journey, commencing in the late afternoon and continuing into the early hours of the following day, always made her uneasy. But she had no alternative if she wanted to get her goods and return home without having to close her market stall for more than a day. A quick turnaround meant more money at the end of the month. Monye's willingness to lend her interest-free seed money for the business had helped, but she had to pay back some of the principal every month. In addition to this she gave money to her parents in the village – her siblings still in secondary school had tuition fees to be paid. And she had expenses of her own.

Out in the parking lot three other buses stood in front of the station. They would be journeying to popular destinations in the north: Abuja, Kaduna, and Kano. All the buses, including the one she sat in, were multicolored. Plastered against diagonals of fluorescent blue and pink on their flanks, bold yellow letters proclaimed LANDJET TRANSPORTERS, INC. Along the top of each bus the prowess of Landjet was advertised with the words CONCORDE OF THE NIGER. Lower down, near the tyres, a biblical passage secured protection from the Almighty: THE LORD IS MY STRENGT & SHIELD, PSALM 28:7. Uloma smiled at the misspelled word and wondered if the phrase actually came from the Book of Psalms.

A short distance from the parked buses people milled around the narrow veranda that fronted Landjet's offices. Latecomers battled for the few remaining tickets at the counter, and a disorderly line stretched from the door.

Uloma patted her belly and felt for the small apron underneath her outer wrappa. Three hundred thousand naira, half the cost of three bales of secondhand clothing, was stitched into its pockets. Earlier in the afternoon, before coming to the bus station, she had divided a further 290,000 into three envelopes and hidden them in her handbag. The cups of her bra were padded with another 10,000.

She looked around the bus. Only a few people were inside. Some of the seats across from her held bags, left by passengers to colonize places for themselves. Most people boarded the bus, secured their seats, and got off to walk around the station's premises in search of snacks and drinks, returning only when the final departure call came.

Out in the Landjet compound a mobile market spread itself among the crowd. Food vendors darted in different directions, hastening to attend to customers. Uloma raised the window beside her. A boy selling bread caught her eye and shoved a loaf high into the air. 'Aunty, touch am,' he called out. 'Na today own, fresh.' She shook her head. A flock of hawkers scuttled over. They clamored for her attention, showing her their wares. A woman held out her tray of boiled eggs and shouted, 'Egg, ten-ten naira, aunty!' A young girl pushed herself in front of the woman, raising two plastic bags of water into the air. 'Pure-water, pure-water,' she sang in a falsetto.

Uloma slipped the strap of her handbag from her shoulder and brought out her wallet. Her late lunch of pounded yam and vegetable soup felt like a stone in her stomach. The snacks she'd brought with her were enough nourishment until the bus stopped for breakfast, at Ore. All she needed was a cold drink and some bottled water to keep with her for the journey. She waved at a woman carrying a bucket of soft drinks and drinking water on her head. When the woman set down her load, Uloma pointed to a bottle of Fanta and a large Eva water bottle swimming around in the melting ice. She paid for her beverages, took hold of the bottles, and shook her head at the woman's offer to wipe them with a dirty rag.

Passengers streamed into the bus in twos and threes. To discourage anyone from approaching her, Uloma kept her arm draped over the bag of snacks on the seat beside her. She looked behind her and tallied the vacant seats on the bus. Other than the one next to her, only two seats remained empty. But once the bus left the station, the conductor would bring out 'attachments' – crude padded stools that fit in the aisle – so he and the driver could earn extra money for themselves by picking up passengers along the way.

Uloma peered into her handbag and checked again for the manila envelopes that contained her cash. A bead of sweat rolled into the valley between her breasts, and she rubbed the front of her blouse. Its stiff lace fabric rustled. Her breasts itched from the damp naira notes in her bra. She untied her outer wrappa and fanned herself with it, twirling the ends while she blew down the neckline of her blouse. The ankle-length fabric of the wrappa still tied around her waist trapped the heat, and her moist thighs slipped against each other. She dressed this way – the lace blouse and double abada wrappas – only to fit in with the other madams who rode the bus. This was not the life she had imagined for herself when she graduated from the university with her French degree. Still, her French came in handy when she bargained with Beninese traders in Cotonou. They thought she was a native.

Uloma checked her watch again: fifteen minutes to go. Perhaps Monye was going to miss the bus. If so, she'd get off and go home. She had not wanted to make the journey in the first place. Carrying all this money made her nervous. And Monye's scheme that they travel as strangers seemed unnecessarily complicated, even though she understood his fear about the money. But if it was so expertly hidden, as he said, why did they have to pretend not to know each other? She'd tried to press him for answers, but he'd brushed aside her concerns. And she'd given in – as he knew she would – when he told her that this deal with the car would provide him with the money he needed so they could get engaged and he could talk to her parents about wedding plans.

Her parents bothered her about Monye all the time. Whenever she visited them, they welcomed her with criticism: 'All your education gone to waste – you are now a common trader kept by a man,' her mother would say. 'When is he going to bring his people to see us?' her father would ask. Yet every month they accepted the money she gave them without questioning where it came from.

Monye helped her out with the monthly stipend she gave her parents. If it weren't for him, she'd probably be a prostitute by now. Many of the girls she knew openly flaunted their sugar daddies, the older married men who kept them clothed and housed in return for services. At least Monye loved her and provided her with an independent income.

A year before, she'd been unemployed and living off her small savings, shuttling between the homes of friends and worrying about how to support her parents and five younger siblings. It was a terrible time. Monye came to her aid when all seemed hopeless. They'd met up again at a party given by a mutual friend. All night, Monye danced only with her; when he held her close, his body told her what he wanted. Barely a month after their reunion, he asked her to move in with him. He vowed his love and promised to marry her when he had enough money to support a family.

And now, with only minutes to spare, Monye boarded the bus and looked down the aisle. He spotted Uloma, walked up to her, and pointed to the seat beside her. 'Excuse me – is this taken?'

Uloma indicated the bag resting there and shrugged her shoulders. She gestured in the direction of a vacant window seat farther down the aisle.

Monye smiled. 'Madam, please, I would prefer sitting by the aisle.'

Uloma sighed and moved her bag of snacks. She exaggerated her annoyance, hoping that the other passengers wouldn't suspect she and Monye knew each other.

A few minutes later the driver climbed into his seat and revved the engine. A volley of gunshots punctuated the air. The security officer boarded the bus and strode down the aisle. He stumbled on a red-and-blue GHANA MUST GO bag and poked it with the barrel of his gun. 'Madam, move dis ting,' he ordered its owner. The woman spread her feet and squeezed the bag between them.

Uloma tugged at Monye's arm. She bent down, fiddled with the duffel, and whispered, 'What took you so long?'

Monye looked over the seat in front of him and said, 'Okwudili called.'

Uloma couldn't match the name with a face. Monye had many friends, but they came to the house late in the evenings, and she never saw them. She prepared the fried meat and pepper soup he requested for their entertainment, but he did the serving. He insisted that she stay in the bedroom whenever his friends visited. While she waited for them to leave, bits of their conversation filtered through to her. Arguments often broke out. Sometimes she picked up a word or two from an angry raised voice, but most of the time she dozed, the sound of garbled voices lulling her into a fitful sleep until Monye came to bed.

'What did he want?' Uloma asked.

Monye pressed a finger to his lips and jerked his thumb toward the aisle.

The security officer stood beside their row. Uloma bent her head and looked at him out of the corner of her eye.

The officer tapped Monye on the shoulder. 'You know dis woman?'

Monye shook his head.

'De way you dey lean to am, e be say like you wan know am.'

Monye grinned. 'Ah-ah, officer, no be like dat. De bag wey im keep for under, I just dey move am small make my leg fit.'

'Anyway my man, make you no touch am. Na me wey get dis lady.' The officer blinked at Uloma, pursed his lips, and laughed. Monye joined in.

Still chuckling, the officer walked off and continued his inspection of the bus. On his way back he stopped beside Uloma and Monye, slung his automatic over his shoulder, and spread his arms wide. The odor of his body wafted over them. Uloma looked at the dark sweat rings spreading from under his sleeves and held her breath.

'My people, Aba–Onitsha direct!' the officer declared.

'What of Lagos?' a voice from the back of the bus queried.

'Wetin, my friend? I never finish.' The officer cleared his throat and announced, 'Aba–Onitsha–Lagos direct!'

Laughter filled the bus.

The driver revved the engine and tooted the horn. The bus jerked forward, and the officer steadied himself against Monye's seat. Somehow he managed to push his face next to Uloma's. His lips brushed against her forehead.

'Don't touch me!' Uloma flung her hand in his face.

The officer backed away and looked at her with mock alarm. 'Madam, de madam. No be me wey do am.' He held both palms up, straightened himself, and called out, 'Draiva, softly oh! Dis bus don make me do romance.' The officer chuckled and looked around.

A few passengers applauded.

Tears welled up in Uloma's eyes, and she dabbed them with a tissue. All these people cared about was being entertained. It didn't matter at whose expense. Monye's elbow jabbed her waist, and she wiped her eyes. She couldn't understand why he allowed her to be humiliated, and why he even joined in making fun of her.

The horn sounded again, a grinding of gears set the wheels going, and the Landjet lumbered out of the station. Monye sat back in his seat and flipped through a magazine. Uloma felt a stroke on her thigh. Monye's fingers circled and lifted the hem of her wrappa. She wanted him to comfort her, not this. She squeezed her eyes shut against the tears she felt returning.

'Ulo, don't cry now,' Monye whispered, and stroked her thigh again.

On the highway, wind rushed through the windows. The bus hummed with conversations. Several passengers dozed. But Uloma was unable to sleep. She leaned against the window and watched the blue of the sky deepen into indigo.

Halfway to Onitsha a voice rang out from the back of the bus: 'Brothers, sisters, let us pray.' An itinerant peddler stood in the aisle. He wore a knee-length patchwork jacket of black, red, and white triangles over a pair of baggy white pants. Holding up a worn Bible, he executed the sign of the cross and said, 'in the name of Jesus, Jehovah, and all the saints, Professor Bede Nsofor is my name.' When no one responded, the professor strode down the aisle, turned halfway, glared at the people before him, and said, 'repent, brothers and sisters, for the devil is among us tonight.'

Conversation in the bus stalled. Passengers craned their necks and looked at one another, exchanging glances. The unacknowledged tension that had been suppressed in the daylight darted from face to face. Uloma looked out uneasily at the darkening horizon. In an hour, after they passed Asaba, the worst part of the journey would begin. Vague forms flashed by her window while the bus careered over the road, slowing only at bad stretches, when it was forced to carefully navigate the pothole-riddled terrain.

Professor Bede jumped forward and launched into a lengthy prayer. A chorus of voices rose in protest and urged him to hasten to his mission. He responded by waving a tube of toothpaste in the air. Walking back up the aisle, he called out, 'special from India, with full protection from de condition of bad breath, odawise known as halitosis. N'only hundred naira for one.' He did a brisk business, then retired to his seat.

'Onitsha-Onitsha,' the conductor announced.

The Landjet stopped behind another bus that was parked by the roadside. Within minutes two more buses arrived and pulled up on the opposite side of the road. Beyond them a motor park – devoid of vehicles – bustled with the trade of a night market. Flames flickered atop the wicks of oil lamps and illuminated the faces of patrons seated at tables in makeshift restaurants. Along the outer perimeter of the low wall encircling the park, women sat behind large pans balanced over glowing coals, tending to balls of akara bobbing in hot oil. The aroma of the frying bean cakes permeated the bus as windows opened and passengers called down to make purchases. Here and there, between the akara sellers, children were visible, hovering over grills to tend roast corn and ube. Uloma's mouth watered. Roast ube, with its soft, buttery green flesh, was one of her favorite foods.

Fifteen minutes later engines revved and the convoy moved off. It crossed the Niger Bridge in a slow procession. In Asaba a twisted line of backed-up traffic blocked the road. The head-on collision of two vehicles obstructed one lane. A lorry lay on its side, baskets of tomatoes scattered around it, and the wooden frame of its carriage perched precariously over a small car.

The Landjet driver maneuvered around the accident site, half the bus's wheels on the road and half on the shoulder. The bus tilted, wheels grinding in the sandy soil. It circumvented broken glass on the bloodstained tarmac, and a hush fell over the passengers. Two bodies covered with wrappas lay in the road. An upturned palm stuck out from one, a twisted foot from the other.

Away from the obstruction the driver accelerated. Uloma stared into the night sky. She gazed at her reflection, took her rosary from her handbag, and fingered its beads. She draped her second wrappa around her shoulders and settled back in her seat.

The snores of sleeping passengers and an occasional whispered conversation rippled in the dark cabin as the bus sped through a desolate landscape on its way to Benin City. Uloma feared this part of the journey most. From now until the Umunede rest stop, only bush and the silhouettes of roadside buildings would be visible.

Monye slipped his hand under her inner wrappa. He lifted the armrest between them and placed Uloma's hand on his crotch. She leaned her head on his shoulder, and her fingers worked as he demanded. The heat of Monye's arousal excited her, and she felt herself swelling. But after she satisfied him, Monye turned away and fell asleep.

Uloma woke to the sound of gunshots. She reached for Monye, but he shrugged her off. Explosions rent the air. The driver stepped on the brake, and the Landjet swayed from side to side. When the bus swerved off the road and stopped, panicked cries of 'Wetin happen?' and 'A beg oh!' came from all over.

'Make all of una remain in your seats,' the officer demanded. He opened the window beside him and fired shots into the bush.

Incoherent prayers rolled through the bus. Sobs broke from several women; they wailed and called on God to protect them. No one knew for sure what had happened, but they all suspected armed robbers.

Someone banged on the front of the bus. The driver cowered in his seat.

'Stop or I shoot,' the officer said, and aimed his gun at the door.

'No shoot. Na Sergeant Okoye from first bus,' a voice replied.

On hearing this, the driver opened the door, and the security detail from the convoy's lead bus entered.

The aisle lights came on.

Blinking at the faces before him, the man said, 'Armed robber dey for operation. First bus tire don blow. Driver say make I bring two strong men, make dem help remove barrier for road.' The staccato beat of his voice reverberated through the bus.

A breathy silence fell over the Landjet. No male passengers stirred from their seats. The security officer stepped up to the rows nearest him and hustled two men down the steps.

Uloma crossed herself, thankful that Monye had not been chosen. She looked out the window. From all sides the bush closed in on them. Night noises were magnified, echoing strangely. A branch cracked; another answered. Leaves swished in the wind, chattering to one another.

Goosebumps rose on Uloma's arms, and she shivered.

When several minutes had passed without any sign of the men who'd left the bus, the security officer and the driver disembarked. The beams of their flashlights flitted across the road and disappeared.

Monye grabbed the duffel strap and pulled the bag from under Uloma's feet.

He pushed her things aside and pried the bottom of the bag loose. A pistol lay among the packets of money. Uloma's eyes widened. Monye put a finger to his lips and slipped the gun into his pocket.

Gunshots broke out around the bus. Monye stood, and Uloma clawed at him. He shoved her back into her seat and rushed toward the front of the bus. As he left, shots rang out.

'Monye, oh,' Uloma wailed in a hoarse whisper.

Fists banged on the front door. An armed man entered the bus; within seconds another joined him. Both wore masks, leaving only their eyes and mouths visible. They waved their weapons in the air and called out, 'all rise.' They went down the aisle, moving swiftly, stopping at each row to demand cash and valuables. Uloma watched her fellow passengers mutely remove watches and jewelry.

One of the robbers stood before Uloma. Urine trickled down her leg. He held his hand out. She loosened her watch and slid the rings off her fingers. She gave up her handbag. The robber pointed to the duffel. She reached for it. The muzzle of his gun rested at her temple; the raised veins on his hand and trigger finger pulsed beside her face. She rose in a panic, lost her balance, and fell back against the seat.

In the row across from her the other robber turned. Uloma's eyes locked with his. 'Monye,' she whispered in disbelief at what she saw – the scar over the man's left eyebrow.

The man ignored her, but his companion pulled him back. 'Okoro, you know dis woman?'

The robber Okoro shook his head.

Looking from Okoro back to Uloma, the robber beside her said, 'E be say like she reconize you.'

Okoro turned away. 'No be me wey im call, na Monye. You fit hear the woman.'

'I fit, botu we no fit take chance,' the other robber replied. He turned to Uloma. 'Oya, madam, out!'

'Please, sir,' Uloma stammered. She stared at the man's face, mesmerized by his red eyes. Her feet refused to carry her, and the robber pulled her into the aisle.

Okoro spoke: 'Jaja, stop now, make we continue operation. Time for enjoyment still dey.'

Jaja spat and said, 'You talk true.' He drew Uloma to him, ground against her, and announced, 'Jaja go poke tonite.' He released her, cupped a palm over his crotch, and hitched his trousers up.

Okoro grinned, slapped Jaja on the back, and whispered something. The two of them continued their work down the bus.

Uloma sat down. Doubts filled her. That man – he sounded nothing like Monye. There was no way he could be Monye. She had heard the shots when they killed him. A sob rose in her throat.

On their way back to the front of the bus the robbers pulled Uloma from her seat and shoved her ahead of them. All down the aisle her fellow passengers averted their eyes. She descended the steps and stumbled to the ground, pushed by the robber Jaja.

Moonlight illuminated the road. The bodies of the driver and the security officer lay to one side. Uloma rose to her feet and gravitated toward a third, facedown in the dirt. Jaja grabbed her and pushed her across the road. Okoro followed.

The night's silence amplified bursts of gunfire from the operations going on behind them. With each shot and cry Uloma's chest felt close to bursting. They trekked on; the tarmac stretched far beyond them. Some distance past the last bus in the convoy, swaths of overgrown elephant grass leaned over the road. Uloma waited fearfully for the order to stop. It never came.

At a small clearing laughter broke out. Uloma started. A man emerged from behind a tree and stuffed his penis back into his trousers. The robber Jaja cackled and circled Uloma's waist with his arm. He pulled her to him and humped against her.

'Space dey there?' Jaja asked.

'Eh, but Moses dey for am now,' the man in the clearing replied. He noticed Uloma's gaze on his open zipper and pushed his hips at her.

Uloma struggled in Jaja's arms, and the men laughed.

A muffled moan came from the bushes. It was followed by a shot.

'E don tire,' the man standing before them said, by way of explanation.

Uloma's bowels churned. Please, God, she prayed to herself, let them kill me. She jerked her elbows into Jaja's ribs, twisted out of his grasp, and turned to run. Okoro grabbed her.

Jaja came up to Uloma and slapped her face. He spat, wiped his mouth, and said, 'I go show you today.'

Hustling her to a tree beyond the clearing, he pushed Uloma to the ground and stripped her. He inspected the money in her apron and bra. When he wrenched off her panties, Uloma tried to cover herself, and Jaja giggled uncontrollably. He shoved himself into her and collapsed. He rose and pumped into her again. At the end, when he squeezed her breasts and pinched her nipples, she groaned.

As he stood up, Jaja kicked her and said, 'Okoro, finish am, I go return small time.'

Okoro bent over Uloma, peered into her face, and whispered, 'Ulo.'

Uloma flinched. Only Monye called her that. She gazed into the eyes that met hers, confused now. 'Monye,' she murmured.

The man hesitated. A branch snapped. Figures converged. They egged Okoro on, telling him to hurry so they could take their turns.

Ada Udechukwu was born in Enugu, Nigeria. Ada holds an MFA in Creative Writing and Literature from Bennington College, USA and has a BA in English and Literature from the University of Nigeria. She is the author of *Woman, Me*, a collection of poems and drawings. Her fiction has appeared in *The Atlantic Monthly* and *Callaloo*. Her drawings, paintings and textiles have been exhibited in Nigeria and the United States, most notably in *The Poetics of Line: Seven Artists of the Nsukka Group* (1997), National Museum of African Art, Smithsonian Institution, Washington, DC.

Celtel Caine Prize African Writers'
Workshop Stories 2008

Night Commuter

Monica Arac de Nyeko

I DO NOT WANT you to think that things have always been like this. Things have not always been like this. Things used to be safe. We used to remain home with our parents. That time is gone. Gone like my Baba. My Baba who used to sing *feel it hot hot hot* with high laughter as he rode on his Honda motorcycle. Baba was a skinny, tall man with the best moustache ever. I call it best because no one in Mucwini had a moustache as thick and as long as his. Many people said Baba did not look like the kind of person who should have such a moustache. They said it made him look old. But how could Baba be Baba without his moustache?

Anyway, Baba loved his Honda as much as he loved me. When he sat on it, it was like he was getting ready to fly. Baba's Honda was one of the only three in Mucwini. Baba, being in charge of the immunization campaigns for the sub-counties within and around Mucwini, got the Honda to help his work of monitoring health centres in the more distant sub-counties. It took Baba only a week to learn how to ride it. In the beginning when he had just started riding it, the Honda got all of us children excited. After we had seen it around for six months, it became like a small stain on the wall. No one except Ma and me noticed it.

Baba's Honda must have been like his tail. He went with it everywhere. He rode it to church, to distant sub-country meetings and to the bar at Mucwini centre. In his big grey jacket, Baba always rode his Honda at full speed. The Honda was blue and black. It was not as big as a dudu car, but it made the biggest vum vuuum vuuuuuuum sound I had ever heard. The first time I heard it, I almost wet my pants. I was right behind it and Baba had not warned me. When he saw the way I was startled, Baba laughed a long hearty laugh that made me feel very stupid.

'Don't run away now. Don't run away.' He said holding me back. 'This thing is not like a woman. It does not bite. Eh.' He laughed again. 'It does not cry and it does not quarrel,' he added more seriously. Well if you know my Baba at all then you will know that he said these things only when Ma was not there. When she was there, he said the Honda was as beautiful as she was and that its fuel

73

consumption was as good as Ma's beer intake.

My fascination with Baba's Honda I must say was like a bad cough. It did not go away. In the night when I lay in bed I thought about it. I could almost touch its fine blue shine. I could almost smell the scent of petrol it left on its tail just as it sped off. When Baba went to work in the morning, I always made sure I was awake. If I was lucky, I got a ride on it to school. But the best, bestest part of Baba's Honda, was in the evening. Every evening, when Baba returned home, with no worry about immunized babies on his mind, he took me for a ride on it around Mucwini. As soon as Baba sat me down on the Honda, he did something and there came the vum vuuum vuuuuuuum sound. Soon after, the smoke went helter-skelter out of the exhaust and me and my Baba flew away on the tarmac road down the hill. If I know Mucwini now as well as I do, if I know now the charred brown and spotted green of its landscape, it is because I saw it all behind Baba's Honda. Mucwini on the Honda was not just Mucwini. It was moving trees, shifting hills and brown houses so quick, so beautiful. On the Honda, the church at Wii Gweng was a large stone structure. In the distance it looked unshakable like a strong memory. On the Honda, the Aringa River was more white than green. At full speed, you caught the true sandy smell of its belly. You did not catch the stench of pupu and susu rising off the banks. And so, that is how it was every evening for me and Baba. It was always a boastful bare-chested me in my dirty khaki shorts with the holes showing my pitiful behind and Baba laughing or singing *feel it hot hot hot*.

Now, if the speed at which Baba rode the Honda down the tarred hill made me feel a mixture of fear and excitement, all Ma felt was anxiety. Ma hated the Honda as much as she hated burnt meat. In the beginning Baba laughed at her because he thought she would give up pestering him about it. If there was going to be any giving up on anyone's part, it was not going to be on Ma's. She had simply gotten tired of the Honda, while Baba was still laughing and thinking Ma was fooling around. She demanded that if he still wanted to keep riding it, then he must stop taking me along. After much repetition, Baba did stop taking me with him. You see, if Ma demanded something hard enough from Baba, he always gave it to her. He always did it. That is just the way things were. He had after all named her after the calypso song of their days, 'oh my commanding wife…'

Yes, Baba always did what Ma wanted, but he never did buy that helmet as Ma had demanded. You see, Ma was a policewoman before she got married and moved to live with Baba in Mucwini. In her days, I hear she was as hot as a charcoal stove. A mere glance at her was enough to turn your pants into flames, Baba said. When she marched on parade in her khaki police uniform and those stiff smelly boots they made them wear, I hear she made the officers swallow gulps of saliva with longing written all over their faces. But, however much they wanted her, they did not get to even as much as touch her hand. It was my Baba who got that honour. I am told that, the day they met, Baba had come to apply for the position of a junior medical trainee at the police barracks health facility in Naguru. Baba, in his stiff bell bottoms and big Afro, did not get the job he had applied for, but he got Ma. A year after they met, they married and moved to Kitgum, and then to Mucwini where jobs were abundant and the district gave bonuses as big as Hondas to ease the hardship of rural health work. But Mucwini was too far from Kampala. Ma's parents were not happy about her giving up the city and its excitements for Baba. In the beginning Ma reasoned with them. After I was born, she told them, they would be able to see me frequently even if I was far away. That was not enough for my grandparents. They insisted she reconsider taking her job back. Ma did not want to reconsider anything. All she wanted was to speak her mind. This is why her fire mouth jumped into action. Ma told her parents to stop making empty noises like a bunch of senile dogs. She told them they should stop bickering about her marriage like they are the ones going to live it. She told her parents (straight and proper) that if Baba was going to end up as far as Sudan with the Dinkas, she would follow him there. Now, like you probably already know, Baba did not end up in Sudan. My Baba ended up in Mucwini with a 1985 Honda CB400 that came without a helmet.

'You need to buy that helmet. You need to.' Ma said to Baba the first time he rode home on the Honda. She continued to say this to him time and time again. Whenever she talked about the helmet, the policewoman in Ma came into her voice. It turned her voice into something worse than an angry sow.

'That is a waste of money!' Baba said.

Now, despite the little squabbles they sometimes got into, my parents never did get into serious fights. If they did, it was when I was not around. I liked to boast about this at school. I told the children that my father did not shout at Ma and he did not whip me. I told them that even when I took home a bad report card, he talked to me in a kind but serious voice.

'You have to put more effort into numbers and show this math teacher you are a man. Okay?'

'Yes,' I said and asked him if he would take me on a ride on the Honda.

'Not today. Not today.' Baba said and left home.

That evening, the evening that Baba refused to take me for a ride, a man came home. He told Ma that Baba had fallen off his Honda. 'There was no chance he could have made it,' he said. I was ten.

'It is a waste of money, huh?' Ma said and went inside the house. Ma asked Baba the same question throughout the time the mourners started arriving home for the funeral. During the funeral ceremony people got tired of telling Ma to stop talking to Baba like he was alive. They told her to start being strong for me. I sat under the mango tree and watched Ma. She was not crying. When they brought Baba home that night, the women rolled in the red sand. They cried for my Baba like he was the district head. 'Why did you not bid us farewell? Why did you die so soon? Why why why?'

'It is a waste of money, huh?' Ma said. She did not stop saying that. She did not cry. When the funeral was over, after everyone who had come to mourn my Baba left, they told Ma that time heals these things. They told her that she should take heart and trust in the Lord. 'He holds the future and He alone knows why He took your husband away.' Then they hugged Ma hard. They looked into her eyes. They promised her she would be okay. But Ma was not okay. She stared at the Honda at the spot it was resting by the mango tree in the compound for several days. Tired of seeing the thing there, Ma took our five litre paraffin jerry can. She poured paraffin over it. She set it on fire. The day after she burnt the Honda, Ma held me by my shoulders.

'Me and you are going to be fine. You hear me?' she said. I nodded my head. I looked Ma straight in the eyes to make her know that I had heard her and that I truly meant it. But, like you will learn later, even if Ma said we were going to be fine, we were not going to be fine. We could not. The war had started.

I remember now how we knew the war had really really started. The radio said there were fighters hiding in the lush vegetation. They said it just like that – there are fighters hiding in the lush vegetation. Ma, my mother, the tall woman with loss still in her eyes stood with the radio in one hand. She had wrapped a lesu around her waist. The purple fabric clumped her hips and the knot on her waist looked too tight. Ma put the radio down on the veranda where she was seated. She slapped her thighs twice then she shifted her small hands to her face. The smell of firewood was still in her plaited hair. I could smell it from where I stood. I was just from school. In my blue polyester shirt, khaki shorts and bare feet I stood there. I held four books under my arm and just stood there. I watched Ma. I heard her beat her lips. Ma did not speak immediately, when she did, it was only to lament. It was only to say 'madoo'.

* * *

It is now two years and three months since Baba died. It is two years and three months since Ma stood under the mango tree to tell me we shall be okay. Two years and three months since the war started. When it had just begun, people talked about it like it would end tomorrow. They said the fighters would get tired. We would all go back to school. But month after month, the fighters have not gotten tired. We have not gone back to school. The radio has not stopped broadcasting bulletins about the war. Ma has not stopped listening to the news on her veranda.

And now, everyday all Ma does is sit on her veranda. Ma gets up to leave only late in the evening when the sun's gaze is almost gone. When she lifts herself up from her spot, she goes inside the house. She takes out her hoe. Ma heads to her cassava garden. By getting her hoe from the kitchen and going to the garden late every evening like that, Ma refuses to acknowledge the arrival of the night. She refuses to believe the day has ended. She refuses to see the darkness.

Always, when Ma makes her way to the garden, I stand there and watch her. I stand there and watch her grow smaller and smaller until she is completely one with the grass. When she is gone, I get inside the house. I take my blanket out. I join the other children who go to town every day to sleep there. You see, ever since the fighters started taking children away from their homes to teach them how to use guns and be *kadogos*, all of us children now go to town. Kitgum town is fourteen miles away on foot. The fighters cannot get us. Soldiers guard it with machine guns.

In town, every evening when we arrive, we head straight to our veranda. Children from different areas have taken up different verandas. Me and the boys and girls from Mucwini have the veranda of Savannah Restaurant to ourselves. We did not get it by accident. We stoned, pinched and beat up the other Ayul boys. They were too few and could not stand up against us in a real fight. We were men. Real men.

As you probably already know, Kitgum is a small town. This means there are not so many verandas for all of us. The ones that are there are for the strongest gangs like us. Because there are not enough verandas for all the children to sleep in, the people who work for some children's organizations have set up blue tents in the football fields in Y Y Okot Memorial College. This is where the other children sleep. I hate it there. The children there are too many and they all have lice and they stink of susu. They come with bedbugs in their blankets and these bedbugs are so hard to get rid of. But that is not why the blue tents are bad. The truth is that the tent camp is not exactly in town so even if the fighters have never come to fetch children from there, they could come one day. I hear one day a boy made a frightened sound in his dream in the biggest tent. That boy slept at the tent entrance and everyone imagined he was giving them a signal to run because the fighters had finally come. There were no fighters that day, there was only a stampede and many little children who would not be seeing their Mamas again.

Anyway, our veranda is not like that. It is in the centre of town and for us there is no worry at all. It is also more fun. We have no rules like the other tent children.

77

We can tell stories up to late in the night and laugh as loud as we want. Savannah Restaurant closes early so the owner of the veranda does not hush us all the time. He is a nice man anyway except that his stomach makes him look pregnant and he talks like he has burning porridge in his mouth. He calls us 'my little rats'. Don't ask me to explain what he means. I do not know why and none of us looks like a rat.

This man, the owner of the shop, we call him Ninja. He is our Ninja but he is also as dark as the real Ninjas. Ninja, our Ninja I mean, does not smack us like the owners of the other verandas. All he asks of us is to leave the veranda clean and not to do any susu or pupu in the gutters in front of his restaurant. Whenever he gives these instructions, he talks to Ofwono. Well Ofwono is not our leader but because he is the biggest, the baddest and loudest everyone thinks he is the leader. For a nickname he took on the name of Ofwono: the tallest man in Uganda. Maybe that is why everyone thinks he is a leader and real giant.

To be honest with you, I do not like Ofwono very much. I am not sure many of the boys like him either. He stinks like toilet and his teeth look like rotting corn. But the girls among us must be blind. They like him as much as they like sugarcane and they do not see these things about him. Every night when Ofwono tells us stories, the girls sit next to him. They like to hear him tell some of his exaggerated stories. His most famous is the restaurant one. He likes to repeat it every time even if we have all heard it like a million times. This is how the story goes: one day, Ofwono went to a restaurant and met some white man having lunch. The white man was eating a strawberry and vanilla ice cream. Ofwono was eating chicken. Because he enjoys chicken so much Ofwono was consuming even the bones. The white man looked at Ofwono and said, 'what do dogs in Kitgum eat if you eat all the chicken bones?' Ofwono turned to him and said ice cream.

After this particular restaurant story, the girls on the veranda always get very excited.

'Give us more. Give us more,' they say. When the girls talk like that, Ofwono starts to say that he is tired of them. He says they are like houseflies. When he is in those moods he comes over to us the boys. He starts to give us tips on how to seduce girls and how to do bad manners with them. He also likes to give us biology lessons because he calls us ignorant nincompoops. His favourite biology lesson is the one about where babies come from. The first time he told it to us, I looked at him. I was so confused. I got up from under my blanket.

'Do you mean to say they come from the umbilical cord?' I said to him.

'They are not from the umbilical cord, you green locust!' He said. 'They come from somewhere in a woman. Every woman has that thing, your mother too!'

I looked at him. He wanted me to ask him more questions. I did not but he started laughing out loud anyway. Ofwono slapped my back so hard I nearly bit my tongue. I did not laugh with him. But he was not giving up.

'Ask me and I will tell you all about these adult things,' he said.

I did not ask him and because I refused to, he slapped me twice. To tell you the truth, I wanted to be brave with Ofwono this time. I wanted to tell him he was a bad person and that is why his children would inherit his bad teeth. But I did not. I just turned my back from him and curled up in the warmth of the blanket. I started to think of Ma. And that night like all nights, I dreamt of her. But this time, unlike the other nights, there was Baba in my dream too. He was in the middle of our compound in his 1985 Honda CB400. He was taking me for a ride. Baba had a blue helmet. I had a blue helmet too. Ma was sitting on the veranda when we sped off. She was not afraid. I was not afraid. There was no Ofwono. There were no fighters. There was no war.

Monica Arac de Nyeko is a Ugandan writer of fiction. She studied at Makerere University and the University of Groningen. In 2007, she won the Caine Prize for the story *Jambula Tree*.

Lost

Ellen Banda-Aaku

THE SECOND ORCHESTRATED BLOW to the door wasn't necessary; it flew off its hinges with the first. The policeman who swung expecting to strike wood, cut through the air and stumbled through the doorway. His fellow officers tumbled in close behind.

Tobias's scream was drowned by the door's thunderous tumble. It crashed beside him, an axe caught in its splintered wood, like a man hacked in the back. The blinding light from the police torches filled the small living room, humbled the yellow flame that burnt off a string in a jar of paraffin.

Shock hit Tobias in the stomach. It stirred, the smell and taste of the maize corn he had eaten earlier surfaced. He swallowed. Trouble! His father was in trouble. Tobias knew full well that when the police raided a house in Chilenge, they were looking for freedom activists or criminals. His father wasn't involved in the struggle for independence. Tangled in his orange and brown checked blanket, he scuffled backwards on his bottom, out of their way. Wide-eyed, he hunched against the wall, cornered, cradling his folded knees.

He counted seven of them, white men in starched khaki, with matching long ribbed socks that came to within an inch of the hem of their shorts. They moved fast. One carried the door outside; another dropped to his knees, and started to roll the plastic mat off the floor. The shortest of them, the one who looked as if he had a football stuck under his short sleeved shirt, stormed up to an inner door and kicked it open.

'Everyone get up and stand aside!'

Tangu, Tobias's baby sister, burst into a high-pitched wail.

Tobias peered from behind a chair and watched, while his father, in a vest and pyjama trousers, was led from his room. The white handkerchief he tied over his greased hair every night, sat on his head at an angle.

'Let me dress, *napapata*, please let me dress!' Tobias heard his mother's pleas. She stepped out of her bedroom, a *chitenge* tied around her waist, her breasts hanging free. The police officer standing nearest to her stepped back, startled. He waved her away and she disappeared back into the room.

'We have been informed that you are in possession of goods that do not belong to you.' The police officer grinned into Tobias's father's blank face. The officer turned to the bedroom and shouted, 'Get dressed and get out!' He waved his officers into the room.

Tobias's mother emerged again, her chitenge slung over her shoulder. She had pulled a skirt over a pink nightdress, and Tangu was tied to her back with a bath towel.

A policeman pulled out a sharp blade and rammed it into the brown plastic sofa. Tobias stifled his gasp. Two other officers joined in. They sliced chairs open, dug their hands into the openings, and ripped out the white foam stuffing the way Tobias had seen his mother pull intestines out of a chicken. A loud slashing came from the bedroom. Tobias grimaced at the thought of his parents' new mattress, its plastic wrapper still intact, being disembowelled. His mother kept the wrapper on it to prevent Tangu's yellow urine stains.

'It's cold. Take this.' Tobias's mother held her chitenge out to him. He stayed in his corner, scared. His mother surprised him. Her pitch was unusually low and calm. No trace of the fierceness she unleashed on her husband when he wobbled home on his bicycle, slurring a Jim Reeves song, long after the last candle in the neighbourhood had been blown out. Now, gently bouncing up and down, she lulled Tangu, while she surveyed the chaos. She tiptoed politely round the men who were ravaging her home, as if they were visiting in-laws.

A fifty kilogram sack of maize meal was dragged from the kitchen across the small veranda and shaken out onto the living room floor. The white mountain of flour was then flattened with a shovel. Then they dragged in a sack of charcoal and overturned it onto the floor. A blackish grey cloud of dust filled the room as they scattered the heap of coal.

'We know it's somewhere in this house. Just keep looking! Search everywhere!' The fat policeman spurred his officers on.

Sounds of destruction filled Tobias's head. Ripping fabric, rapping knuckles, thumping of fists on walls and floors. Doors slamming, tables and chairs crashing to the floor. A table toppled and Tobias's father's face smiled up at him from the floor through shattered glass and splinters from a wooden picture frame. The black and white image marked with a print of a police boot.

From the corner of his eye Tobias watched his father standing a few paces away. He stood still, statue-like, with his head cocked one side as if listening out for a sound in the distance. He gave the impression the sound he listened for was more important than watching the destruction of the hard work he put into his journeys. Journeys through the bush, bypassing border posts, and into the Katanga mines of Congo.

'Tobias!' His mother called him again. This time he struggled to his feet, cupped both his hands over the front of his navy underpants. He was relieved; surprised he hadn't wet them. To reach his mother, Tobias climbed over a chair that lay on its side.

'You!' The officer pointed at Tobias's mother. 'Get out!' He nodded in the direction of Tobias's father. 'You stay here!'

Out on the veranda Tobias's mother wrapped her chitenge around his shoulders like a cloak. The cloth carried her scent; the intoxicating fume charcoal gives off before the blue flame turns yellow.

'It's cold,' his mother whispered dropping to her knees, her breath stale from sleep.

Tobias could make out figures around him, neighbours lurking just out of reach of the torch beam. Two Land Rovers, with Northern Rhodesia Police Service stencilled in white across the front, were parked on either side of the house. Tobias's mother pulled the edges of the cloth together and tied a knot at his neck.

'I'll tie it tight because it's cold.' She spoke to him but her eyes were on the policeman squatting by Tobias's father's bicycle, feeling his way along the tyres.

'You have to keep warm otherwise I'll have to take you back to the doctor.' Tobias looked up at her. What did she mean? He hadn't been to the doctor. His mother looked back.

'You don't want to go to the doctor again, do you?' she asked. Her eyes held his. She reached for his hand and placed it over the knot she had just tied. He felt a tight ball inside the knot. It was the size of an egg. Before he could react she palmed his cheek, the feel of her calloused skin against his, gentle, brief, unfamiliar.

She stood up. 'Keep warm. I don't want you to catch cold. Don't worry. Everything will be okay.'

Tobias's mouth suddenly felt dry.

'Tobias you'll be okay,' she said again and tuned away.

The police officer on the veranda tossed the bicycle aside and stood up. He peered into the dark then shouted.

'I know! Let's check in there!' He pointed at a small brick shack that stood away from the main house. 'Bring torches!' He ran towards it. Three officers emerged from the house and followed him. The short officer walked sideways through the narrow opening. A second officer, a torch in his hand, ducked and squeezed in behind him. Light spilled out of the gaps between the top of the brick wall and the tin roof, streaking the black night with rays of white.

'Bring more light! Bring more light!' More torches were lit. The policemen ran back and forth with sticks and torches. No one seemed to be watching Tobias. He stepped off the veranda slowly.

Holding the knot in his cloak tight, humming, his voice shaky, he walked away. Slowly, he walked alongside the house. Slower, he crossed the vegetable patch, trampled over the sweet potato leaves his mother cooked in groundnut sauce. His heart thumped in his chest, deafeningly in his ears. He took this path to school every day, but now he felt he was walking it for the first time. Tobias started running. Without his school canvas shoes, he felt the bite of the sharp stones in the gravel. The wind screamed in his face blowing away the icy tears it brought to his eyes. Although he couldn't see, he knew where he was going. Tobias was comforted, and for the first time grateful, that his skin was the hue of the night.

Tobias wove through the small houses built in uniform rows. All painted in white emulsion at the top and brown enamel at the bottom, the way the municipality stipulated. The houses huddled close. When a child sneezed in one house, a neighbour could be heard clapping their tongue against the top of their mouth. Chasing away the evil spirits.

When Tobias got to the undeveloped land behind the estate he slowed again. Grass whipped at his legs, his feet tangled in unruly roots and thorn shrubs, prickly and wet with dew. With every quick step he lifted his feet high off the ground; scared of the snakes he thought he heard rustling around his feet.

He burst through the shrubs and into the vegetable allotments. Groundnuts, pumpkins, maize, and sweet potatoes were grown. The earth along the path between the crops was smooth, stamped and moulded by the feet of the women who worked their fields. It soothed Tobias's feet. He dropped to his knees exhausted. Someone had once told him that there weren't any snakes in the allotment because they didn't like to be disturbed.

He unclenched his fist. He had run the whole way with his hand clamped over the knot in his cloth. He started to untie it with shaky hands. Then he stopped. His mother hadn't told him to open it. Her eyes had pleaded with him to take it away. He didn't know whether he was supposed to hide it, or throw it away.

Tobias stood up. He knew that whatever he held in his hand was valuable. Or dangerous. Or even evil. Why else would police officers shine torches down the latrine? Only recently, when he turned nine, his mother said he was too old to use the bucket and he was forced to go inside the small shack with no windows. Tobias wondered what the police saw inside when they flashed their torches down the deep dark hole. It was a hole he tried hard not to look into because he couldn't stop thinking what would happen to him if he slipped. He imagined himself at the bottom of the pit surrounded by darkness. Sometimes when he was inside and he coughed, the echo of his cough came back to him through the hole.

The tall trees standing beyond the allotments had changed their mood. They moved angrily, their intertwined branches howled and rustled for space. No more the soothing breeze on a hot day. Sometimes after school Tobias and his classmates came to the trees to settle scores; test who was the strongest boy in the class. Teach someone a lesson for writing down the names of those who spoke Nyanja instead of English. Other times, he came with his friends, because they were certain to find three or four unsuspecting birds to catapult out of the trees.

Weighed down by fear, Tobias approached the nearest tree and crouched by it. He untied the knot. Inside was a cloth that felt as soft as Tangu's nappy. It was too dark to see its colour. It clinked and grated in his hand like a tiny pillow filled with stones. He pulled at its edges. It didn't tear open. He used his teeth. He gnawed at it a few times. It didn't tear. He gave up, dropped it and ran off. A few paces. Then he stopped. It was too near the allotments. What if someone found it? What if they opened it and somehow found out it belonged to his father?

Tobias didn't allow himself to imagine life without his father; he ran back and picked the bundle up. He had to hide it in a place where no one would find it. Behind the trees was a big open drain that carried the rain water away. In the rainy season the water gushed light brown, like milky tea. In the dry season, it trickled grey, like dirty bath water. And all year round, the rims of the drain were lined with thick green slime. Once Tobias and his friends had walked through the trees and reached the drain. The second time they went to play at the drain was the last time. Because Tobias's classmate Joe, the strongest swimmer in the school, had been washed away. Since then, the thought of the drain made Tobias feel cold and nauseous at the same time.

Now he considered the drain. Relieved, he reminded himself it was the dry season so there wasn't enough water to wash the little pillow away. And besides, even if it did wash away like Joe did, it could still be found like he was, lying stiff some miles away. At least that's what Tobias heard his mother say happened to Joe.

Tobias fidgeted with it. What was it worth? What plans did his father have for it? Would he buy the new gramophone he had been talking about? Or would he send Tobias to the bigger school near town? Tobias, for a passing second pictured a shiny metal trunk with brass hinges, filled with new uniforms, a blanket or two, and cans of corned beef and sweetened condensed milk. He saw himself standing beside the trunk in shiny black shoes and white socks.

The thought passed quickly, brushed away by the cold wind and a vision of his father in jail. Because that's where his father would go if the police ever found it. Tobias couldn't even start to imagine what would happen to him without his father. And what would his father do in jail? Who would starch his trousers, or iron his hair flat with a hot stone?

Tobias knelt and clawed at the earth a few times. His finger nails filled with soil but he couldn't dig into the ground. He stood up again and looked round. No place seemed safe enough to hide it. He had to think fast. The cold numbed his feet and his chest felt like a fire was burning inside it. He spun back and forth a few times, ended up in the same place; scared, confused, undecided.

Then from the distance the sound of a car engine reached him. He saw beams of light flash in the distance. The police were leaving. It was over. Tobias felt a wave of relief sweep over him, he also felt urine trickle warmly down his inner leg and sink into the soil. It was then, he decided.

* * *

'Here or there? Where Tobias? Where is it? Tobias's father asks.

It's three nights since the police search and Tobias is in the fields with his father and his uncle Yama.

'Leave the boy.' Uncle Yama waves his hands at his brother. Anger and frustration etched in both their faces. The two men are getting tired. The dark patches in the underarms of their shirts are getting bigger. They have been searching for hours. Lifting creepers off the ground, upturning stones. Raking the earth in small heaps of stones, loose leaves, soil and fallen fruits. Combing through the debris with their hands, the men search with the same diligence that the police officers searched their house.

'Are you sure we're in the right place?' Tobias's father glances at his wrist watch and then up at the sky. The black sky is slowly turning grey.

Tobias nods. He's combing through a crevice beside a root.

Both men wipe their faces with their handkerchiefs as they rummage through the field. They murmur to one another. Tobias knows they don't want him to hear what they are saying. But he knows. If they are seen out in the field, it will be obvious what they are looking for. They have to leave before people come out to tend to their allotments. They come as soon as the sun comes up.

'Okay, think again,' Tobias's father rests his elbow on the rake. 'Did you run up to here, or there?'

Tobias points to where they are standing.

'Talk boy, talk!' His father flings the rake to the ground.

'Easy on the boy.' Uncle Yama claps loose soil off his hands. 'We will find it.'

Tobias is hungry and scared. He knows his father is angry with him because they can't find the pillow of stones. They are all referring to it as 'it'. As if none of them know what 'it' is. Or if they do, as if they are too scared to admit they know.

Uncle Yama is wrong. They don't find it. When the sky turns a milky grey they head home. Balancing a rake, a slash, and a hoe on his shoulder, Tobias trails behind his father and Uncle Yama. His father is a head taller than balding Uncle Yama. Both are wearing black trousers and their shoes are covered in dust. They are arguing; their voices are low and gruff; their shirts stick to their backs in wet patches. The neighbourhood is waking up. Smoke rises lazily from firewood, white nappies hang on a washing line, chickens are out roaming.

They find Tobias's mother outside, kneeling beside a chair. She's sewing foam back into a chair.

'Your son can't find it!' Tobias' father says. He storms past her and into the house. Tobias knows that if the police hadn't removed the door, his father would have slammed it.

'We didn't find it.' Uncle Yama sinks onto a stool on the veranda.

Tobias stands away from them.

'Put the tools down, and take a bath,' his mother says to him. 'Porridge will be ready soon.'

Tobias puts the tools down and walks towards the shack.

The room doesn't seem as dark or as cold as that night. He places his hand against the wall to support himself and squats next to the hole. He peers inside it; just as he had done the night he returned from the field and snuck in unnoticed.

Darkness stares back at him.

'Tobias!' He hears his mother call.

'Yes ma!' His voice echoes through the walls. Tobias smiles into the black hole.

It's gone for good. And his Tata is going nowhere. Tobias has made sure of that.

Ellen Banda-Aaku is Zambian, born in the UK. Her first book, *Wandi's Little Voice*, won the 2004 Macmillan Writers' Prize for Africa, New Children's Writer Award. She sat on the judging panel for the 2006 Macmillan Writers' Prize for Africa competition. In 2007 she won the Commonwealth Short Story Competition for her story, '*Sozi's Box*.' She lived and worked in Zambia, the UK, and Ghana before moving to South Africa where she is currently studying for an MA in Creative Writing at the University of Cape Town.

Where You Came From

Karen Hurt

POLICE OFFICER SANDRA VAN Wyk strides into her office. Her dark blue cap is pulled low over her eyes. A bunch of flowers, as always after a night like the one they had last night, stands brightly in a jar in the middle of her desk. She drops her handbag next to it. The jar rocks slightly. She frowns at the flowers. Opening the top drawer, she picks up a large pair of scissors. She pauses for a moment. Charmaine, her junior officer, is watching her.

Sandra draws a flower out of the bunch by its stem, and snips its head off. She watches it drop into the bin. Her pace increases. Pulling and snipping. Yellow, orange, red, yellow, red, orange. They make dull thuds in the metal bin, each one like a final heartbeat.

'I'll make you a cup of tea,' says Charmaine nervously. She goes to the office door and closes it and then switches the kettle on. She's uncertain what to do, or say. Sandra has never done this with the flowers before. It is not a pattern Charmaine is used to. There are just green stems left in Sandra's clenched hand. She dumps the scissors on the top file in her neat in-tray. Drops of water slide off the metal blades and soak into the file, turning the words blotchy. She bends the stems and twists them until each one is broken. She tosses the lot into the bin, and smiles. It is a strange smile; one that she hasn't worn before.

Charmaine holds out a mug of tea to Sandra. Sandra looks at the mug but does not take it. The mug has 'We catch the criminals' printed on it, in confident lettering. A laugh bursts from her throat.

'*Ja*, and some of us live with them,' she mutters.

Charmaine blinks. 'I'll leave your tea on the desk then,' she says. Sandra does not seem to hear.

She grabs her handbag and rummages in it. She pulls out a pot of eye gel and walks over to the small mirror on the wall where she examines her face. Her fingers dab – jab – gel around her puffy eyes. She scrutinizes her face for physical signs of what happened last night. She stands there for a moment, just looking.

Charmaine's concerned eyes are there in the corner of the mirror. Sandra has never spoken to her about these things. But Charmaine is no fool. She is in on the station's gossip.

Returning to her desk, Sandra throws the gel into her handbag and takes out her sunglasses. She puts them on. She sits down, and stands up. It is as if every cell in her body has an electric current vibrating within it. Her boots squeak every time she turns, marching to and fro in the small office. Her right arm brushes the metal in her holster. It feels like the buckle on her husband's belt.

The pacing is getting faster and faster.

'Why is she so moody?' thinks Charmaine. 'Is she going to pace here all day?' She finds the confidence to ask a question; to break the pacing.

'Did something happen last night?'

Sandra grips the back of her chair, and nods at the scattered blossoms in her bin. Last night, *ja*. She stands up and rubs her arm. She sways and purses her lips back and forth. Something definitely happened last night.

Watching TV in her pyjamas on the sofa. His car pulls up. A glance at the clock. Just past midnight. She pulls the light blanket off, unfolds her legs. Gets up. Reaches the front door before he does. She quickly turns the key in the lock. Slides back the chain. Opens the door. There he is: her husband. Standing directly under the beam of the veranda light. His uniform's crumpled. His belt's loose. His cap sits at an angle too jaunty for his age. He looks across at her with that slack mouth.

'Waiting for someone?' he jeers. 'Oops, sorry! My mistake! With a body like yours you'd be lucky attracting anyone.' He finds this extremely funny, and guffaws until he coughs. He becomes offended by her silence. 'Sheesh woman, where's your sense of humour? Did you lose it with your sex appeal?'

She follows him into the house and closes the door. She does not ask where he's been. That question dried up on her tongue many years ago. The night their fight had woken the children. Silent, frozen at the lounge door, their frightened eyes looked straight into hers. She had ushered them quickly back to her daughter's bedroom, and lay there all night with them, stroking their hair, soaking them with tears, unable to answer their anxious questions.

'Since you're up, make yourself useful. Get me some food. But not your usual tasteless stuff.'

'You'll get what you get,' she tells him, risking it. The children are not here tonight. They are at her mother's house down the road. She feels a strange sense of freedom.

His complaints started soon after they got married, when she became pregnant with her daughter. Her food, her looks, her anything. She'd gone to cooking classes. She tried in every way to please him.

Now, tonight, disgust and shame rise in her, filling her chest right up to her throat. She walks down the passage and into the kitchen.

'No, lady. *You'll* get what *you* get,' he roars. She hears the squeak of his boots behind her. He wrenches her arm back and spins her around. His thick fingers steady her, the way a striker positions a soccer ball for a penalty goal. He pushes her. She manages not to lose balance but she is not balanced enough to stop things. Again. She falls heavily on the tiled floor. A spray of white lights explodes in her brain. He is down, over her. His fingers poke into her upper arms, gripping and shaking and cursing her, adding deep red marks to the old mustard yellow and brown bruises. She knows that he knows that her uniform will cover this secret bouquet.

The smell of unwashed sex and nicotine laced with brandy makes her want to vomit. But she also wants to survive. She wants her children to survive.

He grinds a smile into her face, and bears his mouth down on hers. Suddenly he pulls back, surveying her.

'Hell man. Actually, I'm not in the mood.' He belches, lets go of her, and stands up.

Sandra rolls onto her side, and pulls her legs up to cradle her knees with her arms. She stays like this for half a minute. She releases her knees and pushes herself up to sit. Stands up. Reaches out to the kitchen counter to steady herself. Notices where he is standing. Moves out of his reach. He's watching her.

She opens the fridge door and removes a plate of food covered with cling wrap. She closes the door and slides the plate in the microwave. She takes longer than necessary to set the timer. She wants to keep her back to him for as long as possible. For some reason, he has never tackled her from behind. It's the front of her he goes for, like a person who prefers a particular cut of meat.

'You can bring it to me in the lounge.' He is bored with it all now. 'I'm gonna watch TV.'

Sandra climbs into her daughter's empty bed and is comforted by the soft toys and her daughter's scent on the pillow. She holds her breath when she hears him come down the passage. His footsteps turn into their bedroom. The bed squeaks, boots hit the ground, and the bedside lamp no longer throws a beam of light into the passage. She waits. Snores rasp through the air. Sandra wonders what other sounds her daughter has heard from their bedroom over these years. What ideas about being a wife are taking shape in her mind? She does not fall asleep. Each snore cuts through her attempts to drift off, like a metal saw, back and forth. Sleepless hours pass until it is time to get up and ready for work. She pulls open the curtains. It is still dark outside. And chilly.

'Sorry, hey,' he says to her at breakfast, touching her arm. 'Had a helluva day yesterday. This new job's stressful. Me and the guys went for a few beers after work. I'll make it up to you, babe. You know I always do.' He frowns. She does not seem to be listening.

There is a knock on the office door and Sandra's patrol partner opens it before being invited to. He winks at Charmaine and ambles over to Sandra's desk. Sandra sees Charmaine rolling her eyes and shaking her head. He sees the empty jar and then the stalks and flower heads in the bin.

'So what have you got against flowers, Sandra?' He gives her a light tap on her upper arm with the file he is holding. She winces. Sandra doesn't doubt that it is this man, her husband's drinking and whatever-else partner, who put the flowers on the desk this morning. She cannot bear to exchange words with this collaborator with whom she has to spend the day. She wants to flare up at him like a cobra, and spit venom into his eyes.

'Okay, so it's like that, is it? The silent treatment, hey?' These are phrases that her husband also uses and they rasp on her nerves like insomnia.

'Where're we going today?' Sandra asks him in a level tone.

'Zapping illegals again,' he tells her with glee, patting his pistol. His jaw is swinging, mouth open, chewing gum. He flaps the file again, far too close to her. She resists the urge to swat at it. To swat him.

'So what are you waiting for?' she snaps. 'Let's go. I'll drive. Give me the keys.'

He frowns, as if she is asking him to give up his manhood. But he can't quite fathom Sandra today. He drops the keys into her open palm. They are cold and metallic. Like the buckle on her husband's belt.

En route to the freeway, Sandra takes a detour past the neighbourhood where she grew up. She has not come this way for many years. She drives here today, but unsure why, and deaf to his irritated sighs. She recognizes the low semi-detached houses set close to the road. The waist-high fences. The corner shop that used to be called 'Anything Goes' is now called 'Nomsa's Nice Foods'. She drives past the small park where she and her friends used to swing so high that they could touch the dazzling blue sky with their toes, and feel their tummies turn. It was in this park in this street that she learnt snatches of Portuguese. How to greet. And, when she was older, how to say, 'Does he like me?' to a trustworthy go-between. How to say, 'I love you too'.

Sandra pushes down on the accelerator and quickly finds her way to the main road that will lead to the freeway.

* * *

From the warmth of his bed, Eduardo hears the radio crackle of a police van passing. Even though his work permit is in order, panic always stabs him when police are around. He has had some bad experiences. He takes a deep breath and exhales slowly. He reaches out and stifles the alarm clock. He wants Karabo to be able to sleep a little longer. Her shift at the supermarket starts at ten today, and ends at six. But he must be waiting on the street by seven. It is still dark outside and bustling. Their bedroom is so close to the pavement that he could easily join in conversations.

He feels Karabo's gentle finger stroke up and down his back. Her foot draws his leg towards her. He wishes it was a weekend morning.

'I can't be late.' He reaches for her hand and kisses the tip of each finger.

'Saturday's just around the corner,' she murmurs. They will both be day-off tomorrow. Eduardo can feel her smile. He shaves, takes a shower, and gets dressed. In the kitchen, he lays the table for three, and makes himself some breakfast.

Opening his son's curtains he warns him that he must get up in five minutes, or risk being late for school.

'Play hard at your practice today,' Eduardo tells his son. 'I'm sure you're going to score a goal on Saturday.'

'I will, *Pai.*'

On his way out, Eduardo puts a cup of coffee down next to Karabo's bed. She'll rise just after he has gone, make breakfast and walk their son to school. He goes to wait outside, closing the door on his way. His opposite neighbour is sweeping her yard. Despite being retired, she does this early every day, no matter the weather. He and Karabo are sure it is because she likes the passing company.

'*Bom dia,*' she calls across to him in her quavering old lady voice.

'*Bom dia,*' he replies. 'How are you?'

'Fine, thanks. Tell your son I have sweets for him. His favourites.' She has a permanent stoop in her body, like a tree that has grown in the direction of a prevailing wind. She was born in this street and has seen its many changes. Most of the white people have left.

Eduardo sees his boss's large bakkie turning into his street.

'Thanks, *senhora*. See you this evening,' he calls across to her. The bakkie pulls up next to him. The boss gives him a brusque greeting and revs the engine. There is much work to get done today. From the back, Lesego stands and offers his hand. Eduardo grips it and climbs up. Everyone shifts a bit to make room for him. Conversations are paused for greetings. It's a long drive out to the building site, and there will be plenty of time to talk.

Once there they jump out of the bakkie. There's ten of them working on this site. They stand around, each making their final point about politics, sport, or relationships, teasing each other, taking last drags on cigarettes.

Beside them a large house is emerging from the deep foundations they have laid. In the rose-tinted light of this morning, with mist mingling, the jagged outline of walls and window frames look surreal. They become quiet and survey it. They breathe in the smell of damp cement.

'One day I'll have some land and build a house of my own,' says Eduardo to the guys.

'In your dreams,' laughs Lesego. 'You foreigners will be last in the queue. You can help me build mine first.'

The boss comes over and they gather in front of him for the day's instructions. Eduardo and Lesego will be laying bricks together on the far side of the house. The boss has noticed that they work fast as a team. But he does not know that they are related. It was Lesego who got him this job. Karabo and Lesego's wife are sisters.

The boss says, 'I'm off to the bank and to see a new client. Let's get some good work done while I'm gone.'

* * *

'So you got a protection order this morning?'

'*Ja.*' She stares ahead. She'd been wondering how long it would take him to begin this conversation.

'It will affect his career. His salary. You're making a mistake.'

She changes gear. 'You're a mistake yourself,' she thinks.

'He loves you. You know that, don't you?' he says, chewing his gum.

'Here's the turn off,' says Sandra.

They pass the warehouses that overlook the freeway, the housing complexes, the expansive malls with their Woolworths, Jets, Mr Prices, and Pick 'n Pays. They pass the nurseries with their autumn specials.

'A lot is at stake. Years of marriage. The kids.'

Sandra wonders how many cases of beer are at stake between this man and the man she married. The two men begin to merge in her mind. She flicks the indicator down. The traffic is heavy this morning. She waits, the indicator goes tick-tick-tick-tick. She grips the steering wheel tighter. Her knuckles gleam white. There is a small break between a large truck and a bus. She takes it. Tyres squeal on tar.

'*Jussus* Sandra. What the hell are you trying to do?' He wipes his forehead.

She is not sure what she is trying to do. But she likes that he is sweating.

'Watch the road for Chrissake!' he shouts at her. He frowns and broods.

'Why must I sit here talking to myself?' he whines. 'Aren't you listening? Don't you care?'

It feels as if there are insects crawling under every inch of her skin. Mosquitoes, high-pitched in her ears.

Wood smoke rises from the building site they are driving to. It reminds her of the braais she's had to endure; the suffocating afternoons her husband and 'the boys' all love so much. Last Saturday. At their house. He's even invited *her*. Men turning meat, beers in hand. He's boozing and bragging and flirting. She feels the sympathetic eyes of other wives. But she's to-ing and fro-ing and keeping going. Get this. Get that. Avoiding the children's anxious looks. Much later, in the garden, she's taking a break. Glance back at the house. Her bedroom curtains are closed.

Sandra swings the steering wheel sharply, veering onto the dirt track that leads to the building site. They are going to arrest any illegal immigrant they can find. She brakes. The van skids, scattering loose stones. She pulls up the handbrake.

'I'll take the lead here,' he tells her, slamming the door. She opens hers, gets out, and watches and listens to this man who collaborates with her husband.

'Hey you! Where's your boss?' she hears his barking voice. She sees his rolling stride. He hitches up his pants. Pulls his service pistol. He is set for action.

'You! The lot of you! Line up here!' he yells. 'Make it fast! Unless you want a bullet in your backside to take back to wherever you came from!' There is a line of men with yellow safety helmets on their heads, blue overalls tucked into boots. Her arm is crooked back. Her hand rests on her pistol. Its cold metal feels like the buckle on her husband's belt. Her arm is sore at the shoulder. The arm her husband wrenched last night.

She hears a worker telling him that their boss has their work permits. That he has gone off to see to business in the city. He turns his head and yells at her: 'Check no one's hiding!' But he thinks *he* is the boss here now. She frowns. The insects are crawling again. She walks past him and all the lined-up men. She draws her pistol from its holster.

'Snip, snip, snip,' she thinks.

She finds no one in the unfinished house. No one lurking along the outside walls. She scans the property and spots a portable toilet set back in the veld, behind a tree. Burnt stubble crunches under her boots. The mosquitoes are high-pitched in her head. She pulls open the door. There is no one inside. She walks around it. A man is crouched there. She levels her pistol at his head.

'Show me your papers,' she shouts.

He is sweating, and Sandra likes that she can do this to a man. Her finger tightens on the trigger.

'My boss has it,' he tells her in a soft voice.

'Again? I can't hear you!'

He clears his throat. 'My boss has it. He will not be back here until late.'

'Why are you hiding if you're so damn legal?'

'The last time I was picked up they kept me for a week.'

'Show me ID. But don't pull a fast one. I swear I'll kill you if you do.'

Eduardo slowly puts his hand in the gap in his overalls and pulls his wallet out of his back pocket. He pauses. He gives her a small photograph, instead of his ID. It is of Karabo, his son and him.

'My son is in a soccer match tomorrow,' he tells her. 'I promised to watch him play.'

She grabs the photograph and studies it. The young boy's smile, or maybe his eyes, reminds her of someone she played with in her childhood park. Of a time when she could swing so high her toes could touch the sky. When she could say, 'I love you too'.

She gives him the photograph, and returns to the van. He has handcuffed three men. She looks at him.

'Let them go,' she orders. 'They have told you where their papers are.'

He stares at her, incredulous.

'You fucking mad, d'you know that?'

'Not any more,' she replies.

Karen Hurt is a Zambian-born South African. While working as a teacher in Durban in the early 1980s, she got involved in teacher, worker and women's organisations. She was a founder member and editor of *SPEAK* women's magazine, for which she wrote articles and features. She lives in Johannesburg and, since the mid 1990s, has worked as a freelance writer, materials developer, editor and trainer. She is currently completing her MA in Writing at the University of the Witwatersrand. *Where You Came From* is her first short story, and, along with her novel in progress, her first venture into fiction.

The Cost

Kingwa Kamencu

'SWEETIE, I HAVE A surprise for you! Guess what?'

Shadrack Mugambi paused slightly, exchanging the cell phone into his right hand as he put the syringe down. In front of him the girl on the bed squirmed slightly. A smile played on his lips as he wondered what his fiancée was planning this time. Perhaps a new dish for dinner that evening?

'Eh… I can't guess. What?'

'I'm on the ground floor; in the building where your new clinic is. I'm just coming up to see you.'

'What!!! No!! Where are you? Stay where you are. I'm very busy, you can't come up, under no circumstances… where are you?'

'Aren't you happy I'm here?' Her voice turned suspicious. 'Are you with someone else?'

'Yes,' he replied unthinkingly, glancing at the girl on the bed, 'I mean no, I mean, I'm busy. Are you downstairs? Let me join you there,' he said hurriedly.

'I can't believe you would cheat on me a few months before the wedding!'

'Darling, I'm not cheating on you.'

'Then are you ashamed of me? How come you never let me meet your workmates.'

'Nkatha, you know I'm not ashamed of you, I'm just a bit busy. Let me finish what I'm doing and I'll come and uh… buy you lunch.'

'Okay, I'll wait for you at Seasons.'

He grimaced, wondering if he had enough money on him to cover lunch at Seasons but told her it was okay. Lunch at Seasons would placate her, at least for now.

He finished with the patient, writing the date for her next appointment on her card. She snatched the card from him ungraciously and stalked off. She probably had not cared to have been kept in the cold for so long as he was on the phone. Just then his phone began to ring, rudely interrupting his thoughts. It was his mother. He sighed; another woman putting him through strife and grief. It was just a normal working day.

'*Mugambi inaa uray*? We are at the hospital with Aunt Grace. You said you would deposit some money for the surgery. The doctors are still waiting. You know they can't do the surgery without that 250,000 shillings deposit.'

That was five months ago. He had winced. He had forgotten. His mother had called him two days before about it but seeing as he didn't have any money, he had somewhat blacked it out of his mind. His father had been in hospital for almost a month now. His hospital bill almost depleted Mugambi's bank balance and he, being the first born and only child working, was expected to shoulder the brunt of it. His remaining bank balance had been diminished by the car loan he had taken barely two months ago, rent for his one bedroom studio and supporting his last two siblings' high school fees. And then, there was the cost of the upcoming wedding, and even much worse, dowry for Nkatha. Things were thick.

'Mum I don't have any money. I'm really stretched, I'm late in paying rent, these people might take my car 'cause I'm late in paying it back. I really don't have any money.'

'Mugambi, you can't be broke, you're a doctor! You make so much money! Surely Mugambi how can you be mean to your parents, parents who brought you up and clothed you and fed you, sacrificed so much for you. And now you're here, you can't even help your poor father who is dying!' His mother wailed. 'Ungrateful children like these I have never seen!' she said and hung up. She knew he would call back eventually with some solution or another. That was him, the model first-born son. Obedient, dutiful, reliable and conscientious.

He was seized by a sudden rage. He counted to ten. Ungrateful? He had already spent more than 300,000 for his dad's medical fees. From his own contribution. And he, a mere 26-year-old medic that was barely out of his internship. And his mother said he was being ungrateful? The rage subsided into self pity. It was like the whole world was ganging up against him. Give, give, give, everyone around him seemed to be saying. All around him were outstretched hands. They viewed him as an endless well that never ran dry. All they had to do was ask. His mother, his fiancée, his siblings.

He racked his head. What was he going to do? He had already taken out one loan and was late in payments. He had no money to pay rent and keep his car and other daily needs going. And Dad was in hospital. He couldn't just say to hell with it. Being a first-born came with its perks, but it also had its responsibilities. Big responsibilities. He sat in his tiny office at the National Hospital, resting his head on his table. What were the options? There were two. Take another loan, use it to settle his bills for the month, the repayments on the last loan and for his dad's surgery. It might even cover the dowry and wedding costs for him and Nkatha. Option two was, call up his friends working abroad and ask them to hook him up with a job there and he could then run away from all this. But he was not that kind of person. Responsibility had been ingrained in him. His thoughts shifted back to the first option. If he saved extra hard that month and the next, he just might make it. Having decided this, he felt better.

Things were moving progressively from bad to worse. It was now three months later and things were no better. By now, he was knee-deep in debt and behind on his bills. He had not paid his rent the last two months. He had to be up and out of his house way before the crack of dawn to escape his landlord's nagging, rattling and raving. His landlord was already wisening up and coming earlier to demand his pay. Only the day before, he had narrowly missed him. Mugambi had seen him on the road and jumped into shrubbery on the roadside to hide. His electricity in the house had already been cut off and he appeared at work in crumpled and creased shirts; a sharp contrast to his fellow doctors who cruised the wards in well-pressed shirts and trousers, looking sleek, professional and up to their task. He could imagine the fright he gave his patients, appearing red-eyed and scruffy. Far from professional. He had refused to let Nkatha into his place for a long time now, lest she see him in this pathetic state. Thoughts of Nkatha just drove in the fact of his penury. He shuddered at the recollection of the last meeting at his future in-laws, Nkatha's parents, a while ago.

They had arrived at Nkatha's parents' house two hours late for lunch. It would have passed for the usual African timing but it was not. They had stopped at a hotel on the way to discuss the issue of her dowry, or bride-price as his witty younger brother gleefully called it. On the mission was Mugambi, his father, his mother, his brother Marete and their last-born brother Gitonga. His two sisters Kathambi and Kanana were in boarding school and not able to join them for this auspicious meeting. Mugambi's father was of the view that the family should tell them outright that they had a rather modest amount for the dowry but they could agree on a sum which Mugambi would pay in future. Mugambi's mother thought it would be rude to even bring the subject up and would prefer it lay quiet till the other party brought it up. Mugambi however thought the deliberations should take place on another day. It was the first time Mugambi's and Nkatha's parents ever met and according to the Tigania custom, this was the meeting during which the dowry was negotiated. Nkatha's family was from Chuka however and they, Mugambi had been told, did the bride-price negotiations towards the end of all the wedding arrangements.

And so they had driven through the gates of their future in-laws; and what wondrous gates and house they were. Gitonga had whistled in disbelief on stepping out of Mugambi's half paid for car, as he gaped at the mansion in front of them. At its front was a courtyard, huge white pillars supporting it, giving the house the look of a Grecian temple. Exquisitely arranged flowering shrubs escorted them up on the walkway from the parking area to the courtyard. The functional brick house they had always taken pride in back at home, and which made them a fairly respected family, compared to this, was but a shed.

'Eh, Mugambi! *Enyewe hapa utalipa!* Here you will pay. If you don't drop at least half a million here, ask me!' Gitonga the loud-mouth wit had predicted.

Mugambi frowned, as his father pressed on the doorbell while his mother inspected her shoes and everyone else's for any signs of dust. Despite a spectacular performance from the family (they had all behaved inordinately well), it had not gone on as Mugambi had hoped. True to Gitonga's dire prediction, the words half a million had crept into the conversation with Nkatha's parents. They had all grumbled that her family was such a mercenary bunch. Wasn't that talk supposed to come towards the end of the negotiations?

And so Mugambi was meant to shoulder that amount on top of all the other bills. His father had suffered a heart attack shortly after that which had taken the bulk of Mugambi's savings. The 300,000 had been the aggregate of his savings since before campus. It had been earmarked for the down payment of a mortgage for what he hoped to be his first house. And of course he was almost defaulting on his car loan so he had to take another loan on top of that. The wedding would cost a further 300,000 shillings; Nkatha had flipped through all the glossy wedding magazines and duly given him the cost. It was now five months to the wedding and he had neither the dowry nor money for the wedding costs, nor money for his father's bill nor money to pay his rent, loans and other bills. Things were bleak, he was knee-deep in trouble.

He was leaving the government hospital where he worked when his phone rang. He grimaced. It was his mother. She wanted more money as always. He had stopped guessing the reason for her phone calls by now, it had become a ritual.

'We need more money.'

He sighed and resignedly asked. 'What for now Mum?'

'You know your brothers are going back to school, they need some shopping, your sisters' visiting day is coming up, your Dad...'

'Mum,' he cut in wearily. 'I have no money, I swear Mum. I have taken so many loans I don't know what to do anymore. I haven't paid rent for two months, I can't even move anywhere with my car, I can't afford fuel. I'm doing so badly mum.'

'But these are your siblings, you can't let them stay at home. Now if we can't turn to you when Dad is sick and dying, who else can help the family?'

Tears came to his eyes, a sob choked in his throat which suddenly felt dry and constricted.

'Mum, it's bad... it's just bad. I can't help now. I already took an advance on two months' salary, I don't know how I'm going to survive the next two months. Please, just leave me alone, I'm tired!' he shouted and hung up.

God, I'm tired, he thought. I'm really, really tired. I can't do much for them right now. I can't even do enough for myself right now!

He trudged to the bus stop heading to his studio home in Langata. He expected to find heavies at his gate every day, demanding the rent. There were none today. What he did find was his girlfriend Nkatha, tut tutting at the contents of his fridge.

'Sweetie, there's no electricity, what's going on? And your fridge is empty. What do you eat in this house? Surely, you can't be doing that badly. What's that you have, chips?'

He had stopped off at the local chip shop to get some takeaway. At 35 shillings, chips were a saviour at this time.

'And you haven't been driving your car? What's wrong, is it spoilt?'

He sat on the sofa, staring into the darkness. He had kept his financial troubles away from her, not wanting to scare her.

Nkatha was the happiest, most angelic, most content person in the world – when everything was okay. According to him, she wasn't good with handling crises and so he was afraid of how she would take it to realize the truth of his present circumstances. In truth, theirs was a rather flaky relationship. She was in love with him because he was a doctor, and he was in love with her because she was in love with him. She was the kind of woman he was always drawn to, empty headed and a tad fickle. The hero-worship and seeming awe, reverence and respect she provided due to his status made him feel so much bigger in the world. It had never troubled him how she would always introduce him to her friends as a doctor, sometimes even forgetting to mention his name. Her family was of old wealth, wealth carefully made from business and investing and saving for many long, hard years. All of her siblings had gone into business; none of them had been particularly bright at school with many dropping off right after secondary. And so, her bagging a doctor was hitting jackpot in her eyes.

'Things have been a bit rough,' he told her, there's so much pressure from so many places, I'm a bit broke.'

Nkatha's eyes widened. This was not a good sign, she did not like the direction the conversation was taking.

'Sooooo... you don't even have money for food?' she asked hesitantly.

101

He nodded. 'But that's okay, don't worry, we'll share my fries.'

Her eyebrows went up, her mouth pursed as she looked around the room softly illuminated by candle light.

The sitting room was a fairly attractive affair; cream sofa seats, cream flowered carpet, flowers at one corner, a large flat-screen TV in a nice walnut brown wall unit. She had helped arrange this room, helped buy furniture and arrange it. Now there was no money.

'So how will we get married?' she asked.

'That's another thing I was meaning to tell you. We might have to postpone the dates.'

'Postpone the dates?! We can't, I've already told everyone! How can you do this to us? This is so unfair!' She stalked off into the bedroom and he heard her throw herself on the bed. She always went to bed when she got upset. She tended to do drastic things. He would not be surprised if she even told him she had decided to break off the engagement. His present poverty might be reason enough to scare her off.

He sat in the living room and opened the black paper bag with chips inside it. He didn't feel like going to the kitchen and putting them on one of his nice white arcoroc plates; he ate inelegantly, straight out of the packet.

'What will I do man, what will I do?' he groaned to himself. 'I need money, and I need money fast.'

Slowly, hazily, the thought drifted into his mind and settled.

'No I can't do that, I just can't do that. If people find out I'll lose everything, my reputation, my license, my friends, the lot!'

But he had to do something about his situation. Any day now he would be thrown out of the house and his furniture auctioned; or the bank would come and repossess his car, or Nkatha would go for good.

He knew where he would go the following morning. He knew he would do it. Life was about taking risks. The odds were stacked against him already; this little decision would mean nothing. He had to save himself from penury and shame.

He appeared at the clinic on the fifth floor at 8 am sharp the following morning. It was smack bang in the middle of town in a respectable 20-floor building that housed government offices, dental clinics, advocates' practices, among many other respectable trades. It was the kind of place the police and nosy media fellows would never think of visiting; the media to unearth sensational stories on illegal trades and the police to catch culprits. The belief was that they all practiced in dingy back street slums.

'I'm here to see Dr Mogere. Tell him it's Dr Mugambi,' he told the lady at the reception.

The first ten minutes wait was bearable but when it got to half an hour, he was edgy. He had been joined by a few people, people he presumed were patients. They were all women, seated beside him and across from him, some looking nervous and taut, others in cool, sophisticated repose. These would be some of his clients he thought. His gaze shifted to the wall. The room was painted in cheery pastel colors of cream and blue, flowers were placed on almost every corner of the room. It looked bright, sunshiny and wholesome. Not the place where such things happened. To his left were two young girls; they looked about 16 or 17; like they should have been in school instead of here. They sat together, backs hunched and faces down, their bodies still. One of them kept tapping at her knee with her fingers. The other stared blankly at the wall. To Mugambi's right was a woman who looked like she was in her mid-twenties. She was in a black formal business suit and time and again she glanced at her watch impatiently. She kept on walking outside to answer her snazzy Nokia phone. Next to her was a plump, brown-skinned woman. She looked like a housewife in her brown, shapeless trousers and large red sweater, and well scrubbed face with no makeup on it. He wondered how far advanced she was.

An hour later, he was ushered in to see the doctor.

'*Daktari*, good to see you. How've you been?'

The other doctor boomed warmly as he rose to greet Mugambi. This was meant to put Mugambi at ease but it intimidated him more. Dr Mogere was a plump, dark-skinned man. His Issey Miyake aftershave filled the room. He had that shine that professionals in their thirties get when they are making money and eating well. He had on a pink and black striped shirt, under his white hospital coat. They looked worlds apart. As the other doctor shut the door and walked back to his seat, Mugambi's doubts lessened by the moment. This world the other doctor was in, of shiny-faced contentment, free from debts, was a world he knew he would soon cross to.

Kingwa Kamencu lives in Nairobi. She is the author of the book *To Grasp at a Star* which won the Jomo Kenyatta Prize for Literature, youth fiction category in 2007 and the Wahome Mutahi Literary prize in 2006.

Valley of Voices

Russell H Kaschula

THE OLD FARMHOUSE WAS crumbling. Generations of Jameses had lived at Melrose. Stripped of her white-wash by decades of Eastern Cape storms, she stood bare. The tin roof rattled in the wind, unpainted, rusted. Varnish peeled in strips from the heavy front door. A creaky yellow-wood passage led deep inside. On the wall hung an old black phone in a wooden box, with a handle that no longer turned. There were gaping holes in the ceiling boards. At the end of the passage was a hall stand, laden with felt hats, tweed caps, wool-knitted jackets and hand-made walking sticks; vestiges of the elders who had come and gone. Dark-framed photographs of women in stuffy frocks and men in black suits adorned the passage walls. Formal brooding lines of relatives, standing stoically, staring straight ahead, unsmiling.

The rooms of the farmhouse were large. Elegant English furniture filled these airy spaces. The delicately carved dining room sideboard came by ship in 1857, the year of the Xhosa cattle-killing, *ngunongqawuse!* – White bones littering the rolling hills, burnt-out granaries, famine. Nonetheless, the ancestors failed to answer. As prophesied, the sun rose red on the given day, but the cattle were not reborn and there was no grain. The ancestors did not arise from their graves. Ancestors. This morning's sun glinted on silverware with the James family crest. Yet a darkness governed in the kitchen, walls blackened with smoke from the wood-fired Aga stove, the plates now cracked, but still in use.

A scrawny, red, bare-necked rooster pecked about for scraps outside the front door, as ill-tempered as if he were master of the farm. An aged sheepdog with knotted fur lay on the step, his job long done. It was years since the red *stoep* had been polished.

'Why did our forefathers have to come here? Why?' Dunford asks this rhetorical question on a daily basis. The place is unforgiving; so inviting, yet so unforgiving – ready to spit one out at any time.

'Come on then, drink your tea, dear, before it gets cold,' Priscilla responds impatiently.

And as for the neighbours – a black spot. That's how Priscilla James refers to the people of near-by *Eluxolweni* village, Place of Forgiveness. Dunford, together with his wife Priscilla, has worked Melrose farm for many years, deep in the heart of the Belmont Valley near Grahamstown. They endured apartheid. Now they are enduring a freedom that is trammeled by thieves, thugs and new laws. Daily, Dunford's inherited certitudes wrangle with change.

Within walking-distance from the farm lives the Mfengu community. They were given title to the land by King George VI of England in recognition for fighting alongside the British in the Second World War. Already in those bitter frontier wars of the 1800s, the Mfengu sold out their own people, settling closer to Grahamstown. Not even apartheid could remove them from *Eluxolweni*. Those title deeds stand strong. Dunford draws friendship from those people; also loss and pain.

From the veranda, covered with gnarled purple wisteria, Dunford observes his little empire. The aloes burn red on the hills and koppies, the euphorbias prickly in their deadly poisonous beauty. It has rained and the smell of freshly tilled red earth fills the air. But truth to tell, the only planting that is still being done is some green-feed oats for the merino wool sheep.

Over the centuries these flocks had thrived and grown. Proud prize-winning rams ran with the ewes. Lambing season was once a time of abundance. Rich flocks passed through the green and fertile valley as they were brought to the shearing shed for inoculation and shearing.

But times have changed. The flocks are now reduced from thousands to a mere hundred. They roam around the farmhouse where Dunford keeps an eye on them as best he can. In the evenings they're kraaled. A few days before, the old ram's throat was slit – all that was found of him was a skin, draped over a thorn-bush.

The shed stands forlorn, patiently waiting for those long gone shearers. The clippers hang from rusty nails. The once full wool-bins stand empty, hollow vessels where rats play. Sheets of roof zinc bent upwards by the wind, leaving bare the trusses.

The silo is empty next to the shearing shed – a tall, lonely sentinel overlooking the other buildings, it takes the brunt of storms and wind. It was once home to grain and silage. Now the roof has blown off, it is filled with green, smelly, stagnant water – a place for frogs.

* * *

A wizened old Mfengu walks up to the electric fence that surrounds the tired homestead; oily blue overalls, battered army boots from yesteryear, calloused hands. An emaciated rib-racked dog follows him. Dunford walks up to the gate to meet the old man.

'*Iigusha ziphelele*, the sheeps are all counted, Tata.'

'*Enkosi* Johnson, *ungahamba ngoku*, you can go now.'

Johnson refers to Dunford as *Tata*, father, though they are much the same age – it is a question of authority. They nod in familiar recognition, two old hardened landsmen.

Ah! Zanemvula!
Great Grandfather of Johnson Mavuso, directly descended from Chief Davidson Mavuso;
Ah! Zweliyashukuma, Shaker of the earth!
Ah! Zanemvula! Bringer of rain!
Ah! Jongilizwe! Bhele! Caretaker of the earth!
Greetings to you, Chiefs of the house of Mabandla!
Greetings to you, Chiefs of the house of Mavuso!
Nkunz' emnyama, Black Bull of Gaga!
Black bull that kicks up dust and stones, breaking antheaps!
Bull that runs with other bulls!
Ayashukum' amathamb' ez'nyanya, the bones of the ancestors are shaking!
Guybon Mavuso, Father of Johnson Mavuso;
Johnson Mavuso, Father of Zamuxolo!
Ah Jongilizwe!
Ah! Zanemvula!

Dunford and Priscilla sit on their veranda. Dunford mutters:

'*Ja* well, Johnson - he's the only one I trust you know. He's the only one I trust.'

Priscilla sighs:

'It's good that we sent Zam to school with Guy. He had a good education, and he's doing so well in his job. The old man won't forget that.' She primly holds her little English porcelain cup in her tiny hand – second-generation South African, spouse of Dunford, mother of Guy.

Johnson's wife died many years ago. He's been a faithful servant and Dunford has no reason to complain. Zamuxolo is like his own child. He's seen him grow from boy to man.

'I just can't pronounce that name,' Priscilla said when he was born.

They called him Zam. He and Guy had attended the elite St Andrews College together; bowling, batting, rowing, rugby. At the age of seventeen they both underwent the ritual of *ukwaluka*, circumcision. They descended from the mountain four weeks later, *amakrwala*, smeared with red ochre.

'Why do you need to do this heathen thing? Many young people die from it you know?' Priscilla questioned Guy. But Dunford had made a decision in support of his own son and there was no going back.

* * *

'Today, it's only education that'll set this country free...' Dunford remarks, steadily sucking on his pipe. The smell of rum-flavoured tobacco fills the air. But freedom is an enigma. Johnson is free. Free, though, from what, from whom? Just the other day he returned to his cottage to find his chickens stolen.

Priscilla turns her face away, staring into the distance:

'Education... look what it did for Guy... a no-good drug addict whom you never see or hear from. With all that education he's just a driver – driving other people's cars. He doesn't even own one,' her response sour. 'Oh, and do stop smoking that darn thing,' Priscilla scolds him.

'It's too late to stop. It is just too late.'

Dunford and Priscilla had met through the *Farmer's Weekly* magazine 'hitching post' column. They wrote letters and sent photographs to one another. It was an odd arrangement, but now it works in a functional way, even though she's thirty years his junior.

'Scrawny's back again, just look at the poor thing...' Priscilla remarks, getting up from her wattle-tree bench. 'When will those blacks ever learn to look after their animals?'

'He pitched up here this morning with Johnson,' Dunford says.

They'd named him Scrawny-Scar-Face as he's an old dog. His body's covered in scars from human beatings and dog-fights. He only has one eye. Children from Eluxolweni follow him, shooting at him constantly with their slings-shots. Every time a stone strikes home Scrawny yelps in pain and the kids laugh, victorious.

Priscilla emerges and moves towards the gate. She tosses some kitchen scraps and bones over the electric fence and the dog hurriedly gobbles them up, as if this is his last meal.

'There you go...' Priscilla reassures him.

'One day you'll go to heaven my dear,' Dunford commends her, coughing to the point of choking and then regaining his composure. 'If it weren't for you that dog would long be dead.' Scrawny-Scar-Face peers at him curiously before disappearing like a ghost into the dense scrubby khakibos, as sly as a jackal in the night. No-one ever touches Scrawny-Scar-Face. Is he so untouchable?

The dog doesn't belong to Johnson – it just follows him around.

Johnson is back behind the electric fence, this time standing at the gate.

'*Yintoni ngoku?* What's it now?'

'*Ndicela ukuthetha nawe…* I need to talk about something important...'

Dunford knows that when Johnson speaks like this he's had a premonition. Johnson's been a *thwasa* all his life, though he's never graduated. Wearing his white beads, he exists comfortably with the living-dead, *abantu basemlanjeni, izinyanya*. Johnson is a seer.

A storm is brewing. Heavy dark clouds hang low over the Belmont Valley. Rumbling thunder bounces from the granite koppies surrounding the farmhouse. Flashes of bright lightning play tricks up above. They lick across the sky, twitching, a heavenly serpent's forked tongue of fire. When the rain drops come they are fat and deliberate. Dunford loves watching these Eastern Cape thunder storms, they are part of his soul. But Priscilla turns her back and goes inside.

* * *

Paul James of Sussex, Henry James, son of Harold James, ancestors of Dunford James,
Peter James, Grandfather of Dunford James,
John James, Father of Dunford James,
Dunford James, fourth generation South African,
Proprietor of Melrose farm,
Holder of the James Family Crest,
Father of Guy James,
Old and young Bulls running together.

Dunford James and Johnson Mavuso sitting on the stoep in silence.

Then Johnson begins to speak in slow, measured, deliberate *isiXhosa*:

'*Tata, ikhon' into endifuna ukukuxelela…* there is something I want to tell you. I had a dream last night. I dreamt that the lands were green with oats, the sheep fat. The shearing shed was full again. The bales were many and the wool was clean. Do you remember those days?'

'Oh, yes, those times were good.'

The smell of oily wool; the throwing of pure white blanketed fleeces, deft fingers sorting wool classes into piles. Zamuxolo and Guy pressing the bales with their bare feet, filling the air with innocent laughter. Wool-bins; the old steel press clanking down hard, and finally the bale, stitched and sealed and ready for market. Millionaires were made in those good times. This farmhouse is built on wool.

'Well, those days are no more…' Johnson continues. 'What the thieves have not taken the dogs and jackals have killed. You and I have now grown old. Your son is gone from the farm. My son works in the city. They have no interest in this place. They no longer even talk to each other.'

'My son has brought me much grief, but your son, *Tata*, he's a good boy,' Dunford responds. 'He has his degree, and he works in the city and sees you often. He is what a son should be.'

'Yes, *Tat' omkhulu*, I cannot complain. Thanks to you he's a clever boy.'

The conversation turns to other matters:

'There's something I want you to have. It's been in my pine-box at the end of my bed for all these years,' Johnson says. 'I bought it even before I came to work for you. I thought to be a fence-maker in those days. I was barely a man then. Do you remember how you used to shout at me when I first arrived? *Yho*, how impatient you were!'

'Yes, we worked hard in those days. Things had to be done properly. People had to learn. But now we are used to one another. We are old friends, *"mhlobo wam"*, isn't it?' Dunford says.

Johnson pulls out a brand new set of fencing pliers from his bag and gives them to Dunford.

'These are for you.'

'Johnson, thank you, *enkosi*.' Dunford is moved. 'But does this mean you are preparing to leave me, old friend?' he asks in a sad voice. He looks bent and aged, hair grey and tangled. Is this what it all comes down to? He touches the set of steel pliers. Life is unforgiving.

'I'll go when I can no longer cope. I will know when that time has come...'

'Any one of us could leave at any time,' Johnson replies. He rises from his bench to return to his labourer's cottage.

* * *

This night it rains. Johnson tosses and turns as he sleeps. He dreams uneasily:

There is a thin sheep stranded on a high rocky scarp overlooking the Blaaukrantz River. A wire is tightly tied around its neck. There is blood as the wire has chafed away the wool. Johnson tries to crawl along the rock-ledge towards the sheep. He wants to save it. He holds out his hand. The sheep moves away, closer to the precipice. He does not want to frighten it, lest it jumps. He looks down and he feels dizzy. He does not want to fall. Full of fear he moves backwards to where it is safer. The sheep stares at him, hollow with hunger. He just cannot reach it. It is too close to the edge.

This very night they come. They come in savage, unforgiving roaming packs. Perhaps Scrawny-Scar-Face is one of them. The rain is deafening and nothing can be heard.

At first light Johnson stands at the electrified gate. He cuts a forlorn figure, leaning on his *knobkerrie*. Dunford now relies on his Grandfather's walking stick. Leaning heavily on the stick, he comes out of the front door at seven sharp, as he has done for years. With one hand he holds onto the sand-stone wall as he labours down the veranda steps. Johnson sees him. Step by step, Dunford slowly descends. It takes a while before he gets to the gate. He opens it.

Johnson limps slowly forward through the open gate and into the farm-yard.

'*Kugqityiwe*, it is done.'

They walk slowly. Two old men, side by side, they walk out of the gate towards the kraal and into the Valley. What has chased the sheep down into the Valley? There they lay – dead and mauled – a battlefield. Stomachs and necks punctured by sharp teeth; ears shredded and bitten from the faces of lambs. There is no bleating. An eerie silence hangs over the grey-green thorn-bushes, the euphorbias and granite koppies covered in prickly pear – silent witnesses.

Dunford places his hand in his khaki trouser pocket. He takes out his knife. A sheep is breathing, entrails lying next to it. The knife open, he kneels down on both knees next to the sheep. He carefully places his walking stick on the ground. With one deft movement he slits the throat. He doesn't count, but he will kneel another thirty times. Johnson staggers around in a bent-over daze. The vultures circle, their long, bare necks extended. Some have landed. Ghoulish mourners, they stand erect in dark suits. They respectfully wait for all to leave before they begin their feast.

Wasted meat – only the red earth will drink this blood. None but the vultures can feed on these torn, ripped carcasses. All that will remain are the bones, turning white in the hot blistering sun. *Ngunongqawuse*, this is beyond belief!

'*Kugqityiwe ngoku*,' a mantra repeated. The ancestors, *izinyanya*, have spoken, their bones are shaking.

Clouds gather, thunder rumbles – echoing, resounding voices from one side of the Belmont Valley to the other.

Dunford and Johnson sit together for a while in stunned silence. Each holds his walking stick.

'*Mas'goduke*, let's go home.'

Slowly they make their way back to the farmhouse.

'Where've you been? The toast is cold,' Priscilla calls as she hears the thud, thud, thud, of his walking stick coming down the long passage.

The ancestors look on. She hears the bedroom door close.

Dunford picks up his precious gift from where he'd placed it on his bedside cabinet. He gently holds the fencing pliers, weighs them in his hand, trying their grip, before carefully placing them down. His anthology of Yeats poetry, a gift

111

from his late Grandfather, lies open on the bedside table. He reads silently from his favourite poem:

I will arise and go now, and go to Innisfree,
And a small cabin build there, of clay and wattles made;
Nine bean rows will I have there, a hive for the honey bee,
And live alone in the bee-loud glade.

And I shall have some peace there, for peace comes dropping slow,

Dunford sighs. What peace? It's all over. He takes the double-barrel shotgun from the cupboard. Grandfather, Father, men who've held this gun, hunting guinea fowl and bushbuck... He sits down on the solitary chair. He positions the gun between his legs. He feels the cold steel in his mouth. He lowers his head, as if in prayer. He is numb. His left hand on the trigger...

Izinyanya ziyabuya. A mist appears on the horizon. There are hidden faces, familiar faces, peeping through yellow-woods, round boulders, between thorn-bush and prickly pear. Faces covered with white ochre, bodies dancing in unison. They have come up from the River, through the forest, and to the Belmont Valley. What do they want? They clap and sing, moving with the rhythm – and a steady drumming all the while. They lift their bare feet higher and higher into the air – *amagqirha*, bringing them down with resounding rattling thuds onto the barren earth – *umxhentso* – the grey mist turns orange-red with dust.

And now they are gone. And Dunford James is gone.

Russell H Kaschula is professor of African Language Studies and Head of the School of Languages at Rhodes University, Grahamstown, South Africa. He holds a PhD in African literature. He has been the recipient of the Young African Leaders Award, the Nulton International Scholarship for Study in the USA, and the Ernst Oppenheimer Scholarship for study at SOAS, University of London. He is the author of a number of short stories, novels, and academic works in English and isiXhosa. His novels include *The Tsitsa River and Beyond* and *Mama, I Sing to You*. His academic works include *The Bones of the Ancestors are Shaking: Xhosa Oral Poetry in Context* and *Communicating across Cultures in South Africa: Toward a Critical Language Awareness*. Previously he has been awarded the Nadine Gordimer/COSAW prize for short story writing and the Nasou-Via Afrika literature prize. In 2008 his novel *Emthonjeni*, published in English as *Take me to the River*, was placed on the International Board of Books for Young People's Honour list.

Mrs Siro's Harvest

Jacqueline Lebo

AT NO TIME DURING the fighting did Mrs Siro look for her passport. There were more important things on her mind. The maize harvest was stacked in a thousand burlap sacks in the store, in the garage, on the veranda, outside on the lawn covered by a tarp – basically anywhere there was an inch of space. For two days, dark clouds had threatened in the east and the afternoons were blistering hot, a sure sign of rain. The last thing she needed was rain. She needed the dry weather to hold so she could fix the sheller, shell the maize, take it to the silo in Maili Saba, get a deposit on it, pay the workers, repair the two lorries and put them back to work. The lorries represented her only source of income for the next three months: the silo owner paid in full sometime between March and April, but he gave a fair price and did not deduct taxes. If you sold to the government depot, the check had a tagline, just below the line where they took their 30-per-cent cut, stating *Kulipa Ushuru ni Kujitegemea* – she did not believe it quite yet.

For the hundredth time Mrs Siro wondered why she did this every year, banking her money in the land, hoping to get it back nine months later with a profit. She should sell up and buy a nice house in Nairobi. With land prices so high she could make a killing, better still, sub-divide into plots and sell as a residential development. But what would she do in Nairobi? Just sit around, drink whiskey, turn into a polite alcoholic and die.

A few months before, Mrs Siro visited her friend Mrs Saina in the city. Mrs Saina headed for the city two years before, when people started getting killed in Maili Saba; she had leased out her land, packed her things and left. It seemed Maili Saba had turned overnight into a dangerous place. Most residents blamed the rise in crime on the hordes of people running away from the land battles in Mt Elgon. Mrs Saina insisted on being called Catherine and had taken to referring to herself as a merry widow. She lived in an old spacious apartment in Kileleshwa, the kind often described as having lots of character, not like the numerous new apartments coming up in crowded lots where single-family homes once stood.

113

The homes were now being sold and demolished to develop apartments. Mrs Siro went outside to smoke and found a live chicken on the balcony of Mrs Saina's otherwise city apartment. Maize grains were scattered on the floor, blending in with the terrazzo pattern. The chicken clucked and weaved apprehensively when she approached. It briefly attained flight before the piece of beige sisal rope tying its leg to the balcony rail brought it down.

'I am afraid to kill it,' Mrs Saina said, stepping cautiously to avoid the green and white-flecked shit from the bird. 'You live in the city long enough and you cannot slaughter...' She told Mrs Siro some upcountry relative had brought her the chicken, and taking it to the butcher would cost an amount of money not proportional to the task. It might also mess her sporty new Subaru. So while she stewed in dilemma the chicken got reprieve and lived another day.

'This is what happens when you live in the air,' said Mrs Siro, twisting her mouth and referring to Mrs Saina's upstairs apartment. 'How can you live in the air?'

Mrs Siro believed in Terra Firma, a patch of earth to call her own. She was the one who insisted they buy shares in the Sirindet Land Buying Company when the old Briton farmer decided to go back home in 1972. She was of the generation that believed no one was from the city, and so she made appropriate plans for a place to retire when she and John got to that age. John had said they were not peasants anymore and never understood her attachment to the farm. In the divorce (better described as the keeping-away-from-each-other, since there was no legal proceeding) the only thing she wanted was the land in Sirindet. John took a local government job in Botswana and she heard there was a woman with a small child living in his house.

The phone rang and Mrs Siro ran towards it, praying it was the mechanic calling about the sheller. A quick look at the caller ID showed it was her neighbour. Kip Naibei had been calling her almost every hour since the fighting broke out. He worked for an NGO somewhere in West Africa and had five recreational acres of land bordering the far end of her farm. He had come home for Christmas, and to vote, and his hysteria was beginning to get to her. She let it ring four times before picking up the call.

'Have you seen what is happening?' he said without greeting, 'the commissioners are now saying it was rigged. Can you imagine?'

She moved towards the TV and switched it on, keeping the volume low. There were four electoral commissioners addressing a press conference.

'They are saying they don't know what happened. That they are not sure of the outcome,' said Mrs Siro.

'Rigged!' he said emphatically. For him there was no doubt. 'Those old fellows need to go home and leave it for the young men. Is it that salary they want? *Si* there is a pension.'

The line beeped. It was the mechanic.

'Listen… let me call you back,' she said. He was still talking when she hung up.

'Madam,' said the mechanic. 'I hear they are still blocking the road. *Sitaki kubahatisha,*'

I don't want to test my luck.

'Can you use the back route?' Mrs Siro said.

'I don't know if I can pass that forest. I hear there are men hiding there.'

'Try and make it at least to town. I can send someone to meet you and bring you here.'

'*Kesho… kesho.* Maybe by tomorrow it will have cooled down.'

Mrs Siro disconnected the phone and shook her head. Maybe it would have cooled down tomorrow. And the university school fees would need to be paid, the borehole pump replaced. It might all go to hell, but then again it might not.

Early the next morning, there was a loud knock on her window. Mrs Siro shot from sleep to wakefulness in an instant. She had slept fitfully, willing the rain not to fall. She opened the window as much to see who it was as to see if she had slept through a predawn shower. She was surprised to see Charles Maina, her neighbour to the east, and his teenage son. Most of the Kikuyu neighbours had fled within two days of fighting breaking out in Eldoret, one hour south of Maili Saba. Rumour, innuendo and frantic text messages had combined and now the word was the fighters were moving north to finish the work they had started. There had been small pockets of fighting in Maili Saba town but it had not reached Sirindet, and it was nothing like what happened around Eldoret. It seemed even the land wars in Mt Elgon had stopped, like a car waiting for a particularly long train to pass, recognizing a much bigger war that could flatten them all was coming.

Mrs Siro opened the door slowly, almost expecting Mr Maina and his son had been followed. They were shivering as if they had walked far and dew clung to the bottom of their trousers. After they greeted, she left them sitting on the sofa and went to make tea. Even in times of imminent danger, the guests must have tea.

'Things are bad,' said Mr Maina, his hand shaking slightly as he reached for the teacup.

'Things are very bad.'

'Yes,' she said, shaking her head.

Before they voted, he always told her they should give the old man another chance. Let him return. He has done really well for the country. The farming sector is doing really well. Look at how much we are getting for milk and maize. These other ones don't know about the economy. It will go down completely. Us, we know one shilling is better than none. One shilling from one hundred customers you are starting to go somewhere. These guys are still young. They can come back in 2012.

Mr Maina gathered himself, and asked what he had come to ask. 'We need to get to the airstrip, we can't go by ourselves. I don't know what will happen to us. We can't go by ourselves.'

She looked at him steadily and did not answer for a long time. She could probably get them to town. She knew her immediate neighbours and those beyond that. If there was anyone blocking the road she would probably know who they were and talk her way out of it. Beyond town was the problem. The twelve kilometre stretch to the airport worried her. They would be fair game to anyone manning that stretch of road. Mrs Siro went to the kitchen and called the Area Chief. She always called him when she thought thugs were in the area, which was often. He told her to go the District Commissioner's office. They could probably get an escort to the airstrip from there.

Mr Maina should sit in the middle, they decided, the farm manager on the passenger side, so he could be the one to talk if they found any roadblocks. They would only show their IDs as a last resort. Mrs Siro would drive. Mr Maina's son would sit at the back of the pickup in the middle of two young workers hired for the harvest. When Mrs Siro looked at the three young men at the back of the pick-up, she couldn't point to any discernable thing that made them different. They left through the field at the bottom of the farm, a shortcut that came out right near the tarmac road. It was still cold and the grass was slippery with dew. The silence inside the car only served to make the diesel engine seem louder. She drove slowly as they did not want to attract attention. It was an uncomfortable ride with three adults at the front. Mr Maina had to sit skewed to one side so Mrs Siro could reach the gear. Just when they reached the tarmac, Mrs Siro's phone beeped. It was a message from Mrs Saina. 'Hi dear,' it said. 'Hope you are keeping safe. Take care, Catherine.' Mrs Siro grimaced.

They passed farms where the maize was still stalked, gathered into round bunches, waiting for harvest. If it rained the stalks would absorb water and cobs would fall and rot. The farmland ended and they reached the outer limits of Maili Saba. There were houses on one side of the road and forest on the other. The tall eucalyptus trees rustled in the wind, leaves making menacing shadows. The sweet smell of the eucalyptus worked its way into the edges of Mrs Siro's fear and she knew with a strange resolve that even if someone came out of the forest and stopped them not the slightest tremor would shake her voice. At the edge of the town, six-story grain silos towered over everything, testament to the driving force of the region: maize and its accompaniments – the seed shop, the fertilizer shop and the tractor shop. The dusty street where lorries lined up was empty. Any other December and turn-boys would be hustling for potential customers looking to haul maize to the depots. Any other December and the town would have turned festive and in a bar in town there would be a man slapping large wads of harvest money on the table saying, 'lock the door, the whole bar is drinking until we finish this money.'

Mrs Siro accelerated when she saw the District Commissioner's office. The renewed energy of a runner seeing the finish line. Inside the compound were families sitting forlorn on every stoop and veranda of the building. On one side were families, better dressed, quite distinct, in cars waiting for an escort to the airstrip. These were the ones who could afford to get out. They were there for twenty minutes when two Land-Rovers with red-beret policemen came to the compound. One lead the convoy, one brought up the rear of this sombre procession. After a slow, excruciating drive, the airstrip could be seen from the road, indicated by the black and white striped windsock flapping in the stiff wind. There was a building that looked less like a control tower than a shaky two-storey structure of the kind spectators sit in to watch horse races. Five white planes were lined up on one side and one was on the small runway, preparing to take off.

They got out and Mr Maina clasped Mrs Siro's hand in both of his.

'Thank you,' he said.

She nodded. He was looking behind her at the planes, contemplating the next portion of his journey. Already the police escort was turning to return to the District Commissioner's office. On the way back, fat raindrops started to fall on the windscreen.

'Shit!' Mrs Siro exclaimed. 'There are some plastic bags under the seat. Remove them for the boys to cover themselves,' she said to the farm manager.

The rain started slowly, the fat drops falling. It took a while for it to come down in earnest. She prayed it was one of those December storms, heavy but brief. She took her phone and called the house. They were covering the maize as best they could.

When they got home the rain had stopped, but the clouds had not completely dissipated. It was as if the storm was regrouping for another attack. Kip Naibei was there with the workers.

'We covered most of it. You should be able to dry the ones that were rained on,' he said. He walked with her to inspect how much maize had been rained on. A little water had seeped in through the bottom of the sacks. If they took the maize, shelled and dried it right now, they could save the crop.

Her phone rang as she went into the house. It was the mechanic. He was in town. The farm manager took the pickup and went to get him. Kip Naibei went to the liquor cabinet, took two glasses from the shelf and poured the Teacher's. Even now she noticed his over familiarity, but it did not irritate her as it usually did. She drank and felt her chest warmed up.

'You know my mother sold *chang'a* to put me through university,' he said.

'Please,' she said, with a disbelieving look.

'You think I am just this town guy. I grew up in *mashambani kabisa*. I swear!' he said, putting one hand on his heart in an oath-taking gesture. 'I swear to God! *Mungu* one.'

Mrs Siro was laughing now.

'She made some serious brew. Twenty shillings and the whole table was drunk... finished!'

The mechanic arrived, examined the sheller and said it was not something that could be just welded together – he needed a new part. The shops had been closed for several days and there was no sign of them opening anytime soon. When she thought about it later, Mrs Siro could not be sure who suggested it first. Charles Maina had an old sheller in his store, from the time when he leased out farm equipment. Mrs Siro tried to call him several times, but all she got was a message saying the subscriber could not be reached. They went with the pickup and the tractor; the tractor was for hitching the sheller and bringing it back, in case they found it. They cut the barbed wire fence and went through the paddocks – they could not use the road in case they were mistaken for common thieves. They pulled down the metal door to the store with the tractor hitch and a chain and peered through the machinery. The sheller was still there and after a few attempts to get it going, it came to life with a loud whirring sound.

The old sheller was slow. It took two days of working day and night to shell the maize. The whole compound was filled with white chaff and it was stuck to everyone's hair and clothes. They all looked like ghosts. Kip Naibei helped the whole time, and a little Teacher's in the evening had the double effect of making him less irritating and helping her resist the urge to smash his face in. As the last of the shelled maize went into the store, Mrs Siro felt the band that had been wrapped around her heart unclasp.

'I don't even know why I am farming,' she said with a glass of whiskey in her hand.

'You are lucky to have this...' Kip Naibei said, his gesture encompassing the house, the land, everything.

'Lucky! I put everything in here. The money is so bad nowadays. Prices of fertilizer are so high. This land people are fighting over, we need to do other things. I think I should start an amusement park... something with a swimming pool, chips and nyama choma where families can come on weekends. If I knew when I bought it...'

'What do you mean you bought it?' he said, incredulous. 'You people were given this land when Moi was president.'

'I bought it,' she said, a dangerous tone creeping into her voice.

'How? With those settlement schemes? What did you pay? Five thousand shillings an acre. That was a nominal sum. Meanwhile my people are sitting on a rock on the side of the mountain fighting each other.'

'I bought it!' she said. 'If your people were not educated enough to know how to get into the settlement schemes, that is not my fault.'

'How could we know, we had been pushed to the mountain by the colonials.'

'We have all been pushed out of land by colonials. Even me, right now there is a mzungu still living where we come from. You were not the only one who was chased out of your land by colonials. This has happened throughout history.'

'This is not history we are talking about. This is the 50s. My mother still remembers exactly where she was born. She knows exactly what part of this land is theirs. All this Maili Saba is ours and we are fighting each other for a rock on the mountainside.'

'Are you serious? You are an educated man. You should be finding alternatives for your people. There is no way you are going to chase people off their land in Maili Saba.'

'Land is wealth. Land is capital. What do you mean find an alternative? Alternatives!' he exclaimed. 'My mother had to sell *chang'a* to put me through university. Do you know how humiliating that was? You people have land in Keiyo, in Tugen, in Nandi. We don't want hand-outs from the government.'

'We cannot go back. My brothers have divided our father's land. There is nowhere for me to go.'

'Then we should divide the land. All of you should just cut half your land and give it back to the original owners.'

'That is not going to happen. You should find economic alternatives.'

'The only language you people understand is violence. We are killing each other on the mountain and fighting the wrong enemy. The enemy is down here and we can see you enjoying your hundreds of acres while a whole family up there is sitting on a rock.'

'That will be war!' Mrs Siro said.

'Why can't you even give half your land as a gesture of good faith.'

'That will never happen.'

Kip Naibei started laughing hysterically.

'That will never happen. That will never happen!' she said, banging her glass on the table, and raising her voice.

Mrs Siro stilled and looked at the amber liquid in her glass. Somewhere beyond the shouting, she was already thinking about tomorrow, about how to get her harvest to Maili Saba.

Jacqueline Lebo lives in Nairobi, is a writer, photographer and the Managing Editor at *Kass Magazine*. She is currently working on a book about Kenyan athletes in the Rift Valley.

First Time

Kgaogelo Lekota

IT DID NOT MATTER to Gwekerere whether it was Wednesday or Tuesday because he worked in the darkest of places. It was dingy; it reminded me of a shopping centre. Except it was much smaller. In the sense that once you got inside you lost time. I guess they are designed to make you shop until you realize you've got holes in your pockets. Similarly it was easy for you to experience the same when visiting Gwekerere at his place of work, you always left with your pockets empty, drunk and happy. He stayed there so it might as well be his home. He often wondered sometimes, you know like how he ended up there. This was one recurrent thought that went through his head. He could not remember anything. I guess the place became part of him, a subconsciously parasitic part of him. Although he must have had an internal clock, because he miraculously knew when it was time to knock off.

At this point, he was sitting down on a bar stool in the dark place. He seemingly was heavily engaged in deep thought. The kind which makes you step out of your body and experience your past and or your future. He snapped out of it and recalled one of his friends talking about a friend of his who aborted her baby. Apparently it really happened, and a second later she went straight to the bar and ordered two Windhoeks. After that with no shame showing on her face she had herself some Red Square. No shame, that's what Gwekerere repeated to me over and over again. I mean what do you do when someone tells you something like that? Especially when I knew that Gwekerere helped her to do it. The old man across the road only dealt with him when it came to abortion merchandise, which was illegal. Otherwise, the sweet and cigarette stall was just a front. Gwekerere, looked around, and for the first time all he could see was filth. Even though it happened once in a while, all he could smell was aborted babies and the smell of fresh blood. For Gwekerere this was one of the things that he had to face in his occupation. They always came to him, for help; what could he do? Refuse? For some strange reason, he was the only one that the old man in Mandela Park trusted when it came to the abortion merchandise, if you know what I mean.

When I met him, in my eyes he was just an ordinary black kid. His eyes were sunken into his skull, his skin resembled wrinkles but you could see he was very young. And his tongue was as quick as a lizard running away from shade. To me, he somehow had an uncanny resemblance to my grandfather, that's why I thought he was wise and I subsequently befriended him. At that time though, I had thought of him as scum.

The more we grew together, I got to realise that Gwekerere was like a poet, weaving his words carefully while he was covered in dung. In a way he was flung from squalor into a mess. That was Gwekerere, the man I got to know deeply and intimately. I shadowed him like I was indeed his shadow. I got to know his moods, his laughter and his joy. All of this seemed to matter much more than anything else. I was just there to be a witness, don't ask me a witness to what? I don't know, all I know is it was supposed to be something divine and this here is an attempt in a round about way to tell you Gwekerere's story and also happens to be mine in a strange kind of way.

Gwekerere came from a family of three boys. If you really thought about it, everything in that family seemed to come in threes. They had three huts, three pots, three spoons and god knows what else. Maybe one of them was born with three legs, who knows? Except they had to devise a plan about the mattresses because the family was much larger than three. To be exact there were five of them, if you counted the mother and the father. By all accounts this was a normal family. Normal as they come. So normal that you didn't even notice even if you took extreme care to do so. There could be no apologies offered for their circumstances. It was either the weather, always apartheid even though it was never noticed, bad luck etcetera. I am not so sure now that they even had circumstances to complain about. They did not care, but Gwekerere and Raymond did.

Raymond was much more wayward than his brother. So he tried all tricks necessary to lift himself out of what he called self-imposed poverty especially when he was an adolescent. If you asked anyone in that village about the truth of the alleged self-imposed poverty, they would have repeated those exact same words and added *my foot* or *big black behind*. It was not surprising because Raymond believed he had never chosen his destiny. He also believed that when he was born God looked the other way and left Satan to do his will with him. That was what enchanted the young Gwekerere to Raymond. To Gwekerere, Raymond's mind was an exotic place, filled with mysticism and other isms that he hadn't learnt as yet. Either way, then it did not matter.

Lucas was their older brother. He was a friend to both brothers and the biggest culprit when it came to the two brothers' beliefs. With regards to behaviour and doctrine, he was their Pastor Ngidi, a self-righteous soapy character on one of the popular six o'clock shows on South African national television. He was an avid reggae music fan, and Gwekerere, Raymond and I never ever saw him smoke anything or drink anything. He used to tell us all these stories about Haile Selassie the First. I remember how he used to go on about how he knows that Rastas originate from Kimberley. He said that Rastas congregated in Kimberley and decided to crown Selassie and organise a huge pilgrimage to Ethiopia for that reason. So in his mind there was no way that they could have originated from Ethiopia. He also said it was the Babylon system that sought to deny the Rasta the true explanation and that system wanted to make less of the Rastafari. He would pace around the room and say Babylon this and Babylon that. Even the reggae radio that he used was also Babylon; everything in that house was Babylon when he was preaching. According to the brothers, he did this when he had just finished 'jumping the primus stove'. I just thought he was completely mad and never bothered to ask what this 'jumping the primus stove' was.

It was an ordinary day when Gwekerere did it. He sneaked over to the neighbour's house which was oppositely adjacent to his. There he played 'mantlwantlwane' with Small. From where we were hiding, behind a lush bush, we could see that Small was the mother and he the father. At some point when they were doing motherly and fatherly things; cooking mud and having invisible tea, he knelt down and touched her thighs for a fleeting second. Small had no chance, particularly because she was so short and so particularly young. It was a dodgy thing to do, and he knew it but somehow he was drawn to it. I don't know how to explain it; like have you ever had the urge to go into a bank and rob it blind? Better still, that urge you get when you are on a high bridge, like what would happen if I jumped off that bridge? Except neither you or I have that urge within us. We might think about it and you may actually be thinking about it round about now.

Stop.

Think…

And maybe do it?

Gwekwerere would have just jumped, he just did things. So, he touched the young girl's innocent thighs and felt a tingle somewhere. Yes he did, and he was not ashamed. It was a revelation to him and he never turned back. He never looked back, never back-tracked. It was like a dream unravelling itself before his eyes. Twisting, turning and twirling till he was blinded with its vividness. He never woke up from it.

We grew up, troubled our parents and when they retaliated, we sought an escape. So Gwekerere's solution was to drag me along to Little Hillbrow. Yes, those were the nights. We were free from parents except for Joseph whom we happened to befriend. We were kings, yah neh! We were once kings. But we were slowly drifting apart like cigarette smoke puffed into the air by an overly eager smoker, especially when it was Camel that was being smoked. It happened and when we realised it we just embraced it. Gwekerere was like that, though. I guess he had seen too much and lost too much to care. So we parted like a banana peels and our friendship, well, became just that, a word. Gwekerere did not care, but I admit, I did. I gave a damn and that's why I never gave up. I looked for him and searched for his soul. I looked everywhere until I found him again. He was still the Gwekerere I knew and he was still in Little Hillbrow. I think I should be honest here and say that, he was a revised edition this time; he was surrounded by women. Now and again he would pass my vegetable stall with one of these beauties and demand I give him free merchandise.

One night as we were doing our usual ritual of partaking in necessary and unnecessary evils, a sister came to us. Beuaty not Beauty. I mean capital B-E-U-A-T-Y. She was just too beautiful to be spelled correctly. Sat down and ordered herself some hard poison. She started talking about how the police were on a rampage, *Gaties* that's what she called them. They had closed down several places, they had started with Hillbrow Inn, Diplomat, another hotel, then moved to Yellow Rose Motel; this was dangerously close to where we were, I felt dubious. We could see her nervousness through her pearl-shaped eyes. My one guess was that she was in a ganjarised state of consciousness. What I do remember though, is that her lips moved like a Jamaican ripe pear. Eish, she was a Jamaican for sure. Anyway she wasn't going to get any work tonight, this was her last drink and she had decided to call it an early night. I felt for her, but Gwekerere looked at me with that look that he always had. So I knew there was no time for pity.

'Time to get some bargains for you, my friend.'

Gwekerere must have been joking, what with the fact that I was broke. Either way I wasn't going to protest, the liquor did not allow me to. I mean he was the chief negotiator after all. Yet I had sensed what he was saying; in my language there is a saying that goes like, well the anglicised version is; 'when you decide to iron, you must iron the shirt while it's hot'. I checked the contents of my wallet and signalled to the chief negotiator. He kicked into action like a reliable old engine. He turned around, and stroked Beuaty's thigh; this must have been a ritual, I thought. Her eyes lit up with a certain hope, the desperation diminished.

124

'You can come to my room, in case they come you will be safe there,' he said.

'Who? The *Gaties*?'

'Yah, plus me and my friend will take good care of you. *Or kanjani my Bra?*'

I nodded, saliva beginning to fill in my mouth. I took another swig of my Black Label to wash it down. I looked at her again repeatedly. She was there all right, another human being; would she do it?

'I need to rest!'

'*Ah wa tseba montwana, mina nawe* you and us – with my brother from my other mother; nice time what do you say? Listen we just have to see eye to eye here. A tit for a tit, butter for fat, hmm? I am there for you, here and there whatever you need and especially when people give you problems. I go the extra mile; I am like a Toyota to you my baby. You know *mos ne*?'

'You help me and everything, but really take a chill pill.'

I was listening to the conversation but I switched off and drifted, it felt like sinking. It ponged pungently but I was drawn to it. Flying, drifting, dawdling, crawling, hiding, imbibing. It was salt. I brawled. Deliberated. Impregnated my thoughts like an expired inspired dreamcatcher. I felt fancy but dirty. Clint Eastwood, gun at my hip; the fast, the deadly and the definitely dangerous. Colours came to me, running away from the darkness. Blues in hues. Dying dead reds. Slippery silvers. Fluorescents pranced around. I opened up like a rainbow chicken and everything came into me. I was a new being, a sentient of the dark world, make it darkish. All I needed was a cape and I would be a super hero, Beuaty's superhero. I came back to life. Realized I was sitting on a hard bar stool and I was thirsty. So I ordered another Black Label, what used to be America's finest beer, according to South African Breweries. Now it is something else. Sweet not bitter, I wonder what I could compare her to. She would be an Amstel; she would have to cease being a Jamaican and be an Amsterdamian. I mean, I could still hear Gwekerere droning on and on, and Beuaty throwing in something here and there. It was more like she was littering on to the pavement of the conversation, I did not mind. She was around. I was falling into it, that hole no man wants to admit exists. Either it was the liquor, but I must say that her skin started to shine, or there was just light after all in all this darkness.

'Mfana, buy her another one; soften the tongue and loosen the notches.'

'*Sho da*,' I agreed.

We both knew one of us had to do something. Gwekerere was beginning to kick into his highest gear; I noticed Beuaty becoming a single malt scotch whiskey. The chair I was sitting on felt like it was morphing into the ground. Gwekerere pulled her closer to him, as if he was about to cast another spell which needed the subject to be in close proximity of the spell-thrower. She willingly obliged. Either way, she was now very close to him; personal spaces were now shared. I was distilled by my envy; in heavy doses. It must have been the smoke of unmentionable herbs in the air that made me jealous. Even though by now the distance between them was constant, they seemed to be getting closer to each other. My envy grew. Her intermittent smiles were starting to tickle me inside. But how could he do this to me? I resigned myself; I think I might have done that a long time ago. It was time, so I took a resolution. If it was meant to be; my ancestors would take care of it. She looked at me and my eyes sparkled. Gwekerere winked at me, came over and tapped me on the shoulder, as if some kind of conclusion was reached.

More sisters arrived; the bar was one of those long ones that seem like they would never end. There were round tables scattered around with what looked like comfortable chairs. The middle had a stage, rectangular in shape. It had tubing that changed colour on its outskirts. I stared at those colours for a while, they were all warm. No blues, no coldness. I guess we were meant to feel comfortable and homely and wanted. After all this was a place for gentlemen. No gentleman would admit reverently that they visited or knew that such a place existed. Only the brave visit during the day, but the less brave do otherwise; hoping that the darkness would not give them away. For Gwekerere, the place and its doings were inconsequential and maybe convenient because he worked there. He was a man one could depend on if you wanted a favour or two.

She turned. Suddenly. I could feel my eyes turning red. I figured it out. My insides, unstable-volcanic-pockets. Took my hand. I followed my hand out of the bar. No words. Vending machines. Slot machines, women behind reinforced bullet-proof glass, standing women. Men smoking. Games, pacman, pin ball, toilets, left turn and immediate right, security guard sleeping, lift, up-button pressed repeatedly, three men, three women, mini-skirts and ties, uneasy ascending, a jerk, halt, doors open, floor five, longish walk, room 528, door unlocked. Bathroom on the right, television switched off, sat on the bed, she disappeared. Only to reappear as beautiful as those places on television that I am sure I will never see; as naked as nature.

I looked up at her and all I could whisper to her in my mind was: I'm dreaming of you, I plead please lead me to your grass so I can graze, be blessed and blazed and get me to those heights, never ending and cast me away my lows, ending; my prancing princess, obsessed by your incandescent light, translucently soft and dreamy, I can almost taste your creamy words, you fill my worlds with luminescent dream streams, et tu, you would feel it too, hum me my blood sweetly and mellow, bellow softly you rumbling..., what's the point you ask, it doesn't matter; anoint my soul, I am crying a dying song, you saved me, I came to consciousness like thunder from one cloud to another – in tongues, the rogue was and now is the sentient – the second being.

Remembering when Raymond and I were hiding behind the bush watching Gwekerere and Small playing father and mother; Raymond wanted to join, so badly I had to restrain him. I was young then. But now there was no Raymond to return a favor and restrain me. The feeling was like what one would feel wandering around aimlessly in a perfume factory trying very hard not to be a fart. As soon as I had taken the steps downstairs from Beuaty's room, I looked for Gwekerere. What had happened was frightening as I began to dwell on it. My manhood was intact. I did not notice Gwekerere passing me in the foyer and motioning that I should follow him. He had to come back and take my hand. He told me we needed to celebrate this occasion because I had tasted what it was like to do manly things.

Lucas, Gwekerere's older brother; was outside, smoking. The parked cars annoyed me; they were almost suffocating, so I had that feeling of needing more air even though I was outside. My eyes looked down and I concentrated very hard on counting the pebbles that were on the worn out tar. We were going to Lucas's new spot, this was the Rasta stall. Evidently, Little Hillbrow was becoming popular. At least there was one positive, I discovered what jumping the primus stove really meant and I was only too happy to help Lucas to combat and chant down Babylon. The Rasta stall had all kinds of fruits, badges of Bob Marley and generally objects which were green, gold and red. We went on about the world as usual, it felt like old times. Images of Small flashed in front of my eyes.

'After all tell me, Gwekerere, why are we disgusted by our own natural smells?' Lucas broke the silence.

'Smell my hand,' Gwekerere outstretched his hand, 'it smells like shit.'

I smelled it. 'Yes it does smell like shit.'

'Puff and pass please,' Lucas was annoyed because Gwekerere had turned the spliff into a microphone.

Gwekerere licked the top end of the spliff, to make sure the fire didn't smoke too much ganja on its own. This was a learning curve for a novice like me, another first.

'You see brothers, sex smells like shit too. And do you know why they don't want you to smell these things, because they don't want you to realize you are human. Now listen carefully, the shit you smelled on my finger was ganja smell, naturally, hundred percent. Do you see my point, broer?' he said looking at me for support. I had to think about that one.

'So why don't we smoke shit then?' asked Lucas. I thought that was a good question, a long silence followed. Giggles started to fill the stall, even the Rastas started to listen with interest.

'Because ganja can never be shit,' one Rasta with three very long blanket-looking dreadlocks.

We all laughed, it was like old days again.

Gwekerere and I started to meet at the Rasta stall more frequently instead of meeting at his workplace. We had many lovely conversations, some were about flowers, and some were about the tricks of politics; never about women. I continued to see Beuaty. Regularly when the money was good and not so regularly when life was tough; which happened more frequently than I would have liked, but what can a man do?

You see, my friend. Gwekerere was a good man, he helped me out; but every time I see him, I am reminded of Beuaty.

One day, she came to me almost running; I could have sworn that a pack of lions had just escaped from the Kalahari. She was terrified; she came straight into my arms. You know, by the way I wanted to marry her; buy her Chicken Licken on Fridays, Nandos on Saturdays and Sundays I would have to cook her the best chicken breast, beetroot, chakalaka and rice. She reminded me of Small.

'I am pregnant,' she said.

'Fokof! How do you know it's mine?' I said.

'Well, I thought you were different. That you would care. I was obviously mistaken. Next time you go to the toilet downstairs look hard, because you might see your handiwork there.'

That was the last time I saw Beuaty. She turned back to where she came from, looking like a very good western film ending. If you are reading this, please get this to Gwekerere, in Little Hillbrow. Everyone knows him. I am rotting away as I write this. This cell has consumed me and there's no point in living without my eternal dessert, my flu lozenge, my Beuaty. You probably think I am crazy, but I did not murder her, I swear. You know, when I took a careful look at her legs, there was blood streaming down their sides almost everywhere and her stomach was sliced open. She handed me the knife, and told me again that it was my child. She had asked Gwekerere to assist but he refused. He wanted nothing to do with the child's murder, he was done with that business. I told the court everything, I did not do it, but they did not believe me, not even my own lawyer. I told them I went to see Beuaty one last time, to apologise. I had bought KFC. I knew that she liked chicken. I didn't bother going to the bar, I went straight to room 528. Her door was open, so there was no need to knock. Three screams, three steps, I was beside her ready to help. She was sitting on the bed, facing away from me. Already slashed, she gave me the knife. I don't remember how much time passed. Three *Gaties* took me away, with the bloody knife in my hands. I wouldn't let go. You see, I did not do it. Tell Gwekerere, I know and believe that he believes in me. Tell him also that

I am going to be with Beuaty, I am going to smoke ganja and disintegrate, like smoke particles I will trickle upward from these ganja clouds, I am disappearing to a ganja farm in heaven. I come in love and peace and I mean no harm. Beuaty, I'm coming baby. By the way do you know if there is a Chicken Licken or a KFC in heaven?

Kgaogelo Lekota, 'Tswatswari thekgo tsa bo Mochidi' is a South African writer, poet, an aspiring visual artist and playwright. He currently resides in Westdene, Johannesburg and is finishing his Bachelor of Science degree at the University of the Witwatersrand (Wits). He is a senior consultant and Administrative Officer at the Wits Writing Centre.

The Lost Boy

Kaume Marambii

I AM AFRICA… DREAMING. When at last I sleep, I dream…beautiful dreams, fantastic dreams. I am the king of the universe. I laugh as I run, the wind on my face. My sandaled feet kick up little swirling dust devils from the dry grass. I am young and strong and I run lightly, untiring. My smooth long-limbed strides eat up the distance. My second wind kicks in and I breathe easily, steadily. At this pace, I can run forever.

I turn in my vast bed and smile and dream on… but now the screams wake me…

They reach down tearing into my misty rainbow-shrouded world and drag me kicking and clawing back to my waking nightmare. The red soil that is my robe is sodden with tears and blood. The stench of death bites my nostrils, the screams of a thousand lost voices echo in my ears…and I feel the pain – pain beyond measure, pain beyond comprehension.

Here comes the evening news again, News of the World flashes by and there is the familiar clip from the heart of darkness. Young African male on his knees pleading for mercy. This is the Baghdad Boys' territory. Grinning drug-crazed rebel thug, no more than a boy really, waves the sub-machine gun menacingly, and hesitates –

'Kwani? – What's your problem?' another soldier shouts, '*Ua ghasia!*'

Kill the scum!

'UA!'

It's such a simple little word: Ua. Kill.

The boy glances nervously left and right. He licks his lips and squints down the barrel. He tries to remember the training. Control your breathing, breathe out slowly and hold it, steady your hand and squeeze gently, steadily. But still he can hear the breath wheezing out of him in shallow gasps. The barrel is jerking slightly, rhythmically with every thudding beat of his heart. His small chest feels like it will explode from the pressure and there's a metallic taste in his dry mouth. They are all watching him carefully now and there is something in their eyes, the dark promise of brotherhood or retribution.

Choose carefully my son...

The boy feels everything receding, falling away until there is only the two of them now, just him and the kneeling man. The man attempts a pathetic smile and holds his hands out, palms upwards, pleading. Beads of sweat stream off his face and the large vein on his forehead pulses strongly. Strange, the boy thinks, that there are so many muscles in his face. Look at them twitch – ears, nose, lips, eyelids, forehead, even the cheeks. The man is still talking, he is saying something over and over again and the boy strains to understand, but they both know it is beyond that now. Something has changed and he can feel it start coursing through his veins. I decide, the boy marvels, I decide. Me. I'm in charge here.

And then to his surprise, the boy feels the kick of the gun as it begins to jerk in his hands, and the staccato rat-a-tat sound echoes in the empty street. He sees the man's body jerking like a grotesque animated doll, face still frozen in that hopeful pleading grin. The body rolls over, jerks one last time and lies still. A stream of dark blood oozes out mingling with the dirt in the potholed street. Wild cheers erupt from the rebels. Their leader Comrade Senior Sergeant Livondo puts his arm around the boy.

'You're a man now, Kay Kay. From now on your name will be Krazy Killer,' he announces proudly, 'tonight we will drink to your health and find you a woman.'

The new man-boy grins happily, turns and casually fires one last careless blast at the body. The slamming bullets kick it briefly into mock-life again, limbs and torso twisting in one last dance. A shell whistles overhead and smacks into a nearby building blowing apart a large chunk of the already pockmarked façade. The Baghdad Boys lose enthusiasm for their grim sport and dash yelling for nearby cover in a commandeered hotel.

The government tanks are creeping closer. The shelling intensifies. The setting sun casts an eerie glow over the scene, the golden light dancing over the streams of blood that ooze from the nameless victim. Glinting highlights dance in the dark stream, perhaps a reflection of the dreams that once coursed through his veins. All captured in glorious Technicolor, beamed right into your living room. A little light evening's entertainment before your favourite soap comes on. Who was this youth? What were his dreams? Were they as beautiful as these shimmering reflections? What cruel quirk of fate led him down this street at that moment to encounter these thugs spoiling for a fight? Did he ever imagine it would end like this, face down in the gutter, where even the dogs, sated from other flesh, would not touch his? Does his mother wonder where he is, why he doesn't come home? Is there a sweetheart somewhere even now waiting with bated breath and trembling heart for that footstep, that particular knock, that soft voice? You will flick the switch and sleep, soon to forget. Perhaps on some particularly pensive days, these thoughts will flicker briefly through your mind soon to be replaced by more pressing matters of your own.

I cannot forget. I never forget. That is my blessing and my curse. I am the keeper of all our memories, and that scene is forever stamped into my mind. It replays over and over again and wakes me up sweating and gasping. It's me rounding that corner, carrying the scraps of grain I had salvaged from the burnt-out shell of a store. Hurrying now to get home and to shelter before dark...

Darkness is not a friend out here and I curse myself under my breath for leaving it so late to get back home. She will be worried, but I couldn't have returned empty handed again this time could I? I knew what I had to do, as terrified as I was. I did it, and I nearly made it.

I round the corner carelessly and it is too late to duck out of sight when I spot the Baghdad Boys manning the roadblock. There is something in the way that they stare. Usually you get a beating. Of course they will also take all you have but you get to live. I see the young boy approach and not the squad leader and my stomach tenses. I have seen this happen countless times. The boy has to prove himself. There can only be one outcome. My father and uncles have prepared me for this moment. I try to recall what I had been told –

'Shakombo, be a man,' they had told me, 'be defiant to the end. Curse them and spit in their faces. Let them know they've met a real man.'

All that teaching is out the window. My legs tremble and I find myself on my knees. No one has told me to kneel but I know what I must do. He is a young boy and I can see the fear in his eyes. I must appear as non-threatening as possible. I must to try make him feel safe. Yes, I grovel and beg and curse my name and my roots. But it is not for me, dear tribesmen, that I throw away all that is honourable. It is for her. My Fatma. My love. My life. What will happen to her? To see her again, I would kneel and kiss the devil's feet.

These fools, they talk of manhood. What do they know? Had they listened more closely, they would have known he died with her name on his lips.

She knew that something was very wrong when she saw old *Mzee* Hamisi coming towards the hut. She had begged her husband not to go out this morning. She would be fine, she had tried to reassure him. Her hands went to her belly and she felt the child growing inside her. She was five months' pregnant now and showing slightly otherwise he would not have gone into town to look for food. The first time she had seen that look of quiet determination was when he had started courting her. 'You'll be mine,' Shakombo had told her quietly confidently. And so she had been. This morning he had said he would go get food, and he had gone. Even now, just whispering his name brought her a quiet calm – 'Shakombo.' Wasn't love a funny thing?

There was a young man she did not know walking beside the *Mzee* and he talked excitedly, his hands waving. Something had happened to Shakombo, she knew it. She hurried out to meet them. When he saw her, the young man immediately kept quiet and fell behind *Mzee* Hamisi. She tried to meet his eyes but they skittered away looking this way and that until finally he bowed his head and stared down at his feet. She turned her hopeful eyes on the *Mzee*. He had made many such visits in this ghost village of his but this was different. He had known Fatma well, ever since she was a little girl. He had known Shakombo too, the young man who had claimed her for his bride, a good man. And now he must tell her this.

'Tell me Baba, please tell me,' she asked, 'I can take it. It's all right.' She was the one calming *him* now, determined, although her chin quivered and tears began to pool in her eyes.

When he still wouldn't speak, she gave a wail and hurled herself at his feet, her hands clasping at his legs. Her tears stained his long white *Kanzu* and the old man cried with her. There were still some tears left in his dried out body and it seemed he cried them all. He cried for his village and his country. She cried for her lover and the father of her unborn child.

At last, she looked up at him and said quietly, with new resolve, 'we must go get him back Baba.' He did not have the heart to refuse her. He nodded and waited as she went into the hut to get her shawl.

These fools that talk of manhood, what do they know?

The government tanks had ceased their shelling. They'd withdrawn to safer positions in the hills surrounding the town. The narrow town streets were not ideal for manoeuvring the lumbering machines. The attack would resume in the morning. The rebels had a reprieve and they made the most of it. They were well aware how de-motivated the government soldiers were. There would be no surprise attack this night. The rebels had taken over the hotel next to the roadblock and now raucous laughter could be heard through the shattered windows. Comrade Senior Sergeant Livondo was holding court. The flickering light came from lanterns lit with the little paraffin they could find. The supplies were running low and they had to squeeze the remaining civilians harder and harder for hoarded rations. Livondo knew that today's execution was necessary to keep the people in line. Random acts of violence like that were important too for the rest of the band. They had to know who had the power of life and death. There was the constant threat of defections and desertions.

Comrade Senior Sergeant Livondo still had his big arm draped around Kay Kay's shoulders and he led the group in toast after toast of cheap spirits. One of the guards came running in and shouted, 'there's an old man and a woman here. They say they have come to claim the body to bury. Should we let them?'

'Is she beautiful? I know what she could help me bury!' A voice piped up. There was laughter.

'She's very pregnant. I doubt she'd be great fun… though that has never stopped Osama.' More laughter.

'Give them the body,' Livondo barked out. Comrade Senior Sergeant Livondo was feeling magnanimous. The vodka and ganja had made him very mellow. Anyway, it was important that the body go back to the village as an example. Then he burst out in an uncontrollable fit of laughter like he had just remembered a good joke. He laughed so long and hard they all kept quiet, tense, waiting like little children do when they hear thunder rumbling.

'Kay Kay! Where's our Krazy Killer? Go take care of it,' he ordered. That would toughen the kid up.

He rose up careful not to show his fear and walked to the veranda where the old man waited. This was just like Comrade Livondo, always testing them. Why must he be the one to face these snivelling villagers? He had been told to pull the trigger and he did. There was a woman behind the old man but her face was turned away and covered with a shawl.

'I'm Krazy Killer,' he boldly announced, so that his voice carried back into the hall. 'But you can call me Kay Kay,' he quickly added in a quieter tone, as if he recognized that the new name hung on him like an oversize suit. 'What do you want?'

'We have come for Shakombo's body, Kay Kay,' the old man respectfully replied.

Something about the boy sparked a memory in old man Hamisi. It was a happy memory of a singing plump brown woman and a laughing little boy peeking shyly at him from behind her skirts.

'Wait, I know you! You are Khakhame, Swalha's little boy! Of course, Kay Kay. Khakame! I knew your mother well Khakhame. She was a wonderful woman.'

Kay Kay had only vague recollections of his childhood. It was the aroma of the blackened cooking pots that he remembered most. He remembered the sweet smells of roasting maize and boiling sweet potatoes. There had always been something for him to nibble. Try as he could, he could not remember his mother's face, but he remembered feeling safe and warm. He couldn't think why she had left him. Comrade Livondo never talked about her but he said the Baghdad Boys were his family now. They would take care of him. They would never leave him like his mother. Yet he was curious. This old man claimed to have known her well. Despite himself, he felt curiosity and an unfamiliar pang well up. He felt his eyes mist over. He did not like this feeling.

'I'm Krazy Killer! I don't know what you are talking about old man. I killed him, this Shakombo.' He jerked his head in the direction of the roadblock where the body still lay. He started walking, leading them towards the corpse.

'I know what they made you do, Khakhame. That's not who you are.'

Khakhame. Why did the old man keep calling him that? He was Kay Kay now. He had a new family.

'I'm Kay Kay.'

The old man did not reply. He quietly stretched out a trembling hand and pointed towards the distraught woman who had run past them and was now kneeling over the body.

'Look at what they made you do. Look at what you did Khakhame,' the old man said.

The woman was beautiful without her shawl. She was cradling the corpse's head and softly wiping its blood-matted face with the shawl. She was whispering something they could not hear. Then she carefully arranged the clothing trying to cover up the torn flesh. The body must stink by now, he thought, yet she doesn't seem to mind.

Then the old man leaned forward and urgently whispered in Kay Kay's ear. Shocked, Kay Kay jerked his head away, shaking his head. He looked around guiltily but saw that no one was paying them any attention. The old man held his gaze steadily. Kay Kay's hands were trembling. He shook his head again. Then he quickly walked away on unsteady legs.

The little party of mourners left. The boy watched the sad procession from the veranda as it wound its way into the darkness. The two carried the heavy body between them stumbling at every step. He had seen many dead bodies. It was just a piece of meat. Why did they hold it so gently like that? Like it was still alive. Like it meant something.

He looked towards the silent dark hills and shivered. He knew they couldn't hold out much longer. Soon he would be like that man – Shakombo was it? But who would mourn for him? Who would weep over his body? There would have been some comfort in knowing that someone would claim him even in death. He wanted someone whispering over him and wiping his face with a shawl.

The laughter was still going on in the hotel but Kay Kay did not enter. He was suddenly restless. He went back over what the old man had whispered to him and the offer.

'You are not Kay Kay. You are not Krazy Killer. If you can make your way to our village, Khakhame, I'll get you across the border…'

There was something else that the old man had told him. Now that had to be a lie. He sat for long moments hunched over his rifle at the corner of the veranda. Then he stood up and went to the hotel door. His mind was made up. He went inside carefully avoiding Livondo's searching eyes. Sometimes he felt the man could see right into his soul. He could always catch the boys lying. It was uncanny the way he did that. He was looking for Comrade Luta.

Comrade Luta was in charge of the first watch. He couldn't drink right now and was looking on enviously at the wild partying. Kay Kay quietly approached him and pulled him to one side.

'Listen,' he said, 'let me have the first watch. I can't sleep now. The old man and the woman have placed a curse on me or something… I just can't sleep'

'I understand Kay Kay,' Luta assured him, 'My first time was like that too.' The Baghdad Boys now trusted him fully.

Kay Kay waited until the laughter subsided. The alcohol had begun to take effect. Some were asleep snoring loudly. It would be over an hour before anyone came to relieve him. He must do it now.

Kay Kay crept to the end of the veranda and placed his rifle upright against the railing. The light through the window briefly illuminated his face and it was not the face of a boy. It was the face of a man. Unencumbered, he slipped quietly into the darkness in the direction the body had been taken. The night was like the embrace of a mother's arms.

'Stop!' The harsh command echoed in the night. Comrade Luta had begun his patrol earlier than expected. 'Where are you off to, Kay Kay?'

Kay Kay stopped. He was halfway to the bushes at the side of the road and from there he knew of the secret path that would take him past the government encampments to the villages beyond the hills.

Luta's eyes narrowed as he noticed Kay Kay's abandoned rifle, leaning on the veranda. He clutched his own rifle tighter and turned the barrel slowly so that it now pointed at Kay Kay.

'I just needed to take a shit *bwana*,' Kay Kay said calmly. 'You know how those toilets stink in there. I would rather do it out in the fresh air.' Plausible.

Still Luta trained his rifle on him. He was not convinced. Kay Kay had to explain the abandoned gun on the veranda.

'Look, I didn't want that heavy thing with me in the dark. Do you remember when Tyson stumbled while taking a shit? His intestines were coming out of his arse. These safety catches are crazy.'

Luta burst out in laughter at the memory. He doubled over clutching his sides and laughed until tears and snot ran down his face. Maybe the vodka and weed had softened his brains.

'Ok, just hurry up before Livondo comes in.' Luta, still convulsing with laughter, jerked his head in the direction of the bushes.

Kay Kay fought the urge to run for the bushes. He knew so well what happened to traitors. What he had done to Shakombo was nothing. They had a special treat for traitors. He walked deliberately until he reached the edge of the road. His neck was stiff from the effort not to turn and watch Luta. His back tingled anticipating a bullet at any moment.

Then he was in the bushes searching for the path. He almost did not find it in the dark. Panic gripped him and he dropped to his knees groping with his bare hands, letting them feel the ground searching. He forced himself to calm down and as his eyes adjusted to the dark he saw it. He moved on the path walking fast. He started out at a brisk walk then he was jogging lightly. Soon he was running at full stride and laughing, running light and free towards the new horizon. The bushes whipped and scratched at his arms as if trying to stop him but he never looked back. He kept replaying in his mind over and over what the old man had whispered to him so urgently: –

'Khakhame, they killed your mother and took you! I was there! I saw it with my own eyes. They killed her when she refused to give you up. They killed your mother! She loved you more than her own life. You have to remember. You must!'

I am Africa... Waking. I laugh as I run, the wind on my face. My sandaled feet kick up little swirling dust devils from the dry grass. I am young and strong and I run lightly, untiring. My smooth long-limbed strides eat up the distance. My second wind kicks in and I breathe easily, steadily. At this pace, I can run forever, running towards freedom.

Kaume Marambii is a self-employed businessman running an agri-business in Kenya called Golden Acres Ltd. He grows potatoes and other vegetables. His background is varied. He has a degree in Veterinary Medicine from the University of Nairobi, a post-graduate Diploma in Information Technology from the University of Sunderland, UK, and is currently pursuing a MSc in Agribusiness from the University of London, UK. He was also a 2003-2004 Reuters Digital Vision Fellow at Stanford University, USA. He is interested in anything and everything. This is his first work of fiction.

Love is like Botswana Rain

Wame Molefhe

IT WAS MY MOTHER who rang to tell me. She rang at that ungodly hour of night when messages of birth and death were usually conveyed. I felt the vibration of the cell phone that I kept on the bedside table. 'Sethu…' she said. 'I have got sad, sad news for you…' I knew that it was serious. It was rare for my mother to call me by the name she used when I was a little girl.

'Kgomotso has passed away.'

'No Mama… how?... when?' I whispered, pressed the cell phone to my ear, waited for her to speak. I listened to her breathing, and regretted asking the cause of Kgomotso's death. I needed to know, even though I myself despised the way Botswana people probed the cause of a person's death the way a nurse felt your arm, searching for the right vein from which to draw blood.

'She committed suicide… they found her body yesterday… the funeral will be on Saturday… and Sethu… she left you a note.'

A note? I asked myself why. Why did Kgomotso take her life and why did she leave me a note? Fear frothed in my stomach like cola when you drop a pebble in it.

My husband, Thabo, lay fast asleep beside me. He slept like our baby did, mouth slightly open, an arm cradling his head.

What if Kgomotso's note exposed my secret? I stole out of bed, taking care not to wake him, wondering if I would ever sleep so soundly again.

* * *

When I was a little girl, life was well-ordered. Winters were cold and dry; summers were hot and moist, the way my geography textbook said Botswana weather should be. When it rained, I raced outside and squelched the mud between my toes. I waved my fingers in the air shouting, 'rain, rain make me grow,' as I chased after corn crickets that appeared with the rainbow, like

141

marching soldiers.

After the rain, I played football barefoot in the sand, and didn't care that people mistook me for a boy. When the sun got too hot, I rested in the shade with my knees drawn up, my elbows on my knees. Mama would creep up behind me and clap her hands, like crackling lightning, saying, 'Sethunya! Sit properly. You are not a herd boy.' I'd straighten my legs, and press my thighs together, trying to be more of a lady.

Back then Kgomotso was my best friend. I was ten when her family moved into the house on our cul-de-sac. We liked lying on our backs together under the morula tree, holding hands, sucking on its yellow fruit. She was a dreamer, even then. I would tell her a silly story and laugh out loud. She'd say, '*shhhh* Sethunya. Listen. The wind is whispering my future to me... listen... it says one day, I'm going to fly to a faraway land where I'll be whatever I dream.'

When my boy-hips filled out, my buttocks grew rounder and softer and the morula-sized knobs in my chest swelled, Mama said, 'boys are trouble. Run from trouble.'

But she needn't have worried. Boys? They did not interest me. I was happiest when I was with Kgomotso and I did not want to share her. When all the girls in my class were whispering and giggling about boys, wondering who was going to ask whom to the school leavers' ball, I really didn't care. But all the same, I played the game. I did not want to be the odd one out.

* * *

As I grew older, life became a trial. Home. School. Church. Everywhere, it seemed as if I was being cast into a mould. In school I had to memorise what made dust different from dirt. I struggled to remember whether to sweep first then polish. At home, Mama asked, 'What kind of a woman are you going to become?' As I grew older, she graduated to, 'Oh my Lord, what kind of a wife will she make?' I tried hard – to be an obedient daughter, a good woman.

Every Sunday, I dressed up in my floral two-piece to attend the early morning church service. Whenever Pastor Simon warned, 'Hell is hotter than a hell-fire,' and, 'Cast out the devil,' I felt hell's flames singeing my body. I twisted and turned in my seat. I taught Sunday school, sang in the church choir and I feared the Lord. I so wanted to be God's child and I had to go to heaven where everyone was family and everyone was happy.

I tried hard to douse that thing in me that caused me to lie awake at night, longing to be with Kgomotso.

My love for Kgomotso was like Botswana rain. I gave it sparingly. When she responded, like new grass after summer rains, I held my love back. Then she would cling to me, like a clump of grass growing deep in the crack of a rock, trying to suck what moisture it could.

But now Kgomotso was dead. No! She had gone to her faraway land where she would find peace. Yes, this thought consoled me.

I relived my last visit to her house. She'd called me saying she needed someone to talk to. We met at her house. She hugged me, but I stood with my arms hanging down, stiff as slats of wood. She had seemed distant and her words stayed with me after I left, like puddles after the rain, murky and brown, concealing rocks beneath the surface.

'Do you ever think of me?' she wanted to know.

'Sometimes.'

'Do you love him?'

'He is my husband.'

'Maybe you could still come and visit... sometimes?' I did not respond.

'Do you ever think of killing yourself?' Her question had shocked me but I said, 'Never. Suicide is a mortal sin,' using my Sunday school teacher voice. My words stemmed her questions and the silence between us became unbearable. I left.

Although I did not want him to, Thabo went with me to Kgomotso's funeral. He was my husband and he always did what was right; that was his way. We drove in silence from our home to hers. I stared out of the window, worrying about what Kgomotso's note might reveal. Her home seemed further away than I remembered but maybe it was because Thabo drove slowly. Rain had gouged out the surface of the road, creating a patchwork of grit, tar and potholes. As we approached her home, I saw a woman sitting alone in the shade of the morula tree, where I used to sit with Kgomotso, pretending to the world that we were just friends.

I thought I had buried Kgomotso in the deepest crevice of my mind, but ever since I heard she had died, the memory of her had risen to the surface. It faded by day, blanched by the things that demanded my attention: my baby's laughter, a meal to be cooked, Thabo's missing sock.

At night, Kgomotso came alive again.

Sitting beside Thabo as he drove, I thought back to when I met him. I was twenty-three. He had just returned from overseas. He played the organ in church. I fell in love with his voice. When he sang, the notes rose from deep in his throat and filled the church. He laughed easily. His shoulders were broad and he towered over me, I had to tilt my head to look into his eyes. He'd been walking me home after choir practice for a few weeks. One evening he asked,

'Do you have a boyfriend?'

143

'No.'

'How come? Why would a girl named after a beautiful flower not have a boyfriend?'

'Maybe I was waiting for you,' I said and smiled.

He laughed and took my hand and turned it over in his. Then he stroked my palm. My hand seemed so tiny in his but his touch was gentle, like a woman's. 'I like you,' he said, 'a lot.'

I smiled. Thabo liked me. Out of all the women whose dreams he touched, he chose me. I thought of Kgomotso and I snatched my hand away from Thabo's. He looked at me and said, 'Sometimes I look at you, Sethunya, and wonder whether you are here with me.'

'*Ao? Re mmogo*, Thabo. You have never seen me with anyone else have you?'

He shook his head and said, 'One day, Sethunya, you will take me with you, to that place where you go.' I smiled. It seemed the easiest thing to do. In that moment, I learnt that lying was easier done in my mother tongue.

After a year of dating, Thabo sent his uncles to my house. I arrived home to the smell of rum and maple tobacco. Thabo's pipe-smoking uncle had come to our home to tell my uncles that their nephew was looking for a *'segametsi'*, a bearer of water. Even before his aroma had left the room, Mama called Pastor Simon and announced 'Sethunya is to be married.' A month later, ten head of cattle arrived, on the hoof, with Thabo racing behind them. Our families had spoken. I would be Thabo's wife.

I saw pride in the way Mama swung her hips on her way to the front pew in church. She held her head upright as if she was balancing a bucketful of water on her head. I heard it when she trilled her notes higher than everyone else when we sang the final verse. I felt her pleasure as she caressed the soft silks she said would make me a lovely bridal gown.

Her excitement was contagious. I wore a white silk wedding dress with a long zip and darts that lifted my breasts and skimmed my thighs on its way down to my ankles. It had a sweeping train that brushed all my doubts under the red carpet that led into the church. I repeated after Pastor Simon, that I would love and obey my husband, in sickness and in health, and recited all the other words meant to define marriage.

When Pastor Simon said, 'I now pronounce you man and wife,' Thabo eagerly lifted my veil to kiss me. I smiled, a demure smile, befitting of a good woman. With my hand clasped in his, we danced to the song of ululating strangers who converged on us as we greeted the congregation, man and wife. It began to drizzle as we emerged from the church. Tiny raindrops mixed with confetti and everyone agreed we were blessed.

'Remember to thank the Lord for giving you such a wonderful husband,' my mother said.

* * *

It was the first morning of our married life and I lay next to Thabo. Gentle raindrops tapped on the windows like a timid man's knock. It was a change from the Botswana rain I knew that usually boomed and thundered as if God raged.

I twisted my hand this way and that and watched my ring sparkle. I wanted to lie still in bed and listen to the rain; listen to my thoughts. When I closed my eyes I smelt coconut and strawberry. I remembered and smiled sadly.

'Tell me, Sethunya. You know you can tell me what is on your mind,' Thabo whispered as he traced my lips with his finger.

'Ah... I'm just happy for the rain,' I said, but his words stole the smile from my eyes and I slid out of his arms. I would have stayed in bed if he had not spoken and soiled my memories....

When Thabo told me he loved me I held my body in expectation of another feeling. The feeling that swept me up on a wave when Kgomotso skimmed my neck with her lips. I smelt the sweet coconut in her hair, tasted the strawberries on her lips. My nipples stiffened as though pecked by a cold breeze and I felt warm in places whose names I did not say out loud. Then she took my hand in hers and we lay together on her bed, soaring to the lands I had only dreamed of.

I was thinking of Kgomotso as I lay next to my husband; thinking how silence did not threaten her, did not disquiet her like it did Thabo.

I remembered how I had told her about him. It was a Sunday, after church, the day I usually visited. I waited for her to settle into the couch and then I took the chair furthest from her.

'How do I say this? ... You know that I have been seeing Thabo, don't you?'

'Seeing him? You said he was a good friend.'

'He is a good friend... a very good friend. He has asked me to marry him. I have said yes. We are going to move. He's got a job... in Johannesburg.'

She looked away, bewildered as a bird that flew into a window mid-flight. And then she looked at me and said, 'Poor Thabo. You are making the biggest mistake of your life, Sethunya.'

'But, Kgomotso, you knew this would happen one day. How could we go on? I live with the fear of being found out. Imagine the shame. The police... jail...'

'Ah... it's your life. Keep lying to yourself.'

I could not respond. She did not walk me out of the house to the gate like she usually did. She had closed the front door as I stepped out. I don't know if she

145

watched me stride down the path to the gate. I didn't look back. What did she know about legitimate love?

I stopped going to her house after that day, avoiding the places she frequented. When I saw her in the street I greeted her politely, like I did old people, '*Dumela mma. O teng, mma?*' Whenever her name was mentioned, I pretended not to hear; or I echoed the sounds that other people made when they talked about her. They called her terrible names and said she was trying to be a man. She was sick, they said and all she needed was a man to cure her. What was wrong with her?

But when I was alone, thinking of Kgomotso filled me with yearning. I thought of her doe-eyes that made her look sleepy, and imagined stroking her smooth olive skin and kissing her nose that sat small and pointed in her oval face.

At first the sun shone when we arrived at Kgomotso's home. But as the funeral service progressed, rainclouds gathered like cattle being rounded up. Rain pounded the earth and kicked up the smell of freshly turned soil into the air.

I had chosen my outfit carefully, covered my dread in the uniform of respectability. I wore a tent-like dress, a shawl across my shoulders, a *doek* on my head and dark shades. Walking beside my husband, my high heels made squelching sounds, kisses to waterlogged soil. I was a good Motswana woman.

They lowered Kgomotso's coffin into the grave. The rain came down. Bumping, banging it floated, banging the sides of the hole. Men took shovels to fill it and the thud of mud landing on the wood fell on my soul. Thabo took off his jacket and draped it over my shoulders and then he too picked up a shovel. I watched the muscles in his arms bunch as he covered my love with soil and I felt tears sting my eyes. I blinked and blinked to keep them from falling.

Kgomotso's mother gave me the envelope when I went into the house to pay my respects. I felt her watching me as I turned it over in my hand and slipped it into my bag. I took it out again and tore it open, slowly, read the words to myself, folded it away again.

S.
Just couldn't take it. I'm going to a better place.
Kgomotso

She had signed her name with her characteristic giant loop and double lines underneath. I remembered how we used to practise our signatures.

'Don't press down so hard on the paper,' I would say.

'I can't do flowery like you, Sethunya.'

That was all. Her words were as bland as the funeral food we had eaten, but I understood.

I wanted to cry till I gasped for breath. I wanted to wear black and lie prostrate like custom demanded, cocooned in grief so everyone knew that I had lost a part of me. Instead I remained dry-eyed like a man. No one said *'Ao shame. Poor soul. It will be okay. Just be strong,'* to me.

I saw Thabo looking at me but I didn't offer to give him the note. He didn't ask to see it.

I ache for Kgomotso. I know that I should have run away with her, to a place where the sun did not shine so hard that it dried people's hearts and made them unyielding. I hope that one day I will find her in that place, where everyone is happy.

This is what I am thinking when Thabo touches my shoulder. I move away from him and then he whispers, 'Sethunya, come.' I turn towards him and fit my body into his.

Wame Molefhe was born in Francistown, Botswana. She lives in Gaborone with her two children. She is currently studying for a BA in Languages and Literature with the University of South Africa. She recently won the *Woman and Home* South Africa short story competition and was highly commended in the 2007 Commonwealth Short Story Competition. She has a short story forthcoming in AmaBooks, to be published in 2008.

The Boulder

Henrietta Rose-Innes

WHEN THE BOULDER CAME down from the mountainside, it must have made a sound like the end of the world, rocking the ground with each thunderous landing and recoil. It must have sung through the air, thrashing the bush on the slope into a sappy pulp with every bounce, on its way to embed itself in the lawn of the luxury holiday home below.

Dan did not hear or see this passage. He was fast asleep, waking only when the last impact shuddered the foundations of the house. He knew immediately what it was, though: not an earthquake, not a bomb. His first thought on waking was exactly this: *the mountain is falling on top of us.*

In the ensuing silence, he did not leave the bed and make his way through the dark house to the back garden to investigate. The two collie dogs that had slept in the room with him both went to sit at the closed door, as if expecting a visitor, but they did not bark. No other footsteps in the house. Dan lay very very still, playing dead, until the trick seemed to work and he slipped back under, into sleep.

In the light of morning, he let himself out of the glass sliding door into the garden, where half the lawn had been replaced by a giant grey-brown beast, high as a house.

The rock was two-tone, raw side up, stained nicotine brown where it had been wrenched from the earth. It looked like a meteor, something from an alien planet, bringing strange and enigmatic traces of a different world. It still bore a few crushed fronds of mountain vegetation, and the sharp sweet smell of mashed leaves and high places.

The more nervous dog trembled at his heels, while the other snuffled around the base of the boulder. Dan was trembling too. The rock seemed precarious: the lawn, at a slight rake, was on the verge of tipping it towards him. When the dog lifted a leg to pee against the stone, he called it sharply away, as if even that much contact might send the monster sliding again, right over him and through the glass doors and on into the house.

But after he'd stared at the monumental guest for a while longer, it seemed clear that the boulder had chosen its place of rest. It did not steam or creak or shift. He went a little closer.

The rock had not had an easy descent – it was bruised and lacerated, with paler stone showing through on the scuffed edges. One small impact mark, at eye level, was almost perfectly circular, a neat scoop of dove-grey. He thought of Colette: a touch of delicacy on the scarred brow of the stone.

He reached out, then pulled his hand away. The scene should not be disturbed. Because had there not been a crime here somehow? Damage? Looking up, he could see the destructive strides of the boulder, a clear trail all the way up to a patch of exposed rock on the ridge. Surely someone would want to know who was responsible? And here, the evidence looming over him, undeniable.

Dan went back inside. He took the dirty wine glasses into the kitchen and put them in the sink. He picked up Colette's shoes and carried them to the main bedroom. The bed was empty.

He was sixteen and Colette, a year and a half older, was his very first girlfriend. She was a slender girl with light, curling hair. At times her long, fine-boned face, with its delicately flaring nostrils, made him think of an ivory horse in a chess-set. They'd known each other for a few months when she invited him to spend the week's holiday in her family beach house.

'I'll meet your folks?' he asked, nervous.

'No, are you crazy?'

So it would just be the two of them. He hid his amazement.

'Sure,' she said. 'I come here all the time. My parents are cool with it.'

Dan was husky, large for his age; he was reminded that Colette had not yet guessed how young he really was.

The holiday was the most exciting thing that had ever happened to him. Colette, who had her driving licence, came to pick him up in a shiny little car. But once they got to the house – which was huge, white, and filled with light and views of blue water – he was awkward, unsure of what they were there to do. His family had never had holiday houses, or holidays, really, and he didn't know how to behave. In the first few days they had sex several times – which was still astonishing to him, barely believable. Otherwise, all she wanted to do was lie on the beach, which was five minutes away on the other side of the road. He went with her, but secretly he felt a yearning in the other direction: up, to the topmost point of the high rocky ground that lay behind the houses.

The big windows and patio doors woke tingles in his scalp. Once, when he was ten, on a school trip to the swimming pool, he'd run in his bathing trunks towards the glitter of water and instead slammed head-first into the shock of a glass wall.

He remembered the dumb halt of it, and then a blank. Waking up a few moments later, he'd felt first a vague despair, and then embarrassment. It still gave him a quake of strangeness, to think of that missing moment, black as space. *Thick head,* he remembered the teacher saying. *That's what saved you.*

'Great view,' he said to Colette. It was not the first time he'd made this observation.

'Mm,' she said. 'Mom wanted bars, but we prefer it open like this. We've got serious security. Those guys are here in like two minutes, with guns. Plus they cruise past every half hour.'

'Great,' he said. 'I'll try not to look suspicious.'

She gave him a laugh, a full genuine one, and he laughed back in relief. He said to himself: maybe she is waiting for you to be decisive; to show her something new. That is what a boyfriend does. You could just say: *I want to go up the mountain today.* Or better: *Let's go up the mountain.*

'Let's not, and say we did.' She was reading the label on a bottle of sun-tan oil. Already she had on her tangerine-coloured bikini.

He flushed, and then laughed. 'Sure, no, I just thought…'

'You can go, if you want,' she said, smoothing the oil onto her legs. 'Go.'

There was no path. Dan climbed up as high as he could, until he could see over the crest of the hill and almost into the valley beyond. Near the top, the boulders were heaped up against the side of the mountain, waiting their turn like huge slow children on a diving board. You could see where others had already rolled and come to rest on the slope below, caught in a lava flow of bush. Right down at the bottom, some had been built into the fabric of the houses, the road, the seawall.

There was dampness on his upper lip and under his arms. Around him the mountain sweated and shifted too. When he came down he would be smelling, scratched up; he would not want her to see him like that.

One last boulder blocked his way to the summit. He kicked at its base. There was no danger of shifting it: the rock was deeply rooted. It was like kicking at the earth's core. Nonetheless, he thought, with the next rains things would tumble, rearrange. Mountains were always falling down.

He laid his cheek against it, smelling the cool greenish-grey of the stone. Then he gripped and started to climb, finding the holds and ridges by touch, clumsy but strong. Granite was harder to climb than sandstone – not so many cracks. It hurt his fingers. Halfway up, he imagined her watching him from behind and it almost made him slip.

Since they'd arrived here, he'd been holding himself so stiff next to her, terrified of breaking something. Trying to tell when it was okay to touch her and when not.

Now it was good just to move. To sweat, and not worry about sweating.

At the top he stood and looked down. The waves were coming in neatly in thin white rolls. Turquoise lozenges of swimming pools gleamed. From up here, the shapes of the big houses seemed extravagant, eccentric, with whorls and curlicues, like multi-chambered seashells. The fallen boulders seemed so much more solid than the flimsy structures nested between them.

Colette's parents' was one of the larger houses, well placed for sea views. He found the broad driveway, the double garage, the patch of grass at the back and the small pink rectangles of the deckchairs.

There was a pale fleck moving diagonally across the green of the lawn. He deciphered it: Colette, settling herself in a deckchair. It was strange to see her so reduced. Although she was not a large person, usually she loomed over him, close up, filling his vision. Strange also to realize that, for the moment, he was glad not to have his face pressed up against that flesh; just at this moment, to breathe. He hated the smell of sun-tan oil.

She had been growing even more beautiful with the days in the sun. In the evenings, they sat down to eat at the long table in the dining room. She liked to dress for dinner: lipstick, hair up, shoes with a heel. It made her look older, even, than she'd seemed to him before. Usually, she ordered in – but not pizza: exotic restaurant food, always several different dishes. She did not seem to expect him to pay. They ate from porcelain plates with silver cutlery, and drank fine wine from the extensive rack.

The formal dining arrangement made him feel that they should be making conversation, like a man and a woman on a date; but he sat searching for words. Each night he said less and drank more. There were periods of silence, with Colette staring out of the window at the darkening sea, or checking her cell phone for messages.

On the sideboard stood family photos in heavy silver frames. Mother, father, Colette as a baby, an older brother. The whole family had a similar look: lean, pale-eyed, with attractive, slightly elongated features. Dan's eyes, in contrast, were the colour of the dark slate floors in the beach-house bathrooms. This thought occurred to him when he sat on the toilet, guts uneasy. Knowing that Colette was waiting – ablaze, expectant.

Up on the rock, Dan felt a dreamy vertigo. Like he might topple onto her, all the way down there. He imagined something happening to her at that moment: an assault, a seizure, a horrible accident. He would see it all reduced, the kicks and struggles tiny flickers against the green grass. Maybe a fraction of a moment later, a thin cry floating up through the air. He would be too far away to prevent it, to catch or hold her; to be held accountable.

He was much higher up than he'd realised. All at once he was stranded – nothing but blue sky all around, no substance, nothing to lean on. His legs started trembling and he went down on his knees, clutching the rock.

He was able to crawl away from the edge. The back side of the rock turned out to be easier, sloping gently. At its base he crouched in the bushes, legs still shuddering. And all he'd wanted was to be up there, at the top.

That night, miraculously, despite his clumsiness and the constant slight trembling that he was feeling now in her presence, he did not break a thing, or bite a section out of the rim of his glittering wine glass. He drank glass after glass, and the more he drank the brighter and more finely drawn her face seemed on the other side of the polished tabletop. Her eyes so bright he could not look.

She was going to leave him. He knew it absolutely. He looked at the cream and silver surfaces of the house, and felt his wrongness there quite clearly. The house was not able to tolerate his touch. He didn't know how to stand here, how to sit or hold things. Of course this was plain to her as well, and any minute now she would dump him. He was quite drunk.

When her cell phone rang, she stared at the screen for a moment without answering.

'Who is it?' he asked, too loudly.

Instead of replying, she took the phone through into the bedroom to talk.

'Who was it?' he said when she came back.

'What? Dan, god,' she said crossly, dropping into her seat. She kicked off her grown-up shoes and pulled her feet up into the chair.

'Who?'

'It was my dad, okay? Look, I'm sorry, but he wants to come out here tomorrow.' She didn't look at him. 'And anyway I think it's better, don't you? This isn't really working out.'

'What? What do you mean?' He couldn't hear her words, only his own, noisy in his head. 'What's better?'

'If you go.'

She would leave him, she would dump him, she was doing it now: he could see her mouth moving, saying the words.

That night, he ended up in the spare bedroom with the dogs. And by morning, of course, the boulder was there.

The boulder had almost no shadow at this hour, just a thin rim of black around its lower edges. Now Dan recognised the rock – it was the one he'd met before, up on the slope. Here was that particular lip that he'd used to pull himself up with, just canted over a few degrees. He could climb it easily now, but the impulse was gone.

He squatted down and peered into the dark gap underneath the edge of the rock. His thumbs tingled, remembering being hit by hammers, caught in car doors. He lay down on his stomach and put his face as close as he could, but saw nothing in the darkness. When he put his hand flat against the ground and slid it in, not touching the rock, his fingertips touched something rough and dry. He worked it back and forth until he could pull it free. A splintered wooden slat, still attached to a strip of deck-chair canvas, candy pink.

He went into the house. Black spots mottled his vision. The living room was dim but he did not switch on a light. Out the front, her car was still in the drive. He sat for a while on the huge white couch, heart hitting the front of his chest. He picked up the phone to call her cell phone but then put it down again without dialling. When he tried a second time it was off. Swallowing back the sickness, he went outside to peer again at the boulder, underneath it, careful not to touch it with any part of his body. The dogs, anxious, trailed him silently back and forth, wagging their tails uncertainly.

He sat on the couch, big as a queen-size bed. He'd kicked at that thing, up there on the mountain, only yesterday.

He felt the sweat cooling in his palms, and wiped them every now and then on the white fabric. Waiting for them to come and find him there.

All at once there were cars drawing up outside, a clatter at the door, a strange man's voice. Without thinking he was up from the couch, through the glass doors and out, not looking back as he ducked behind the boulder. Here the neat beds and boundaries of the garden had been mangled: he saw uprooted tree stumps, split stems, mashed petals. The garden wall had been smashed through, but it was impossible to climb out over the big shards of pre-cast concrete; and anyway, directly behind the property an overgrown bank rose steeply, impassable.

He squeezed in behind the boulder. It was the first time he'd actually touched it since its fall. Smells of dog-shit and damp soil. He could see only a strip of lawn from where he stood. There was a moment of quiet, and then he heard the patio door slide open.

The man's voice again, deep, and shadows moving on the lawn. Shadow people merging, separating; shadow dogs. A man came into sight, pacing backwards across the grass. Lean build, pink polo shirt, thinning sandy hair. He stopped dead and gazed up at the boulder, hand slapped against his forehead in what might be amazement or horror. 'Colette!' he shouted.

Silence. The man remained frozen, staring.

'Bloody hell,' he said more quietly.

Dan recognized him now, from the pictures in the silver frames. Her father.

'Bloody hell!' he said again. 'Colette!'

And then he was shaking his head and – could it be? – laughing, and gesturing towards the house. A slim figure sidled into the crook of his arm. Colette. Arms folded, coy and fidgeting, digging a toe into the grass like a kid. Dan let out the breath that he felt he'd been holding all morning.

'Get that chappie from the *Cape Times* in here,' the father continued. 'Photographer chappie. They'll want this for the front page. Can you climb up there, Col? Get one of you on top – in your bikini. Hey?'

'Dad,' she said, rolling her eyes.

She swivelled out of his clasp, arms still clutched across her chest. Dan could see she was tense – shooting glances back at the house.

It's me, Dan thought. She's worried about me. I'm not supposed to be here.

And for the first time in all the time he'd been with her, he knew that he knew what she was thinking.

He liked the dogs, they were gentle with him and well-trained, never barking, just giving their alert attention where it was needed. Which is what they did now, coming to sit directly in front of him, side by side, pointing their snouts at him with quiet friendly curiosity.

But the father was already going back into the house. 'I need a drink, sweetheart,' Dan heard him rumbling.

Colette remained standing cocked-hip on the lawn, arms crossed, swaying a little left and right as if in a light breeze. As she rocked he saw her eyes take in the dogs, pause, adjust, then follow their gaze to find him there, pressed up against the rock. Her small personal breeze stilled completely.

Only hours before, he would have been mortified, would have shrunk away from those eyes, would have wriggled more deeply into the crack or rolled over onto his back like one of the dogs. But now he simply stood away from the stone.

She gave him a small smile, and for a single moment there was something between them that had never been there before: some kind of recognition. He saw a glimpse of what that might be like, for two people to look at each other frankly, without fear. Perhaps it was possible to show himself to her again, differently. To start over.

He was stepping out from the shade of the boulder, feeling a hesitant gladness, when she glanced at the house and her smile stopped short. Without moving her body she gave a tense shake of the head. *No.* One finger lifted from her forearm, stilling him. Another watchful look at the house, and then she stepped closer.

'We went out for breakfast,' she said in a low voice. 'Dan. What are you doing here?'

He stared at her, wordless.

'You were supposed to be gone already. I told you. I *told* you. Last night.' She

155

looked at the rock with disgust. 'And *this* –'

'Colette,' came a call from the house.

She glanced over her shoulder. 'Just… I don't know. Just don't let him see you. We'll sort it out later, okay?'

She turned her back on him and walked away.

He was still standing like that, one foot forward, pointing like one of the dogs, when he heard the front door open and close again – and then the rhythmic beeping of the alarm setting itself.

He was shaking with anger. He came up to the glass door of the empty house and slammed his fists against it. It bounced his hands back at him. There were no keys, she had never given him a set.

Now the dogs were whimpering by his side, scrabbling at the doorframe. They were not used to this treatment either. Dan backed away blindly, came up against the boulder. He leaned against it, in its growing shade. For one moment he tried to bring it back: her smooth body against his own. But all he could feel now was the stone.

His skin prickled. Like electricity coming through the stone: the energy of its descent, finding a new conduit. Through his shoulders, down his arms and into his chest, his head, his groin, into his feet and back up into his face, which burned with it. Momentum. Forward motion. It kicked him again towards the house. All the rolling motion of the boulder now in him.

His reflection faced him in the patio door, standing against the white and beige shapes and dark-wood furniture inside.

He picked up a heavy plant-pot and threw it and the glass shivered and came down like water. Easy.

The alarm whooped around his ears. But Dan moved steadily, confidently. Nothing could stop him. He was carried by gravity, down through the white spaces of the house. This was the ancient route of boulders; they had always come this way, long before houses. The building was fragile, paper and glass. As he walked he raised his hands and let them trail against things on the shelves, picture frames and vases falling left and right. What broke he could not really say; he did not look back, but he felt that the whole house was coming down behind him.

He touched the front door and it fell open. He went out into the sunlight, over the front lawn and the two lanes of the road and the sea wall, and then down onto the white sand of the beach.

Already he heard the sirens of the security guards, but he knew he was safe; he could not be stopped. The dogs ran to snap at the breakers and then came back to his side; one pushed a muzzle into the palm of his hand.

Dan walked on along the beach until he was out of sight of the house. He would make his own way home.

But first, he reached down to pick up a handful of fine sand and put it in his pocket, to take away. It was what you did when you came on holiday to the sea.

Henrietta Rose-Innes was born in 1971 and lives in Cape Town. She is the author of two novels, *Shark's Egg* (2000) and *The Rock Alphabet* (2004), both published by Kwela Books, and was the compiler of an anthology of South African writing, *Nice Times! A Book of South African Pleasures and Delights* (Double Storey, 2006). Her short stories and essays have appeared in a variety of publications in South Africa and elsewhere. A translated anthology of short pieces will be published in Germany in 2008, and *The Rock Alphabet* has been published in Romanian translation. She was the winner of the 2007 Southern African PEN short story award, and was shortlisted for the Caine Prize in 2007.

Digitalis Lust

Olufemi Terry

HE LOOKS FORWARD TO the second Wednesday of every month, and with the same impatience regardless of his libido. On those afternoons, which his colleagues believe have been set aside for playing squash as his Mondays are, he leaves the office at half past four to drive into town, glad to go against the city traffic.

He turns the car away from the ocean road and goes some distance up the mountain. Here, the streets are close, cobbled in places and uneven. In the sunlight of early summer he sees no one walking. The building he is going to is shouldered on one side by a bed and breakfast; its other neighbour is a town house. He's in the habit of parking directly outside or at the opposite kerb, but today, he finds it necessary to go as far as the next intersection to find a space.

He presses the top buzzer. The door jangles to signal it's unlocked and he lets himself in. On the second floor landing hang etchings of stylized hunters with bent bows meant, he assumes, to connote primitive art. With a short knock at the last door, he enters without waiting for a response. A woman with cocoa brown skin is unhurriedly placing a magazine beneath the bed. In the same motion, she gets to her feet.

'Mr Raymond.' The greeting carries a note of pleased startlement, genuine but practiced. His lips pull into a blank almost-smile, a look of discretion that's part of his ritual for these assignations. Their eyes meet an instant before his slide away. The flowers in the tall thin vase strike him as a peculiar choice; he associates roses with romance. He sets down his case next to the wall before she can take it, but allows her to assist him in removing his jacket.

The small room, with its high, square bed, is cozy rather than cramped and carries a lilyish scent. He sits on the bed to unlace his shoes. From behind him comes the stir and clink of her preparations. Atonal music, faintly Asian, plays.

In nothing but grey undershorts he lies, face in the pillow. The floor squeaks beneath her step and a coverlet, light as lace drops over his prickling skin, draping his body.

159

Warm, greased palms clasp his shoulders, a readying touch. She begins to work oil into the muscles about his shoulder blades, which are, he thinks with pride, knotty from years of swimming. Once or twice, she's told him he is tense but today she moves without pause or comment to press his lower back. He drowses. In the flexing of small strong hands over his torso he detects a rhythm that keeps time with the music. Against her first touch there, close to the buttocks, he clenches a little.

She crosses to the other side and folds back the sheet to expose calves, hamstrings. With a slow movement, as if from an almost-healed injury, he wipes drool from the corner of his mouth, conscious of his erection.

He is on his back now. He watches her movements through half-closed lashes, a pretence which, deceiving no one, is a form of intimacy between them in this room. She gives no sign she's noticed his excitement, not so much as a glance at the bulge of his shorts. Setting down the bottle of oil, she tugs gently at his waistband. He's grateful for the unspoken arrangement they – he and she – have fixed. He need never demand of her the more purposeful touch that is imminent. This would bring him shame. His arousal, visible, insistent, conveys whether the massage is to continue.

How often does she end a session this way? His mind shies from the thought. Her adroit grip, the warm unguent, bring him after a few strokes to climax. He utters no sound, not wishing to embarrass either of them.

She is staunching ejaculate with tissue as one might a flesh wound. In this moment, his body subsiding, surrendering swift heat, he feels vulnerable. He wants a few minutes to himself but forces open his eyes – even now a fresh client might be at the door downstairs.

He sits up, and she brings his shirt, his trousers. Only now that it's done does he permit his eyes to meet hers. She complies in the little game, busying herself with small needless tasks, directing toward him occasional demure glances. At each turn her robe swings open to offer a momentary allure. Even when he does not have a happy ending (the euphemism amuses him) it is a matter of many minutes before he speaks.

'Thank you, Maryam.' He says at last, wary of the false intimacy that might comes with near nakedness and the scent of semen. 'How are things?'

Now she will not turn – he cannot see what holds her attention, perhaps she offers her back simply to safeguard his privacy – but says with a kind of shiver, 'I'm exhausted.'

He does not know what his response should be. Instead, too sharply, he stands to pull on his trousers and blood flees his skull. Puffs of white burst and star before his eyes. He shuts them a moment. Swaying, he decides he must tip her more than usual. As if he were not generous already.

But she faces him, arms folded. 'I have a sister. She can't take care of herself, you know like a vegetable. So we have to do it. My ma and me. But it's work, *ek sê.*' Her voice is flat with suppressed anger.

Is it pity she wants?

'I wish sometimes she'd die. It's no life she has.'

'How did she become that way?' His own curiosity surprises him.

'She's always been. She was born like that. I've been wishing she weren't around since I was ten and I had to help wash her.'

'Does your mother also find her a burden?'

'It's her child. From her body, you know. Maybe I'd feel the same if she were my daughter not my sister.' She leans against the table. The robe, which falls as far as her knee, exposes thighs paler than her face. Before, he's put her age at below thirty but he guesses now she's not more than twenty-five. 'But the effort to take care of her, to clean her... sis, man!'

'Have you heard of mercy killing?' The toe tips of his socked feet rest on the floor but he makes no move to put on his shoes. Incomprehension is apparent on Maryam's face. He doesn't know if he means the question as a joke. The conversation has abruptly become morbid. 'It's for those who'd be better off dead.' He tries to assume his vapid half smile but his cheeks are stiff. A silence has cut between them. Scrubbing a hand through his hair, he ignores the stickiness spreading down his thigh and goes to his coat. From his wallet he removes four notes, trying to conceal that he counts them. He sets the money beneath the pillow and does not look at her.

The next night, he stops to buy Thai food and takes it to Carol's house. Carol is undemanding. Her law career absorbs much of her energy and there's little obligation with respect to sex. He's known her since varsity and although they discussed it idly over breakfast one damp Sunday morning, they do not want to marry each another. They are, he suspects, too alike. Perhaps neither will ever marry.

He watches television. Carol sits close by on the floor, biting her pen, squinting fiercely. She's writing a law brief. At half past ten, she brushes his lips with hers and enters the bedroom. She's already asleep as he ducks beneath the cool tight sheets on her narrow bed. Carol does not like to be held but in the night she rolls against him, snaring his ankles with long feet. Her sibilant breaths do not quite reach the level of a snore. Beside her house stands a forest. The silence is complete. Lying awake, he imagines the trees loom over the little house and peer in with mistrust. He dislikes the quiet and is thankful for the solitary comfort of Carol's noisy exhalations.

Maryam telephones. He is sitting at his desk, the door of his office ajar, and looking at his computer screen. He does not immediately hear. The ring has been turned down very low.

'Hello?'

'Mr Raymond, I'm sorry to bother you. Maryam here.' He shuts the door. How did she get his number? His next appointment with her is a few weeks off.

His voice doesn't waver. 'Maryam.'

'I couldn't.' Her words come to him as from far off. 'I wanted to. I even had the chance. My mother was out to the shops. Memla was sleeping, but I couldn't bring myself to it.'

He interrupts. 'Where do you live?' In her agitation she will say too much. She mutters an address, embarrassed now. He knows the area she mentioned only indistinctly. He gives her the name of a coffee shop. 'I'll see you at six.'

Maryam comes dressed as a woman does to meet a man whose intentions she does not know. Jeans, hair tied back, practical unheeled black shoes. Her face is free of cosmetics. He stands up to greet her. She bends toward him, offering her cheek, then thinks better of it and sits. There is, he observes, no place in our interaction for hugs or cheek kisses. She orders red wine and perhaps to cover awkwardness, looks around. He dislikes this coffee shop, which he's chosen for convenience. It's done up to imitate cafes in films about true love in Seattle or San Francisco. The banisters are blond wood and behind the counter rests a gleaming steel machine that presumably makes coffee.

Before him on the table is an untouched mug of decaffeinated coffee. Maryam waits, taking small sips of a house wine he knows tastes of ash. Leaning forward, he says 'You were telling me about... Memla.' The name has a strange taste on his tongue.

'I couldn't do it. My mother loves her too much. But I also thought, she'll know. Ma, I mean. If I did it I'd have to pretend when she came home... Ma, ma, Memla's not waking. I'm not like those actresses who can make tears come to their eyes just like that.'

'So what will you do?' This is as near as he can come to asking, 'What do you want from me?' His fingers press a spot beneath the inside lining of his coat for reassurance.

'I don't know.' She twists her mouth, which, oddly, makes her prettier. 'Advice, maybe. You know about these things. Mercy killing, you said.'

'Why? Raymond may not even be my real name? I could be with the police for all you know?' Shrewdness colors her gaze a moment. She says nothing. How often one assumes others are fools because they are poor or uneducated.

Again, he puts his hand inside his jacket. Now, he sets down beside his cup a small plastic canister with a click cap. Without looking at it he says, 'In this bottle there are 40 pills. Digitalis.' He drops his voice still more, to a whisper. The cafe will, however, soon be shut for the night and there are no other patrons. Water sluices down the drain as the server rinses off dishes.

Her eyes are intent on his. Foxglove. The name crowds his mouth but she will not understand it. She darts a brief look at the bottle and then resumes staring at him. Her expression is faintly lascivious. He continues, 'I assume you prepare her food? Good. Today, or tomorrow, grind up one half of a tablet into fine powder and mix it into her noon meal. The taste is metallic but only slightly unpleasant. Every five days, increase the dose by a half pill. If you hurry the process, she… Memla may suffer a sudden, sharp heart attack. Maybe fatal, maybe not. She'll certainly experience pain and hallucinations and, being unable to communicate distress, will suffer terribly. In three weeks, if you follow my directions, she'll fall into a deep sleep and die peacefully.'

Maryam's foot brushes his own and he pauses. The contact, he assumes, is not deliberate. Gulping thin, tepid coffee, he waits to be asked to repeat himself. Again, she says nothing, chewing her lip in calculation. Then she shoves the pill canister in her pocket. She has no handbag. 'Thank you… Mr Raymond.' In her inflection is an echo of doubt. She's begun to comprehend how little they know of one another. He's curious but does not ask if Maryam is her real name. Is she a student? Does she work simply to pay tuition? Rather, he too is silent. Surely she has questions to put to him about autopsies. Post-mortems. But she sits back, incurious, at least about the business of poisoning for her eyes do not leave his face. Her wine glass is empty.

He gestures to the server, who comes over with the bill. 'Thank you,' Maryam says again, so tonelessly it might be gratitude for a shared drink. Outside, it is light, the sun stands high enough that their seated forms cast shadows like stumps. He follows her out, but does not offer a lift. Driving home, he ponders the white scar on her cheek, which does not quite mar her face.

He cannot wait for the next month; desire is like an itch on his sole that will not go away. On an impulse, after a weekend of which he recalls few details, he telephones to arrange an appointment with Maryam for that very afternoon, although it is Monday. He is successful and this emboldens him. In a lying voice, which he makes no attempt to disguise he dials a different number and cancels his engagement at the squash court. He leaves in haste a little after half past four. He bumps into Paulsen near the elevator.

'Off for squash?'

Paulsen is a phytotherapist with whom he must sometimes consult. Their relationship is amicable but Paulsen's habit of wearing his white coat outside the lab irks him. There is something knowing in Paulsen's look, or so he thinks. He nods and puts his head down to deter further talk.

The traffic goes more slowly than usual. There has been an accident at some bend of the highway. He drives with a patience he does not feel.

At ten past five, he raps at Maryam's door and then waits. She bids him to enter. Here, inside the room, the rituals are unchanged. She takes his case. He attempts to smile properly, not the imitation that is nothing more than a bland spreading of lips, but he's unsuccessful. No matter, for she turns her eyes from his face. Breathless, he climbs on the bed. Lying on his stomach, hands at his sides, his arousal aches as it is pressed into the mattress by his body's weight. The secret between them invests the air with a charge. The sheet falls across his body. There is no music and this causes a slight irritation.

Then, her fingers clasp his neck and he bites back a shudder. She goes about her work with an unfamiliar delicacy, yet her hands are unconcerned with any stiffness. Instead, her caresses deepen his arousal, as he knows they are meant to, until he feels he must burst. Particular care is lavished on his feet. She chafes each toe, her oiled fingers snaking between so that they tingle when he rubs them together.

Today, it is not by her hand he receives release. He scarcely dares breathe for fear he will whimper. In the moment of greatest intensity and restraint, he opens his eyes. The sensation at the base of his belly is one of physical pain. Once, he calls her name. Afterward, spent as if he's swum against a strong tide, he lies with an arm over his face, wanting the weight of her body on his. He feels no shame.

He looks at his watch. Nearly two hours have elapsed. Maryam sits on a chair in the corner, her robe cinched about her body. She's watching him but he cannot guess her thoughts. He sits to dress. Maryam neither stirs nor averts her eyes. Darkness is settling but a last glare of sunlight illuminates the mountain above him.

He's already inside his car, about to turn the ignition, when he thinks of Memla. He sits, waiting for Maryam to come out. Perhaps her day is finished. But this is foolishness. He drives through quiet streets to his empty, cooling house, too enervated to think of eating. There's nothing on television to hold his interest and it's years since he read a book. In bed the faint film of oil on his skin sticks to the sheets. He falls easily asleep.

Days pass in which he makes no attempt to see Carol. In turn, there is no word from her. Long silences between them are not unusual. In the laboratory or seated before his computer he experiences sharp, sudden recollections of smooth brown skin, and the crescents of fingernails.

At night, his thoughts turn to Memla. He does not know what she looks like, but imagines a bloated and grotesque form listlessly sprawled in a soiled bed; its breathing comes in harsh gasps. The Memla of his imagination has become more inert in recent days. She sleeps deeply and is not easily roused. Her resting heart rate has slowed, and resembles the gait of an old man. In the heat of the day, she dozes. An attentive caregiver might detect the unwonted coolness of Memla's skin. Death approaches with a stealth and placidity he likens to summer's ebb. Maryam's words reel, again and again, through his consciousness: It's no life she has. His dreams are haunted by Maryam herself. Not since he was a teenager has he touched himself so often.

At his desk, he redoes the calculations on a note pad to be sure. It is certain: the dose of digitalis being mixed into the girl's food must now be very high. As if in sympathy, his own limbs grow heavy, lethargic as the day lengthens. He carries out his duties in a fog. There are moments in which his hands shake as if with palsy. Yet he's too adept to break any vials in the laboratory. For him, there can be no mistakes or accidents.

What he wants, as dearly as the touch of her hand, is to hear Maryam's confidential tones over the telephone. He would give much for an opportunity to murmur in her ear the remembered obscenities that are his dreams. Still, no word comes. He scans the papers but there are no stories of poisoning.

It is the second Wednesday of November. The calm he feels in the morning has dissipated by noon. He fears the worst, that when he opens the door in that house, he will see a woman not Maryam. He drives too fast, slowing only when in range of the highway speed cameras. His grip on the steering wheel is like the hold of a madman.

In his eagerness, he does not knock and rushes clattering into the room he thinks of as hers. He's arrived some minutes early. He shuts the door and sets down his case. She's standing over the small table by the window, arranging the flowers in the vase. She knows he is behind her but does not acknowledge his presence in any way. Approaching, he experiences a flare of jealousy. Who has been here? He gathers her hair in his hand and pushes it aside to bare her neck. He stoops to kiss the thin skin, taut over the bones of her spine. She bows her head, offering neither resistance nor invitation. Gently, he turns her about. Her lips meet his. Her eyes are tight shut. 'Your sister?' The question burns in his mind, as if Memla is merely ailing. But there'll be time enough for that.

She's steering him toward the bed, her kisses insistent. Her mouth tastes of nothing at all. His hands are beneath her robe as she tries to undress him. His trousers and his undershorts are gathered about his ankles. There is no friction when she straddles him. Her thighs are warm against his groin. The robe hangs from her shoulders like a cape. He jack-knifes his body so his head comes to rest on her chest. Her posture shifts to accommodate him. A swelling against which he is powerless gathers at the base of his belly. He struggles to sit back, needing to look fully on her. Maryam is unrecognizable, her face a mask. Her eyes are slitted and she bares small jagged teeth. But, he thinks, and the lucidity of the thought is a shock in itself, I too must look like this, in the writhing possession of some demon. Something wrenches from him so sharply he is incapable of crying out. A sensitivity that cannot be borne invades his entire skin and then over his abdomen he feels a spreading numbness.

He starts awake with a yelp. In his dream a beast with a pig's snout has been gnawing at his genitals. He looks about the room with embarrassment but he is alone.

Olufemi Terry was born in Sierra Leone and lives now in Cape Town, where he is completing his first novel. His work has appeared in *Chimurenga* and *New Contrast*.

Harmattan Fires

Ada Udechukwu

NDIDI WELCOMED THE PARALYSIS that spread through her when Malije soaped her limbs, grateful that her body did not betray her. She leaned against the door of the shower cubicle and plotted her escape. Her thoughts filled with what she had done – or failed to do.

Malije caressed her hips. His hand crept closer. She took the bar of soap from him. Her fingers fumbled around its slippery oval. It fell. She knelt to pick it up. When she rose, it was to Malije's manhood.

'Didi... easy.' Malije gripped her shoulder and pressed her back down.

She worked up a thick lather as if to buffer her skin from his. Her fingers fled from Malije's groin, skittered over his belly, and circled his waist. He drew her to him. Their bodies slid against each other, suctioned, and pulled back. He took her hands and placed them on his erection. Waves of shuddering erupted from her and she burst into tears.

Malije towelled Ndidi dry and helped her into her nightdress. He held her, asked what was wrong.

The things she could not say.

He took her hand and traced the lines on her palm. His thumb circled spirals at the base of her wrist. He pulled her closer. He murmured that it would be okay.

But she would not be comforted.

The phone rang, piercing through the wall.

Ndidi pulled out of Malije's arms, crawled over him, tumbled off the bed, and ran to the living room, frantic lest the ringing stop before she got to the phone.

'It's for you... Metu,' she said to Malije who'd followed her.

Malije took the receiver; his eyes quizzed the craziness of what he'd just witnessed.

Ndidi's eyelids fluttered under his gaze. She turned away. Her steps dragged. Tears stung her eyes again and she wiped them, thankful her back was turned to Malije. At the bedroom door, her ears pricked at his words: 'Bro, no let that chick

167

mess with you oh!' His laughter at something shared with his cousin over the phone, followed her into the room.

Ndidi sat up in bed. Fear gnawed at her. She lay down.

Malije did not return. Minutes passed. A chair scraped against the living room floor and the signature tune for the late night news came from the television. *If only she could get up and close the bedroom door. If only.*

Ndidi shivered and wondered if she was coming down with malaria. She pulled the sheets over her head and lay with palms clamped between her thighs, absorbing the warmth of the nest she made. A comforting drowsiness came over her. She sank into her thoughts. Remembered how Kemka's hand covered hers; the swell that overtook her when his fingers strolled back and forth across her palm; and when they walked up and down, stroking each of her long fingers one by one. He skimmed her inner arm, lingered at the crook of her armpit, and slid his hand down the curve of her breast. He wanted her and she wanted what he awakened in her. *Malije was so far away; he would never know, never have to know.* Her body relaxed.

Two weeks later, Ndidi lay in bed, exhausted from the nausea that invaded her body. She pulled the small bucket hidden beneath her side of the bed and threw up. The trickle of bitter bile that left her mouth brought no relief. She gazed at her breasts. Held them; weighed one, and then the other; thought them full, heavy.

It was the fifteenth. She was four weeks late. Ever since her return home from Germany eleven days ago, she'd been unable to conjure the illusion she fortified herself with during her three-month long language course. And each passing day without word from Kemka dimmed the hope that he would call as promised.

She managed to hold Malije off in the beginning, pleading the onset of her period. But when that excuse was over she gave in. The first time she and Malije made love, her betrayal weighed on her for days. But this, too, seemed to pass.

Still, she nearly told him once. They were in bed watching a video. The images flickered in front of them: a husband cheating on his wife, a sex scene. She glanced at Malije, but he stared at the screen, engrossed. She excused herself and went to the bathroom. When she returned, the bedclothes were rearranged, their two pillows pushed together. She got under the sheets and pulled them up to her shoulders. Malije moved his legs to accommodate her. They were both under the covers, hands beside each other and separated only by a flimsy fold. She let him have her. Against the screen of her closed lids, she watched him rise, fall, and rise again for another foray, until sated, he collapsed, soft and flaccid between her legs. But it was Kemka who consumed her. She knew now that it was Kemka she wanted when she lay with Malije. Kemka: his chest bare, his trousers low on his hips, and a trail of curls dipping into his unbuttoned waistband.

One morning after Malije drove off to work Ndidi left the flat and walked toward the centre of town. Rickety danfo buses passed by and scattered ribbons of black exhaust fumes. She moved further to the side and picked her way around trash and other obstacles strewn along the rough laterite shoulder of the road.

A shortcut took her onto a path. Her mind wandered, preoccupied with how to break her news to Kemka. She stumbled. Her sandal scooped a bit of gravel and she arched her foot. A pebble lodged itself between her toes and she bent to pick it out. Blood rushed to her head and the queasy feeling that had been building up in her since early morning crested.

Twenty minutes later, she arrived at the business centre, still debating whether to send an email or to call. She dug into her handbag, brought out her wallet, and peeked at a photo of Kemka she kept hidden there. It was from a strip of four taken in a booth at the railway station on the day of a class trip to Düsseldorf.

The five of them – Iyke, Chetanne, Nkechi, Kemka and herself – agreed to meet on the platform. She arrived first. Travellers skirted her and moved on. At the far end, close to the steps, someone waved. It was Kemka. Sunlight surrounded his dark, lithe form with a halo, setting him apart. The two of them started toward each other. They met midway. And right there she felt something take hold of her. Both of them felt it in the crack of indecision before they embraced. Then their bodies locked, arms searching for the appropriate position befitting friends. But desire was in the layers of fabric between them; it slid from her slender arms flung across Kemka's back. He pulled her to him and they pressed into each other.

Something gave way.

They drew apart, laughing self-consciously.

Later, sitting and facing each other in the train, they were silent. She looked out into the flash of brick walls that skimmed past the windows as they went through a tunnel, and saw Kemka's reflection mirrored in the glass, just as he saw hers. She wondered if he was thinking about what happened at the train station. She replayed the embrace, unable to explain what had come over her.

That night, in the hostel, he came to her room. They talked. She said something. Kemka laughed hard, and she found herself joining him. He sat on the arm of her chair and took her hands in his. After a time, their laughter ebbing, she slowly withdrew her hands. He hesitated. She felt his breath on her face, his lips on hers.

Ndidi paid for her call and stood in line at the booth assigned to her. Urgent voices came from all over, clamoring to be heard over poor connections.

At last she sat with the phone. She unfolded a scrap of paper with Kemka's number, even though she knew it by heart. She whispered a prayer for the line to be clear. She dialed. Static scratched through the receiver. A weak ring began. Six times it rang. He picked up.

'Kem, it's me, Ndidi.'

'What? I can't hear. Who is it?' Kemka's voice wavered.

'It's me, Ndidi. Kem, listen… I'm pregnant.' Ndidi's words tumbled into one another.

'What…?'

'Kem, it's yours.' Ndidi turned away from the frank stare of a man waiting to use the booth beside her.

'Mine? Abi you no get husband?'

Why this? Why was he speaking to her in this way? Sweat pricked the back of Ndidi's neck. Her forehead shone with a shimmer of wetness. She leaned closer to the phone, stunned. Her breasts strained against the buttoned front of her blouse – opening little windows to her bra and belly – and she tightened her grip on the receiver. *It was his. It was.* She knew it. She cupped the mouthpiece, tried to speak, and realized the line was dead.

Ndidi sat in a taxi parked some distance away from a line of danfo buses. She was its sole occupant and waited in the front seat, wishing the car would fill up quickly.

Minutes passed with no sign of another passenger. Most people caught the buses that cruised into the bus stop or hopped onto waiting okada motorcycles. Ndidi twisted in her seat and gazed at the crowd milling around. The mid-morning heat exacerbated her nausea. Hunger gripped her too.

'Onye banana,' she called weakly through the window to a boy.

A flock of food hawkers descended and pushed the banana seller aside. They pitched their wares: 'Aunty, buy akara,' 'Groundnut dey,' 'Coke, Fanta, Sprite, Tonic, cold from fridge.' Their arms shoved through the window, menacing, pushing Ndidi further into her seat.

Horns blared. Engines revved. Two motorcycles shaved past. The hawkers scattered.

Sweat seeped through Ndidi's skirt and her thighs stuck to the car seat. She rehearsed again in her mind the weeks in Hannover – her days with Kemka, afterwards… and before.

At home, Ndidi stood by her chest of drawers with the diary she'd kept in Germany open before her. The cheap newsprint leaves were flimsy, curling at the edges. She read slowly, her index finger followed along. Her words were stale and lacked the passion they once held. She flexed the diary's thin covers and flipped through to the day she wanted. That night. The first. She liked to think the baby had been conceived on that day.

She fingered the page. Her hands closed around the diary. She slipped it back into an old manila envelope. Then she lifted a pile of folded wrappas in the bottom drawer. She shoved her packet under them.

Sunlight filtered through the window louvres and projected itself in parallel lines against the bedroom walls. Ndidi walked into the light. Her frame caught in the horizontal bars. She moved, slipped from the grid, and stepped out.

In the bathroom, she emptied the laundry hamper and turned on the tap connected by a hose to the washing machine. She started the cycle. It broke the silence in the flat.

Ndidi returned to her bedroom and went to the windows. She looked out at the expanse of land beyond the compound wall. A dust-devil of whirling dry leaves, discarded papers and plastic bags, rose in one of the dirt roads to her left. Somewhere in the distance, miles away, a farmland sent out spirals of smoke from the flames of harmattan fires spreading across it. In her mind's eye, she saw the collapsing vegetation; heard small crackling explosions; inhaled the acrid scent of burning grass and shrubs. At the end, only blackened stalks would remain. Only the parched earth.

She felt the window lever on her palm and released her grip. Dust hung in the air, though every window was shut. And, although sheltered from the wind raging outside, she journeyed with it, carried by the gales that lifted, then dropped. She stared, unseeing, caught in memories that took her away, and brought her back.

A low whine and thud told her the wash was done. She went to the machine, flipped the electric switch, turned off the tap, pulled out the damp clothing, and dumped it into a plastic laundry basket. With it on her hip, and clothes pegs in hand, Ndidi walked out onto the balcony at the back of the flat. Grains of sand whipped across her face. She bent and rose, clipping underwear, shirts, and socks, to the line hooked up above her.

Her task ended. She stood with her arms over her breasts.

In the lull of noon, the air tightened around her, drying at the edges. Below, in the deserted compound, a solitary hen strutted along the perimeter wall and four chicks zigzagged behind. Small lizards sped across the stony soil of the yard. The shadow of a circling kite fell as a darkening net. With a burst of squawking, and flapping wings, the hen rounded up her brood.

Ndidi gathered her empty basket and her pegs. She pushed open the kitchen door and walked through to the living room. She saw that all across the floor, her footprints mapped the route of her day in the fine powdering of harmattan dust over the polished red cement.

Lunch must be made. Malije would be home soon.

Ada Udechukwu, born in Nigeria, is a writer and artist. She holds an MFA in creative writing from the Bennington Writing Seminars, Bennington College, Vermont. Her publications include a collection of poems and drawings, *Woman, Me,* and short stories in *The Atlantic Monthly, Callaloo,* and *PMS: Poem.Memoir. Story.* Her drawings, paintings and textiles, have been exhibited in galleries in Nigeria and the United States, including the National Museum of African Art, Smithsonian Institution, Washington, DC.

Caine Prize Stories 2008:
Shortlist

Nothing is harder than to accept oneself. Actually only the naive succeed in doing it, and I have so far met very few people in my world who could be described as naive in this positive sense. – Max Frisch, 'I'm Not Stiller'

Mallam Sile

Mohammed Naseehu Ali

1

HE WAS POPULARLY KNOWN as mai-tea, or the tea-seller. His shop was located right in the navel of Zongo Street – a stone's throw from the chief's assembly shed and adjacent to the kiosk where Mansa BBC, the town gossip, sold her provisions. Along with fried eggs and white butter bread, Mallam Sile carried all kinds of beverages: ordinary black tea, Japanese green tea, milo, bournvita, cocoa drink, instant coffee. But on Zongo Street all hot beverages were referred to as just tea, and it was usual, therefore, to hear people say, 'Mallam Sile, may I have a mug of cocoa tea,' or 'Sile, may I have a cup of coffee tea?'

The teashop had no windows. It was built of wawa, a cheap wood easily infested by termites. The floor was uncemented, and heaps of dust rose in the air anytime a customer walked in. Sile protected his merchandise from the dust by keeping everything in plastic bags. An enormous wooden *chopbox*, the top of which he used as serving table, covered most of the space in the shop. There was a tall chair behind the chopbox for Sile, but he never used it, preferring instead to stand on his feet even when the shop was empty. There were also three benches that were meant to be used only by those who bought tea from Sile, though the idle gossips who crowded the shop occupied the seats most of the time.

Old Sile had an irrational fear of being electrocuted, and so never tapped electricity into his shack, as was usually done on Zongo Street. Instead, he used kerosene lanterns, three of which hung from the low wooden ceiling. Sile kept a small radio near in the shop, and whenever he had no customers listened, in meditative silence, to the English programmes on GBC 2, as though he understood what was being said. Mallam Sile only spoke his northern Sisala tongue, and

175

knew just enough broken Hausa – the language of the Street's inhabitants – to be able to conduct his tea business.

The mornings were usually slow for the tea-seller, as a majority of the streetfolks preferred the traditional breakfast of *kókó da mása*, or corn porridge with rice cake. But come evening the shop was crowded with the Street's young men and women, who gossiped and talked about the 'laytes' neus' in town. Some, however, went to the shop just to meet their loved ones. During the shop's peak hours – from eight in the evening till around midnight – one could hardly hear oneself talk because of the boisterous chatters that went on. But anytime Mallam Sile opened his mouth to add to a conversation people would say to him, 'Shut up, Sile, what do you know about this?' or 'Close your beak, Sile, who told you that?' The tea-seller learned to swallow his words, and eventually, spoke only when he was engaged in a transaction with a customer. But nothing said or even whispered in the shop escaped Sile's quick ears.

Mallam Sile was a loner, without a kin on the Street or anywhere else in the city. He was born in Nanpugu, a small border town in the North. He left home at age sixteen, and all by himself, journeyed more than nine hundred miles in a cow-truck to find work down South in Kumasi – the prosperous and gold-rich capital city of Ghana's Ashanti region.

Within a week of his arrival in the city Sile landed a house-servant job. And even though his monthly wages were meagre, he still relayed a portion of it back home to his poor, ailing parents who lived like destitutes in their drought-stricken village. But Sile's efforts were not enough to save his parents from the claws of Death, who took them away in their sleep one night. They were found tightly clinging to each other, as if one of them had realized that he or she was about to die and had grabbed the other so they could go together.

The young Sile received the death-news with mixed emotions of sadness and joy. He saw it as a deserved rest for his parents, as they were ill and bedridden for many months. Then he made the unusual decision not to attend their funeral, though he sent money for their decent burial. With his parents deceased, Sile suddenly found himself with more money than he usually had. He quit his house-servant job and found another hawking iced kenkey for Papa Acheampong, the Asante kiosk owner on Zongo Street. Sile kept every pesewa he earned, and two years later was able to use his savings to open his tea business. It was the first of such establishments on Zongo Street and remained the only one for many years to come.

Mallam Sile was short. In fact, so short that many claimed he was a pygmy. He stood exactly five feet and one inch tall. Although he didn't have the broad flat nose, poorly developed chin, and round head of the pygmies, he was stout and hairy all over – probably his only resemblance to them. A childhood sickness that deteriorated Sile's vision had continued to plague him throughout his adult life. Yet he refused to go to the hospital and condemned any form of medication – traditional or Western. 'God is the one who brings illness, and He is the only true healer.' That was Sile's simple, if rather mystical explanation. He believed that the human body in which a disease resides will one day give in to Death, 'no matter how long it takes *Her* to catch up with one.'

Sile's small face was covered with a thick, long beard. The wrinkles on his dark face and the moistness of his soft, squinted eyes gave him the appearance of a sage, one who had lived through and conquered many adversities in his life. His smile, which stretched from one wrinkled cheek to the other, baring his cola-stained teeth, attested to his strength, wisdom, and self-confidence.

On any given day Sile wore an identical outfit: a white polyester *danchiki* and its matching *wando*, loose slacks that used strings at the waist. He had eight of these suits, and wore a different one each day of the week. Also, Sile's perpetually-shaven head was never seen without his white embroidered Mecca hat – worn by highly devout Muslims as reflection of their submission to Allah. Like most of the Street's dwellers, Sile had only one pair of slippers at a time, and replaced it only after it was worn-out beyond any feasible repair. An unusual birth defect that caused the tea-seller to grow an additional toe on each foot made it impossible for him to find footwear that fitted him; special slippers were made for him by Anába the cobbler, who used discarded car tires for the soles of shoes he made. The rascals, led by Samadu, the Street's most notorious bully, poked at Sile's feet and his slippers, which they called *kalabilwala*, a nonsensical term no one could understand, let alone translate.

2

At forty-six Mallam Sile was still a virgin. He routinely made passes at the divorcees and widows who came to his shop, but none showed any interest in him whatsoever. 'What is one going to do with a dwarf?' the women would ask, feeling ashamed of having passes made at them by Sile. A couple of them, however, were receptive to tea-seller Sile's advances, though everyone knew the girls flirted with him so they could get free tea.

Eventually, Sile resigned himself to his lack of success with women and was even convinced he would die a virgin. Yet late at night, after all the customers, gossips, idlers, and rumor-mongers had left the shop to seek refuge in their shanties and on their bug-ridden grass mattresses, Sile would be heard singing love songs, hoping that a woman somewhere would respond to his passionate cries.

A beautiful woman, they say,
Is like an elephant's meat.
And only the man with the sharpest knife
Can cut through.
That's what they say.

Young girl, I have no knife,
I am not a hunter of meat,
And I am not savage.
I am only looking for love.
This is what I say.

Up North where I am from,
Young girls are not what they are here.
Up North where I am from,
People don't judge you by your knife.
They look at the size of your heart.

Young girl, I don't know what you look like.
I don't know where to look for you.
I don't even know who you are, young girl.
All I know is: my heart is aching.

Oh, Oh, Oh! My heart is aching for you.

Sile's voice rang with melancholy when he sang his songs. But, still, the rascals derided him. 'When at all are you going to give up, Sile?' they would say. 'Can't you see that no woman would marry you?'

'I have given up on them long, long ago,' he would reply, 'but I am never going to give up on myself!'

'You keep fooling yourself,' they would tell him, laughing.

The rascals' mocking of Sile didn't end just there. Knowing he didn't see properly, they used fake or banned cedi notes to purchase tea from Mallam Sile at night. The tea-seller pinned the useless currency notes on the wall as if they were good luck charms. He believed that it was hunger – and not mischief – that had led the rascals to cheat him. And since he considered it 'inhuman to refuse a hungry person food', Mallam Sile allowed them to get away with their frauds.

When Sile cooled off hot tea for customers, he poured the contents of one mug into another, raising one over the other. The rascals would push Sile's arms in the middle of this process, causing the hot beverage to spill all over his arms. The tea-seller was never angered by such pranks. He merely grinned and flashed his cola-stained teeth, and without saying a word, wiped off the spilt drink and continued to serve his customers.

The rascals did even worse things to the poor tea-seller. They blew out the lanterns in the shop, so as to steal bread and milo while he tried to rekindle the light. He forgave that and many other pranks as they occurred, effectively ridding his heart of any ill-feelings. He waved his short arms to anyone who walked passed his *shopfront*. 'How are the Heavens with you, Boy?' he would shout in greeting. Sile called everyone Boy, including women and older people, and he hardly said a sentence without referring to the Heavens.

He prided himself on his hard work, and smiled anytime he looked in the mirror and saw his dwarfish appearance and ailing eyes, two abnormalities he had grown to accept with an inner joy no one could understand. A few months before the death of his parents, he had come to the conclusion that if Allah had created him any different than how he was, he wouldn't have been *Mallam Sile* – an individual Sile's heart, soul, and spirit had grown to accept and respect. This created an inner peace within him that made it possible for him to not only tolerate the ill treatment meted out to him by the Street's rascals, but to also forgive them their actions. Though in their eyes Sile was only a buffoon.

3

One sunny afternoon during the dry season, Mallam Sile was seen atop the roof of his shack with hammers, saws, pincers, and all kinds of building tools. He tarried there all day long like a lizard, and by dusk he had dismantled all the aluminium roofing-sheets that had once sheltered him and his business. He resumed work early the following morning, and before *azafar*, the first of the two afternoon prayers at one-thirty, Sile had no place to call either home or teashop – he had demolished the shack down to its dusty floor.

After *La-asar*, the second afternoon worship at three-thirty, Mallam Sile moved his personal belongings and all his tea paraphernalia to a room in the servant-quarters of the chief's palace. The room was arranged for him by the chief's *Wazeer*, or right hand man, who was sympathetic to the tea-seller.

During the next two days, Mallam Sile ordered plywood and odum boards, a more superior wood than the wawa used for the old shop. He also ordered a few bags of cement and push-truck loads of sand and stones, and immediately began building a new shack – a much bigger one this time.

The streetfolk were shocked by Sile's new building and wondered where he got the money to embark on such a big enterprise. And even though he had not spoken to anyone about his plans, rumor still carried that Sile was constructing a mini-market store to rub shoulders with Alhaji Saifa, the owner of the Street's provision store. Though Sile categorically denied the rumor, it rapidly gained ground on the Street, eventually creating bad blood between Sile and Alhaji Saifa.

It took three days for Mallam Sile to complete work on the new shop's foundations, and it took an additional three weeks for him to erect the wooden walls and the aluminium roofing sheets. While Sile was busy at work, passers-by would call out, 'how is the provision store coming?' or 'Mai-tea, how is the mansion coming?' Sile would reply simply: 'It is coming well, boy. It will be completed soon, *Insha Allah.'* He would grin his usual wide grin and wave his short hairy arms, and then return to his work.

Meanwhile as the days and weeks passed, the streetfolk grew impatient and somewhat angry at the closure of Sile's shop. The nearest tea shack was three hundred meters away, on Zerikyi Road – and not only that, the owner of the shack, Abongo, was generally abhorred by the streetfolk. And it was for a good reason. Abongo, also a Northerner, was quite unfriendly even to his loyal customers. He maintained a rigid NO CREDIT policy at his shop, and had customers pay him before they were even served. No one was an exception to this policy – even if he or she was dying of hunger. And unlike Sile, Abongo didn't tolerate idlers or loud conversation in his shop. If a customer persisted in chatting, Abongo reached for his mug, poured the content in a plastic basin, and refunded his money to him. He then chased the customer out of the shop, brandishing his bullwhip and cursing after him, 'if your mama and papa never teach you manners, I'll teach you some. I'll sew that careless lips of yours together, you bastard son of a bastard woman!'

It wasn't for another three weeks that Mallam Sile's shop was re-opened, and the streetfolk, much to their disdain, had no other tea option than Abongo's. Immediately after work on the shop was completed Sile had left for his hometown. Soon afterwards, yet another rumor surfaced that the tea-seller had traveled up North to seek black medicine for his bad eyesight.

Sile finally returned one Friday evening, flanked by a stern, fat woman who looked in her late thirties and was three times larger than the tea-seller. The woman, whose name was Abeeba, turned out to be Mallam Sile's wife. Abeeba was tall and massive, with a face as gloomy as that of someone in mourning of a dead relative. Just like her husband, Abeeba said very little to people in and out of the shop. She, too, grinned and waved her huge arms anytime she greeted people, though unlike the tea-seller, a malice seemed to lurk behind Abeeba's cheerful smile. She carried herself with the grace and confidence of a lioness, and covered her head and parts of her face in an Islamic veil, a practice being dropped by most married women on Zongo Street.

The rascals asked Sile: 'From where did you get this elephant? Better not be on her bad side; she'll sit on you till you sink into the ground.' To this, the tea-seller did not vouchsafe a word, knowing his response would only incite more cynical pronouncements.

4

Exactly one week after Sile's return from his village, he and his wife opened the doors of their new shop to their customers. Among the most talked about features of the new shop on opening night was the smooth concrete floor and the bright gas lantern that illuminated every corner of the shop. The streetfolk were equally impressed with the whitewashed odum boards used for the walls, quite a departure from the termite-infested wawa boards of the old shop. And in a small wooden box behind the counter, Sile and his wife burned *tularen mayu*, or witches' lavender, a strong, yet sweet smelling incense that doubled as a jinx-repellent – to drive away bad spirits from the establishment.

On the first night the teashop was so crowded that some customers couldn't even find a seat on the twelve new metal folding chairs Sile had bought. The patrons sang praise songs to the variety of food on the new menu, which included meat-pie, brown bread, custard, and tom brown, an imported, grain porridge. Some of the patrons even went as far as thanking Sile and his wife for relieving them of 'Abongo's nastiness'. But wise, old Sile, who was as familiar with the streetfolks' cynicism as he was with the palm of his hands, merely nodded and grinned his sheepish, innocent grin. He knew that despite the ululations and the numerous smiles being flashed at him, some customers were at that very moment thinking of ways to cheat him. Though unbeknown to both Sile and his future predators, those days of cheating and prank-playing were gone, forever. And it wasn't that Mallam Sile had suddenly metamorphosed into a mean fellow or anything of that sort. It was, instead, because of Abeeba, whose serious, daunting face, coupled with her gigantic presence, scared off those who came to the shop with the intention of cheating the tea-seller.

While Sile prepared the tea and other foods on the menu, Abeeba served and collected the money. Prior to the shop's re-opening, Abeeba had tried to convince her husband that they, too, should adopt Abongo's NO CREDIT policy. Sile had quickly frowned upon the idea, claiming that it was inhumane to do such a thing. Abeeba had pointed out to Sile that most of those who asked for credit and ended up stiffing him were not 'poor and hungry folks,' as Sile expressed it, but cheats who continued to take advantage of his leniency.

The tea-seller and his wife had debated the matter for three days before they came to a compromise. They agreed to extend credit, but only in special cases and also on the condition that the debtor swore by the Qur'an to pay on time; and that if a debtor didn't make a payment, he or she would not be given any credit in the future. But hardly had the tea-seller and his wife resumed extending credit to their patrons, when some of them resorted to the old habit of skipping on their payments. However, an encounter between Abeeba and one of the defaulters helped change everything, including the way Sile was treated on the Street. And what took place was this:

Like most of the city's neighborhoods, Zongo Street had its own *tough guy*, a young man considered the strongest among his peers. Samadu, a pugnacious bully whose fame had reached every corner of the city, was Zongo Street's tough guy. He was of a median height, muscular, and a natural-born athlete. And for nine months running, no kid or neighborhood bully had managed to put Samadu's back to the ground in the haphazard wrestling contests held beside the central market's latrine. Samadu's 'power' was such that parents paid him to protect their children from other bullies at school. He was also known for torturing and even killing the livestock of the adults who denounced him. If they didn't have pets or domestic animals, he harassed their children for several days, until he was appeased in cash or goods. Some parents won Samadu's friendship for their children by dashing him occasional gifts of money, food, or clothing.

One could therefore imagine the stir it caused, when on an early Tuesday morning Mallam Sile's wife showed up at Samadu's house to collect a tea debt. Prior to that, Abeeba had tried amicably to collect the money Samadu owed them, which was eighty cedis – about four dollars. After her third futile attempt, Abeeba had suggested to Sile that they use force to retrieve the money. But Sile had quickly cautioned his wife: 'Stay out of that boy's way, he is dangerous. And if he has decided not to pay, please let him keep the amount. He would be the loser in the end.'

'But, Mallam, it is an insult what he is doing,' Abeeba had argued. 'I think people to whom we have been generous should only be generous in return. I am getting fed up with their ways, and the sooner the folks here know that, even the toad gets sick of filling his belly with the same dirty pond water everyday, the better!' Though Sile was surprised and taken aback by his wife's vehemence, he had decided to allow the matter to die.

When Abeeba arrived at Samadu's house, a number of housewives and young women were busily doing their morning chores in and around the compound – some sweeping and stirring up dust all over the compound, others fetching water from the tap in the center of the compound and pouring it into the barrels in front of their rooms, and a few were lighting up charcoal pots to warm up hot water and their left over food from the previous night. She greeted them politely and asked to be shown to the tough guy's door. The women's intitial response was to turn Abeeba away, as they feared that Samadu would humiliate her once he came out of his room. But Abeeba insisted that it was important business that had brought her, and that she must see the tough guy. Seeing the fire in her eyes, the housewife reluctantly directed the tea-seller's wife to Samadu's room, located outside the main compound – in the boys' quarters of the house.

The usual tactic boys used when fighting girls was to try and strip them of the wrapper around their waist, knowing that they would be reluctant to keep fighting half-naked. But Abeeba had come prepared: She wore a sleeveless ready-to-fight shirt and a pair of tight-fitting khaki shorts, and for the first time ever left her ubiquitous veil at home.

'You rogue, if you call yourself a man come out and pay your debt,' Abeeba shouted, as she pounded her fist at the door.

'Who do you think you are? Ruining my sleep because of some useless eighty cedis,' screamed Samadu from behind the door.

'The money may be useless, but it is certainly worthier than you, and that's why you haven't been able to pay. You rubbish heap of a man!' responded Abeeba. Her voice was coarse and full of menace. The veins on her neck stood erect, like those dervish fighters at the annual wrestling contest. Her eyes looked hard and brutish, and she moved her head in rapid movements as if she was having a fit of some sort.

One of the onlookers, a famished-looking housewife, pleaded with the tea-seller's wife, 'Go back to your house, woman. Don't fight this boy, he would disgrace you in public.' Another woman added in the background, 'What kind of a woman thinks she can fight a man? Be careful O!' Abeeba didn't pay any attention to the women's admonitions, which she considered useless babble. Samadu, meanwhile, was yet to come out.

Abeeba grabbed the door knob and tried to force it open. Then a loud bang was heard from the room. Abeeba retreated and waited for Samadu to emerge from the room.

A few seconds later the door swung open, and Samadu stormed out, his face clearly showing the anger and red malice that was in his heart. 'No one gets away with insulting me. No one!' he screamed. His right cheek was smeared with dried drool, and a whitish-mucus gathered at the ends of his eyes. 'You ugly elephant-woman. After I am done with you today, you'll learn a lesson or two about why women don't grow beards!' he shouted.

'Haa, you teach me a lesson? You?' screamed Abeeba. I too will educate you about the need to have money in your pocket before you flag the candy man!' She immediately lunged at Samadu.

The women placed their palms on their breasts, shaking their bodies in dread of what was about to happen. 'Where are the men on the Street? Come and separate the fight, Oh Men, come out Oh!' they shouted. The children in the compound, though freshly aroused from sleep, jumped excitedly as if in a ritual. Half of them called out, *'prin pirin pi'*, while the other half responded, *'wein son!'*, as they chanted and cheered for Samadu.

Samadu knew immediately that if he engaged Abeeba in a wrestling match, she would use her bulky mass to force him to the ground. His strategy, therefore, was to throw punches and kicks from a safe distance, thereby avoiding direct contact with her. But soon after the fight erupted he realized that Abeeba was a lot quicker than he had presumed, as she managed to dodge the first five punches he had thrown at her. He threw a sixth punch, and missed. He stumbled on his left foot when he tried to connect the seventh blow, and he landed within a foot of Abeeba. With a blinding quickness she seized Samadu by the sleeping wrapper tied around his neck and began to punch him. The crowd's exuberance was dimmed by this unexpected turn of events. No sound was heard anywhere as Abeeba continued her attack on the tough guy.

But Samadu wasn't heralded as the Street's tough guy for nothing. He threw a sharp jab at Abeeba's stomach and somehow managed to release himself from her grip by deftly undoing the knot of his sleeping cloth. He was topless now, and clad only in a pair of corduroy pants. He danced his feet, swung his arms, and moved his chest sideways, like true boxers did. The crowd got excited again. *'Prin pirin pi, wein son! Prin pirin pi, wein son!'* they sang. Some among them shouted 'Ali, Ali, Ali!' as Samadu danced and pranced, tactfully avoiding Abeeba, who watched his movements with the keenness of a hungry lioness, hoping for a slip, so she could tackle him.

The women in the crowd went from holding their breasts to slapping their massive buttocks. They jumped about nervously, their bodies in rhythm to the chants. The boys booed Abeeba, calling her all sorts of names that equated her to the beasts of the jungle. 'Destroy that elephant,' they screamed.

The harder the crowd cheered for Samadu, the fancier his footwork became. He finally threw a punch that landed on Abeeba's left shoulder, though she seemed completely unfazed by the blow, as she continued to chase him around the small circle created by the spectators. With all the might he could muster Samadu threw another fist, but Abeeba had already anticipated it. She dodged, then deftly grabbed Samadu's wrist and twisted his arm with such force that he didn't even know when he let out a high-pitched cry, 'wayyo Allah.' The crowd gasped and watched nervously as the tough guy attempted to extricate himself from Abeeba's tight grip. He tightened all the muscles in his body and moved his head sideways to side – all in an attempt to foil Abeeba's move. But her strength was just too much for Samadu.

The crowd booed, '*Wooh*, ugly rhinoceros.' Then in a sudden, swift movement that many swore later to be as fast as an airplane's lift-off, Abeeba hurled the tough guy off the ground, then lifted him further up above her head (the crowd booed louder), before dumping him on the ground, like a sack of rice. She jumped quickly on top of him and began to whack him violently.

The women jumped about frantically, like scared antelopes. They shouted, 'Where are the men in this house?' Men, come out Oh! There is a fight!'

A few men came running to the scene, followed by many others a minute or so later.

Meanwhile Abeeba continued her offensive. With each punch that landed on Samadu she asked, 'Where is our money?'

'I don't have it, and wouldn't pay even if I had it!' Samadu responded in an attempt to regain his shattered pride and dignity. The men drew nearer and attempted to pull Abeeba away from her victim, but that turned out to be a difficult task; her grip on Samadu's waist band was too firm. The men pleaded on Samadu's behalf and begged Abeeba to let go of her captive. 'I will not release him until he pays us back our money,' she shouted. 'And if he doesn't I'll drag his ass all the way to the Zongo police station,' she added.

On hearing this, an elderly man who lived in Samadu's compound ran inside the house; he returned a few minutes later with eighty cedis, which he placed in the outstretched palm of Abeeba's free hand. She checked to make sure the amount was up to eighty before she finally released Samadu. She gave him a mean, hard look as she walked away. The awestruck crowd watched silently as Abeeba began to walk back to her shack, their mouth agape as if what they had just witnessed was from a cinema reel.

5

Mallam Sile was still engaged in his morning *zikhr*, or meditation, when Abeeba returned to the shack, and of course had no inkling of what had taken place. An hour later, when they were preparing to open the teashop for their customers, Abeeba announced to Sile that Samadu had paid the money he owed them. The tea-seller, though surprised at what he had heard, still didn't see the need to ask how that happened. In his naiveté, he concluded that perhaps Samadu had paid the debt because he had either found himself a vocation or had finally been 'entered by the love and fear of God'. Abeeba's announcement confirmed Mallam Sile's long-standing belief that 'every man is capable of goodness just as he is capable of evil', and that it is only with time and acquired wisdom that people like Samadu would change their bad ways and become good people.

The tea-seller's belief was further solidified when he ran into Samadu a fortnight later. He was greeted politely by the tough guy, something he had never done before. When Mallam Sile told his wife about the unusual encounter with Samadu, she fought hard to restrain herself from telling him what had actually caused the change in Samadu's attitude. Abeeba also knew that Sile would be quite displeased if he found out the method she had used to retrieve the money. Just a week ago, he had spoken to her about 'the uselessness of using fire to put out fire', of how it 'worsens rather than puts out the original flame'. Abeeba only prayed that one of these days someone didn't tell her husband about her duel with Samadu – as the entire city seemed to know about it by now. Tough guys from other neighborhoods even came to the teashop just to steal a glance at the woman who conquered the tough guy of Zongo Street.

Then one night during the fasting month of Ramadan, some two months after the fight, a voice in Mallam Sile's head asked: 'Why is everyone calling my wife the *man-checker*? How come people I give credit suddenly pay me on time? Why am I being treated with such respect, even by the worst and most stubborn rascals on the Street?' Mallam Sile was lying in bed with his wife at the time these questions popped in his head. In his usual fashion, he didn't think any further of the questions or even try to asnwer them. He drew in a deep breath, and began to pray in his heart. He smiled and thanked *Allahu-Raheemu*, the Merciful One, for curing the streetfolk of the prejudice they had nursed against him for so long. Mallam Sile also thanked Allah for giving his neighbors the will and the courage to finally accept him just as he was created. He flashed a grin in the darkness and moved closer to his slumbering wife. He buried his small body in her massive, protective frame and soon fell into a deep, dreamless sleep.

Mohammed Naseehu Ali, a native of Ghana, is a writer and musician. A graduate of the Interlochen Arts Academy and Bennington College, Ali has published fiction and essays in *The New Yorker*, the *New York Times*, *Mississippi Review*, *Bomb*, *Gathering of the Tribes*, and *Essence*. In the Academic year 2006-2007 he was the recipient of the Dorothy and Lewis B Cullman Center for Scholars and Writers Fellowship Award. He lives in Brooklyn, New York, where he has worked since 1996 as a Senior Publishing Operations Analyst for LexisNexis Publishing.

For Honour

Stanley Onjezani Kenani

'MOVE CLOSER,' I TOLD her. It was a cold June night, probably the coldest in the two years Eranive and I had been in matrimony. The thick blanket did not seem enough to block the cold air that seemed to penetrate to one's bone marrow.

To the contrary, she drifted away and faced the other side.

'Did you hear me?' I asked.

'I am not deaf!' she answered curtly. She let a good part of the blanket fall between us, creating a wall between her warm body and my cold self.

I was surprised, very surprised. In the seven hundred and thirty days we had been together, I had never heard her speak in the tone she had just used tonight.

'Is this the best way we can celebrate our wedding anniversary?' I spoke, shivering. I tried to double over, my knees almost touching my chin, to keep warm, but this did not seem to help.

'How else?' she answered me with a question, her voice carrying the same tone which I was not sure was anger or defiance.

I had been away the whole day, looking for a good market for maize. I left her sleeping early morning, having carefully tiptoed from the room. She appeared to be so deep in sleep that I found it unwise to disturb her. After hunting all over Chipiri, with the sad result that I just could not find a buyer willing to take my maize at a good price, I came back home late in the evening. I found her already in the blanket. I joined her immediately after taking my supper, hoping, as usual, to hold each other in our arms and drift to sleep in warmth and comfort – only to have a rude awakening.

'Is anything wrong?' I wanted to find out.

'Of course, everything is wrong, can't you see that for yourself?' she spat out. 'Everything is very wrong. We are "celebrating" the second anniversary of our marriage with no fruit to look at. Tiwonge, who got married the same day as I did, is pregnant again.'

A chill crept up my spine. I took the blanket off my head and sat up. I was tempted to look for a box of matches to light a match so that I could have a look at her. What, exactly, was the matter? We had spoken about this so many times, but it had always been in a friendlier, reasonable way, always concluding the subject by banking our hopes on prayer. Come to think of it, I had even considered her the most understanding woman in the world! Had I been mistaken?

I groped for the box of matches beside the mat, but I could not find it. Frustrated, I lay down on the mat once more. 'How can you talk about our problem like this tonight?' I asked her calmly.

'How else do you want me to talk about this problem? In what tone? Like I am saying "Hail Mary"? I am simply tired of the scorn poured on me every day,' she said.

Anger welled up in me. I wanted to explode and tell her off in an equally harsh tone. But then, just before I could blurt out, she began to weep.

I lifted the part of the blanket that separated us and moved closer to her. I held her in my arms. 'Don't cry, Eranive,' I implored. 'Calm down. Calm down.'

I was confused. I did not know what to do, what to say. Day after day I stared the problem in the eye, without finding an answer.

I had heard them myself, these nuances. Eranive is a strong woman – she had withstood the pressure for two years. But then she was only human. It was just a matter of time before she broke down, which she now had. This was the moment I had always dreaded most.

'I was at the well in the afternoon,' she said, amid sobs. 'Nangondo's mother[1] and Dalitso's mother were there, too. We were all chatting about various issues. When a certain issue arose, Nangondo's mother said: "You know we can't talk about this in the presence of a child who has never given birth before." It pained me!' she cried loudly.

I had never seen her cry like that since we got married. 'Damn Dalitso's mother and Nangondo's mother: how can they say that?' I thought. After all, they had grown up together, my wife being older than both of them by a year or more. Personally, I thought the world was changing. I failed to understand, therefore, why pre-colonial beliefs and values should still preoccupy our minds at that point in time. Why should failure to have a child be regarded as some sort of crime? Why couldn't people leave us alone? I doubted if people in Chipiri had ever heard of adoption. Eranive and I could adopt a child, a beautiful and intelligent one, too, no? And live happily ever after, no?

It was a pity even men seemed to enjoy the pastime of talking about others. I had heard such names as *chumba* or *gojo*[2] muttered under breaths many a time – especially when I was around.

'Don't let a *chumba* touch this mat you are weaving for your child, lest the child be barren, too,' I could hear them say at times, obviously referring to me as I was the only married male in the village who had no child. Quite often, I had strongly resisted the urge to punch the speaker in the face to teach the swine a lesson.

I am a stronger character, I think, stronger than my wife. I couldn't break down. *Children are a gift from God*: that is what I believed in. It just happened that the gift was not in our hands yet. We had, of course, eaten many roots, my wife and I had, from the most famous herbalists in Chipiri. None of these had worked so far. We had gone to the most reputable pastors for prayers. Unfortunately, this route, too, did not seem to work. Where would we go from here?

'Chuma, I want a child,' my wife said. She had stopped weeping now.

'So do I, my dear,' I told her.

'I want to be pregnant within three months from today.'

My heart leapt. 'Is that an ultimatum?'

'Surely there can be a way to do that, no? My pride and honour as a human being, more so as a woman, have eroded away. I must have them restored. Quickly.'

What was she trying to say? For God's sake, I hadn't been deliberately withholding a decision to make her pregnant. I had not had a vasectomy, and neither had she been taking any birth-control pills. It was not just a matter of waking up one day and saying, 'Hey, let us make you pregnant today' – no! Nature was in charge here. It was some unfathomable natural process which was making us fail to have children.

'How do you know you are capable of having children?' I asked her. 'How do you know the problem is not yours?'

'Can't you see that for yourself?' she asked in response. 'It is in your family. Your late brother left no child behind. Yet all the six sisters and two brothers from my family have children – except me. What does that say?'

'It says nothing!'

'It does! It clearly shows you are the problem. You are incapable of making a woman pregnant. You are ...'

'If you know I am the problem, how do you expect me to make you pregnant in the said three months, then?'

She hesitated. 'We haven't run out of options, have we?' she said at length. 'You know there is one last option we have never even contemplated before... one last option.'

'And what is that?' I asked curiously.

'Fisi.'

'What?' I sat bolt upright as if I had been pricked by a needle. What devil had entered my wife's mind?

Throughout my life, it had never crossed my mind that one day I would sink so low as to go to the extent of hiring another man to make my wife pregnant. To imagine another man sleeping with my wife with my full knowledge and permission – I just couldn't do that.

'I just can't do that,' I found myself saying loudly.

'You have to,' she fought back boldly.

'Never ever!' I said emphatically. But I was very surprised by her boldness. The deeply religious person she was, I had always thought she would be the last person to suggest such an unorthodox way of getting pregnant.

'In that case, Chuma, I have no choice but to end the marriage,' she said.

I lay on the mat again, facing our grass-thatched roof. 'What did you just say?' I asked weakly, a meaningless, rhetorical question.

'Don't pretend you didn't hear. I will end the marriage if you can't take my suggestion.'

I tossed and turned on the mat. Suddenly, although it was very cold that night, I was not feeling cold. I didn't want the blanket. I didn't want the warmth of her skin. I wanted to be alone – alone!

'Think about it deeply, Chuma. I could end the marriage, marry another man, get pregnant and give birth to a handsome baby boy. What would that say about you? A proven infertile man, no? It is for honour, Chuma. Yours and mine. My fellow women wouldn't regard me as a child anymore. I would be regarded as an equal. The same with you: you would be treated as a real man in this village.'

She paused, probably waiting for my reaction. Instead, I said nothing. The darkness between us now appeared to be thicker than the blanket that separated us.

'Think about it, Chuma. If you cannot answer now, let me know tomorrow morning, just before starting the new day. Please understand this one thing: I love you. I am doing all this for the love I have for you. I only want our honour restored,' she said and fell silent again. I said nothing.

Instead, my mind wandered into the unknown, asking the supernatural powers that are said to map out each person's fate why they had decided to let me be in such a pathetic situation, unable to make my wife pregnant, no matter how hard I tried. Beside me, my wife had started to snore. Was what she was suggesting an honourable way to restore honour? Yes, it was accepted in our culture, provided it was done in utmost secrecy, but is there any secret under the sun? Even if the man chosen to do the job indeed did keep the secret, the very knowledge of the fact that someone was sleeping with my wife with my consent… oh! I thought it was unbearable. No, I couldn't do that, not even for honour. I couldn't do that!

'I can't do that!' It was morning and I hadn't slept a wink. These were the first and only words that came out of my mouth. I woke up and walked out of the house, away from the house, to continue looking for a market for the maize. I was many, many kilometres away when I realised I did not even say goodbye to my wife.

It had been a long, hard day, made worse by the preceding sleepless night. I walked hurriedly home, all my hopes pinned on the steaming plateful of *nsima*[3] I could clearly see in my mind as waiting for me. I eagerly looked forward to devouring it while updating my wife on the efforts of finding the maize buyers (the prospects still not good, as it were). I would deliberately and skilfully evade any reference to the previous night's sticky issue, that challenge to my capabilities as a man.

I arrived home just at dusk. My heart sank: there was no sign of life. The small, round, grass-thatched house I called home stood lonely in the darkness, its dry-grass door firmly held by a *mpiringidzo*.[4] No fire was burning in the fireplace outside the house, as was normally the case.

'Eranive!' I called. 'Eranive!'

No response.

'Eranive-e-e-e!!' I shouted louder. Instead, it was only my voice that came back to me, not Eranive.

I opened the house to look inside. Of course, it was just a formality, there was no one, anyway.

I paced about like a caged bull. *Where is Eranive?* I asked myself many times. She was always home long before sunset, regardless of whatever she was doing during the day. The pangs of hunger in me had by now worsened, just as they would for a very thirsty man who saw a well from afar and rushed to it hoping to drink water only to find the well dry.

I sat waiting for her for many hours. Later in the night, when total silence descended on the highlands of Chipiri, save for an occasional hooting of an owl, I was convinced Eranive had gone missing. Fear gripped me. This had never happened throughout the two years we had been together as man and wife.

I was confused. I walked out of the house into the night. It was a very long distance to where her parents lived on the banks of Mkaladzi River. It was dangerous to walk in the night at Chipiri. One could meet lions, leopards or hyenas. Sometimes one could be harassed by witches and wizards. I walked on, oblivious to all these dangers. At the second cock-crow, I announced my arrival at the house of my parents-in-law.

'*Odi!*'[5] I said.

'Who is it?' asked my father-in-law, whose voice I recognised.

'It is me, Chuma, your son-in-law,' I announced my identity.

Soon I heard some noise of a bamboo mat crackling as it was stepped on, a match being struck, and, a minute or so later, my father-in-law walked out. I apologised for waking him up in the night, but I asked if my wife was there.

'Yes, she is,' he said, much to my relief. 'Let me ask her mother to go and wake her up, she is sleeping in the small house.'

Ten or so minutes later, she walked to where I sat shivering in the biting June cold, made worse by the even colder breeze being breathed by the Mkaladzi River on the shores of which the houses of my parents-in-law were situated.

'Why are you doing this to me?' was the only question I asked as my teeth rattled due to the cold air slapping my body.

'We already discussed this last night,' she said.

'We never discussed that you would be coming here today,' I pointed out.

'I told you I would be ending the marriage if you don't agree to ...'

'Lower your voice,' I told her. I didn't want her parents to hear this.

'... if you don't agree to hire a *fisi*. I want to have a child,' she continued. 'This is a very serious issue to me, and I mean every single word I say.'

'But we haven't finished discussing this issue yet,' I protested. 'And even if you were to end the marriage, surely there are appropriate channels to follow, no? You don't just walk out of the house, even without telling me, and go back to your parents. Let us be civilised in what we do.'

After arguing for some time, she agreed to come home. We set off that very dawn.

'Who shall be our *fisi*?' I asked in a weak voice. We were holding each other very close under the blankets on a mat. Another day was gone. We had argued about it all day long, since coming back from my parents-in-law. Clearly I was the vanquished, and some faceless guy had prevailed.

'Let us pick him out together,' said Eranive. 'It is as much your responsibility as it is mine. How about Mlingoti?'

He had nine children at the age of thirty. His wife was well-known in the neighbourhood as a 'Child Factory'. People said Mlingoti and his wife bore children at such an alarming speed as if the mission to fill the earth was theirs alone. But the man had other manners – he drank like a fish, and when he was drunk, he hid no secret. Even salient details about how he made love with his wife were common knowledge. Children on the village's playground sometimes imitated how he did it: shame!

'Not that one,' I said. 'Yes, he can make you pregnant in no time, but he won't keep it a secret. The whole village will know about it within a week.'

'Maybe Kamchere will do,' Eranive suggested.

'Not that one!' I objected. 'We have always dreamed to have a handsome son, but I have strong reservations about Kamchere's facial outlook. He can't give us a handsome son. Try someone else.'

After a lot of haggling, we settled for a man called Langi: tall, well-built, nice-looking face, handsome in all respects. He was married and had two children. He had been to school and had read up to the last class of primary school. In fact, he was selected to go for Form One at the famous Robert Blake Secondary School, but his parents could not afford the fees. Reluctantly, he accepted his fate and settled down to start another life. He married a former classmate, a beautiful girl called Elita.

'You must approach him,' Eranive advised.

* * *

It was dark, the moon was not appearing that night. My wife was not yet home. Being the market day, she had gone to sell some sweet potatoes at the market. I seized the chance to try, for a third time, to ask Langi to take over my conjugal rights (on a part-time basis) in accordance with our tradition.

The first time I met him on the issue, I was too shy to say why exactly I had requested a meeting with him. I ended up talking about the weather and other such general matters, completely skirting the real agenda of the meeting. That night I lied to my wife that I had put the request to Langi but he had asked to think about it. When I failed the second time, I told Eranive that he still had not come up with a decision yet. My wife's patience appeared to start waning, which was why I decided to call for a third meeting that night.

'My brother,' I addressed him in the manner we had always addressed each other, although we were not exactly related, 'we have had this problem for two years: we just can't make a child. As they say, one man's head cannot carry a roof. My wife and I have agreed that we should seek your hand in this matter. We want you to be our *fisi*.' I did not mention that I was under unsustainable pressure from my wife to engage a *fisi*, or else.

To my surprise, he accepted the role rather too easily – he didn't even request some time to think about it. Had he been admiring my wife all along? I wondered.

Thus we took no time to discuss the nitty-gritty arrangements of the whole exercise. Every Wednesday, so went the details, I would be coming home late, not earlier than 10 o'clock. He would be expected to come some time around 7 and leave before 9. To avoid being confronted with the harsh reality of it all, we agreed never to meet, so keeping time, a rare virtue among the people of Chipiri, was of the essence.

When we heard my wife approaching from a distance, recognised by her voice as she sang a *chiterere*[6] song that always evoked memories of her childhood, we hastily concluded the meeting.

The deed would start being done the following Wednesday.

Wednesday, 8 p.m. I couldn't bear it any more. I had retraced my steps back to my house. I sat on the *khonde*[7] of the small house made of grass and mud I call home. Although I was outside the house, my mind was inside.

I could hear the tempo of the rattling and crackling of my mat rising, slowly at first, but it rose faster and faster, until it got muffled by cries of lust and shame.

'Oh, where were you? Where were you?' my wife said, panting, as soon as the cries died down. 'You have made me taste real sex for the first time in two years.'

'Sex is an art,' said Langi, 'a profound art. It requires special skills.'

I couldn't stand this! Every word my wife said was totally unbelievable! My heart felt unbearable pain.

I strongly resisted the temptation of bursting in and wrenching the two of them apart. I knew very well what the consequences would be. Thus, to avoid them, I walked away, far away into the bowels of the dark, dark night. I just walked although there was no destination.

I was so confused. I walked on and on. It was only when a cock crowed from a great distance much later into the night that I was jolted to my senses and asked myself, 'where am I going?' I had been walking for many hours. 'And where am I?'

I began tracing my steps back to look for landmarks that could tell me where I was. To my surprise, I recognised the Chipiri Hills and shivered. So I had strayed deep into the Kasungu National Park. The Kasungu National Park where there were plenty of lions and leopards and elephants.

I climbed into a tree and waited for sunrise.

* * *

'Where have you spent the night?'

The sun had just risen as I arrived home, shivering as the cold seemed to bite to the core of my being. My nose was running and my teeth rattled.

'I couldn't…' I said, 'I couldn't stand it.'

'Stand what?' my wife asked. 'Were you spying on us?'

'My imagination was,' I lied.

'Please, free your mind,' she advised. 'Imagine nothing is happening. View this as a temporary solution to a longstanding problem, like swallowing bitter pills to cure a persistent illness – there is no pleasure in doing that. For honour, Chuma, yours and mine.'

I wanted to shout 'To hell with honour! I'll have none of it!' But I knew just what these few words could lead to, so I remained silent.

* * *

After many months of mental torture, my wife told me one early morning: 'I've missed my period.' I looked her in the eye. Her face was bright, very bright. She looked as pleased as a little child could be, the little child that was crying for a packet of biscuits and you had just given it to her.

'Does this mean Langi will stop coming?' I asked.

'Is that all you can say?' she protested, her voice rising. 'For how long have we waited for this moment? And after all that torturous wait, is that all you can say?'

I wanted to tell her that I felt defeated as a man; that she went into an experiment in which I was the control, and she had come out with the findings she was hoping for, thereby vindicating herself; that I couldn't stand all that.

'Congratulations,' I said instead, not really sounding congratulatory.

* * *

Strangely, the child was born on the 29th of February, thus condemned to celebrating a birthday once in four years. My wife's excitement had reached a climax. She called the baby Yankho – Answer, and tried her best to liken me to the baby whenever she was showing it off to her friends. 'Look at the nose – a replica of his father's,' she would say. Some of her over-zealous friends incredibly found that the baby's cheeks looked like mine, and so did the lips. But for all I knew, the only thing common between me and the baby boy was that both of us were male.

At first I didn't like to be associated with the baby in any way. It took me three weeks before I reluctantly agreed to carry the baby in my hands for the first time. I looked at it with disdain, as I might at some specimen of humanity. It began to cry, but I just looked at it. At another time, another place, I could have sung a beautiful lullaby.

As the baby's tears streamed down its cheeks, I asked myself: 'Should the child be hated, this little, innocent child? Or should it be fathered by someone who did not procreate it?' Question chased question in my heart. On the first day, I failed to make a decision.

But as time passed, my love for little Yankho grew on its own. Privately I called him Mphatso – Gift. Someone had given him to me. I carried him around at every opportunity. Some men in the village looked at me with curiosity as men of Chipiri consider carrying babies around a feminine job. Personally, however, I did not mind. My love for this little creature was natural; no traditional beliefs would dissuade me from showing my love to him.

Sometimes, whenever Eranive went to the well to draw water, I prepared some light porridge for Yankho. If the mother was too busy and the nappies needed changing, I did not hesitate to change them. I was not moved by what the people in the village said, that Yankho was 'a lucky child with two mothers under one roof'.

We were all pleased by the progress he was making. When he learnt to crawl, Eranive and I talked about it with glee, cheering him on all the time. Sometimes we would mention it to our visitors: 'Our child has begun to crawl.' In fact, we monitored his crawling efforts with strange enthusiasm, as if we had never seen a child crawl before.

'Da! Da! Da!' he began to utter one day. By this time, he had grown into a big, healthy baby.

Again this was reason to celebrate in the house. 'He has begun to speak!' we said to each other numerous times. It was all so sweet to see him mature from one stage of growth to the next.

* * *

One day, however, little Yankho developed a cough. It was a strange type of cough. Whenever he started, he would cough in spasms for ten minutes or more. At night, he could not sleep adequately – he kept coughing half the time. It was a dry cough in which he only coughed out air and nothing else, no sputum, no mucus. I tried to prepare a concoction of wild herbs. After two weeks of administering the medicine, the situation aggravated rather than waned.

The child had lost his appetite. All attempts to make him eat failed. He vomited whenever he was made to swallow any food.

We tried to take him to Kamboni Health Centre. Unfortunately, like all public hospitals, there were no drugs. They only pacified us with Aspirin. Although we never read medicine, my wife and I knew very well that Aspirin was not the appropriate drug for Yankho's type of cough.

In a matter of weeks, Yankho had lost considerable weight. He was no longer the same healthy baby we had grown to love.

A little while later, even his hair began to lose its texture. It became wavy and pale, you could see each strand standing out separately from the other.

One morning, we woke up to another shock: there were strange sores covering the whole of Yankho's backside. They were big, like blisters. I had never seen anything like that. We summoned Amon, a distant cousin visiting from the city where he worked as a clinical officer.

'These are shingles,' he told us.

I was blank – I had never heard of that disease before. Neither had Eranive. She looked at me for some encouragement, some direction, but could a blind man lead a blind woman?

Yankho's lack of appetite worsened. He had become so thin now, he could not even crawl. He cried most of the time.

The mother, too, had developed the strange cough – I guess it was contagious, like any other cough. Her appetite, too, was gone.

'Eat!' I tried to encourage her. 'You must eat to have a lot of milk in your breasts for the child.' Still she could not eat adequately; she ate like a mouse – just nibbling at the food.

One morning, on a gloomy Saturday, Yankho breathed his last. We could not believe this was happening to us. We, who badly yearned for this fruit, why should it be brutally taken away from us? We, who spent many sleepless nights praying for the gift, why should the wind blow it away from our hands? I cried for a very long time. My grief was indescribable.

We buried him on Sunday, the morning after his death.

'And so dust shall return to dust,' said the minister, Reverend Jekapu, 'and the spirit to Him that gave it. We must not mourn like the hopeless, for we have hope in life after death...' Eranive and I were made to perform the ritual of pouring handfuls of red soil into the grave, just before they started burying the little one, lest his spirit come back to haunt us.

Langi did not attend the funeral. He too had developed the strange sores under his left armpit. Those that had seen him lately said he had become as thin as a bamboo. Was he the one who passed on the flesh-eating disease to the little one? I would never know for sure.

My wife never recovered from the shock of losing Yankho. The grief and the bad cough made her lose weight all the more. In no time, she developed the strange sores, too, around her neck.

And then Langi died. Eranive did not attend the funeral. She was too weak. She could now spend the whole day sleeping on the mat in our home.

A cold hand of fear gripped my heart. Was I next? There seemed to be a strange equation linking the three. Was it some plague unleashed by an angry god?

But recently there has been talk in the village that a strange, incurable, sexually transmitted disease is ravaging the country. They say it is found in blood and that it makes its victims pine away. Already whispers are linking Eranive and Langi to the disease. But can this be true?

These days when I am passing through the village, where two or three people are gathered to chat, talk dies down, only to resume after I have passed. Even the way they look at you, you know there are stories behind those stares. Ours is one of those villages where victims of such a disease as this one are regarded as more sinful and more adulterous than any other.

To survive, therefore, I have developed a thick skin around myself through which no whispers can permeate.

1 Among the Chewa people of Malawi, a woman with child is called by the name of her child. 2 Both words mean a barren person. 3 Very thick porridge made with maize flour, always eaten with something, e.g. meat, eggs, vegetables, etc. 4 A wooden handle (linked to a door by a string) which holds the door firmly from outside the house. 5 Among the Chewa people, one announces one's arrival using this word. 6 A dance for girls. 7 Outer edge of a house.

Stanley Onjezani Kenani was born in 1976 in Malawi. He has read his poems at the Arts Alive Festival in Johannesburg, South Africa, Harare International Festival of the Arts in Zimbabwe, Struga Poetry Evenings in Macedonia and Poetry Africa in Durban, South Africa. His short story, *For Honour*, won third prize in a regional competition organized by the South African PEN of which he is a member. His poems have been published in some prominent literary journals especially in South Africa. A columnist for the *Malawi News*, one of Malawi's leading newspapers, Kenani is an accountant.

Poison

Henrietta Rose-Innes

LYNN HAD ALMOST MADE it to the petrol station when her old Toyota ran dry on the highway. Lucky me, she thought as she pulled on to the verge, seeing the red and yellow flags ahead, the logo on the tall facade. But it was hopeless, she realised as soon as she saw the pile-up of cars on the forecourt. A man in blue overalls caught her eye and made a throat-slitting gesture with the side of his hand as she came walking up: no petrol here either.

There were twenty-odd stranded people, sitting in their cars or leaning against them. They glanced at her without expression before turning their eyes again towards the distant city. In a minibus taxi off to one side, a few travellers sat stiffly, bags on laps. Everyone was quiet, staring down the highway, back at what they'd all been driving away from.

An oily cloud hung over Cape Town, concealing Devil's Peak. It might have been a summer fire, except it was so black, so large. Even as they watched, it boiled up taller and taller into the sky, a plume twice as high as the mountain, leaning towards them like an evil genie.

As afternoon approached, the traffic thinned. Each time a car drew up, the little ceremony was the same: the crowd's eyes switching to the new arrival, the overalled man slicing his throat, the moment of blankness and then comprehension, eyes turning away. Some of the drivers just stood there, looking accusingly at the petrol pumps; others got back into their cars and sat for a while with their hands on the steering wheels, waiting for something to come to them. One man started up his BMW again immediately and headed off, only to coast to a halt a few hundred metres down the drag. He didn't even bother to pull over. Another car came in pushed by three sweating men. Their forearms were pumped from exertion and they stood for a while with their hands hanging at their sides, exchanging brief words in Xhosa with the petrol attendants. There was no traffic at all going into the city.

Over the previous two days, TV news had shown pictures of the N1 and N2 jam-packed for fifty kilometres out of town. It had taken a day for most people to realise the seriousness of the explosion; then everybody who could get out had done so. Now, Lynn supposed, lack of petrol was trapping people in town. She herself had left it terribly late, despite all the warnings. It was typical; she struggled to get things together. The first night she'd got drunk with friends. They'd sat up late, rapt in front of the TV, watching the unfolding news. The second night, she'd done the same, alone. On the morning of this, the third day, she'd woken up with a burning in the back of her throat so horrible that she understood it was no hangover, and that she had to move. By then, everybody she knew had already left.

People were growing fractious, splitting into tribes. The petrol attendants and the car-pushers stood around the taxi. The attendants' body language was ostentatiously off-duty: ignoring the crowd, attending to their own emergency. One, a woman, bent her head into the taxi and addressed the driver in a low voice. He and the *gaardjie* were the only people who seemed relaxed; both were slouched low on the front seats, the driver's baseball cap tilted over his eyes. On the other side of the forecourt was a large Afrikaans family group that seemed to have been travelling in convoy: mother, father, a couple of substantial aunts and uncles, half a dozen blonde kids of different sizes. They had set up camp, cooler bags and folding chairs gathered around them. On their skins, Lynn could see speckles of black grime; everybody coming out of the city had picked up a coating of foul stuff, but on the white people it showed up worse. A group of what looked like students – tattoos, dreadlocks – sat in a silent line along the concrete base of the petrol pumps. One, a dark, barefoot girl with messy black hair down her back, kept springing to her feet and walking out into the road, swivelling this way and that with hands clamped in her armpits, then striding back. She reminded Lynn of herself, ten years earlier. Skinny, impatient. A fit-looking man in a tracksuit hopped out of a huge silver bakkie with *Adil's IT Bonanza* on its door and started pacing alertly back and forth. Eventually the man – Adil himself? – went over to the family group, squatted on his haunches and conferred.

Lynn stood alone, leaning against the glass wall of the petrol-station shop. The sun stewed in a dirty haze. She checked her cellphone, but the service had been down since the day before. Overloaded. There wasn't really anyone she wanted to call. The man in the blue overalls kept staring at her. He had skin the colour and texture of damp clay, a thin, villain's moustache. She looked away.

The black-haired girl jumped up yet again and dashed into the road. A small red car with only one occupant was speeding towards them out of the smoky distance. The others went running out to join their friend, stringing themselves out across the highway to block the car's path. By the time Lynn thought about joining them, it was already too late – the young people had piled in and the car was driving on, wallowing, every window crammed with hands and faces. The girl gave the crowd a thumbs-up as they passed.

A group was clustering around one of the cars. Peering over a woman's shoulder, Lynn could see one of the burly uncles hunkered down in his shorts, expertly wielding a length of hose coming out of the fuel tank. The end was in his mouth. His cheeks hollowed; then with a practised jerk, stopping the spurt of petrol with his thumb, he whipped the hose away from his mouth and plunged it into a jerry-can. He looked up with tense, pale eyes.

'Any more?' he asked, too loud.

The group moved on to the next car.

She went to sit inside, in the fried-egg smell of the cafeteria. The seats were red plastic, the table-tops marbled yellow, just as she remembered them from childhood road trips. Tomato sauce and mustard in squeezy plastic bottles, crusted around the nozzle. She was alone in the gloom of the place. There were racks of chips over the counter, shelves of sweets, display fridges. She pulled down two packets of chips, helped herself to a Coke and made her way to a window booth. She wished strongly for a beer. The sun came through the tinted glass in an end-of-the-world shade of pewter, but that was nothing new; that had always been the colour of the light in places like this.

Through the glass wall, she watched absently as the petrol scavengers filled up the tank of *Adil's IT Bonanza*. They'd taken the canopy off the bakkie to let more people climb on. The uncles and aunts sat around the edge, turning their broad backs on those left behind, with small children and bags piled in the middle and a couple of older children standing up, clinging to the cab. What she'd thought was a group had split: part of the white family was left behind on the tar, revealing itself as a young couple with a single toddler, and one of the sweaty car-pushers was on board. The blue-overalled guy was up front, next to Adil. How wrong she'd been, then, in her reading of alliances. Perhaps she might have scored a berth, if she'd pushed. She sipped her Coke thoughtfully as the bakkie pulled away.

Warm Coke: it seemed the electricity had gone too, now.

Lynn picked distractedly at the strip of aluminium binding the edge of the table. It could be used for something, in an emergency. She opened a packet of cheese and onion chips, surprised by her hunger. She realised she was feeling happy, in a secret, volatile way. It was like bunking school: sitting here where nobody knew her, where no one could find her, on a day cut out of the normal passage of days. Nothing was required of her except to wait. All she wanted to do was sit for another hour, and then another hour after that; at which point she might lie down on the sticky vinyl seat in the tainted sunlight and sleep.

She hadn't eaten a packet of chips for ages. They were excellent. Crunching them up, she felt the salt and fat repairing her headache. Lynn pushed off her heeled shoes, which were hurting, and untucked her fitted shirt. She hadn't dressed practically for mass evacuation.

The female petrol attendant opened the glass door with a clang, then pushed through the wooden counter-flap. She was a plump, pretty young woman with complexly braided hair. Her skin, Lynn noticed, was clear brown, free from the soot that flecked the motorists. She took a small key on a chain from her bosom and opened the till, whacking the side of her fist against the drawer to jump it out. With a glance across at Lynn, she pulled a handful of fifty-rand notes from the till, then hundreds.

'Taxi's going,' she said.

'Really? With what petrol?'

'He's got petrol. He was just waiting to fill the seats. We made a price – for you too, if you want.'

'You're kidding. He was just waiting for people to *pay*? He could have taken us any time?'

The woman shrugged, as if to say, *taxi-drivers*. She stroked a thumb across the edge of the wad of notes. 'So?'

Lynn hesitated. 'I'm sure someone will be here soon. The police will come. Rescue services.'

The woman gave a snort and exited the shop, bumping the door open with her hip. The door sucked slowly shut, and then it was quiet again.

Lynn watched through the tinted window as the money was handed over. The transaction revived the inert *gaardjie*. He straightened up and started striding back and forth, clapping his hands, shouting and hustling like it was Main Road rush hour. The people inside the taxi edged up in the seats and everyone else started pushing in. The driver spotted Lynn through the window and raised his eyebrows, pointing with both forefingers first at her and then at the minibus and then back at her again: coming? When she just smiled, he snapped his fingers and turned his attention elsewhere. People were being made to leave their bags and bundles on the tar.

Lynn realised she was gripping the edge of the table. Her stomach hurt. Getting up this morning, packing her few things, driving all this way… it seemed impossible for her to start it all again. Decision, action, motion. She wanted to curl up on the seat, put her head down. But the taxi was filling up.

Her body delivered her from decision. All at once her digestion seemed to have speeded up dramatically. Guts whining, she trotted to the bathroom.

Earlier, there'd been a queue for the toilets, but now the stalls were empty. In the basin mirror, Lynn's face was startlingly grimed. Her hair was greasy, her eyes pink, as if she'd been weeping. Contamination. Sitting on the black plastic toilet seat, she felt the poisons gush out of her. She wiped her face with paper and looked closely at the black specks smeared on to the tissue. Her skin was oozing it. She held the wadded paper to her nose. A faint coppery smell. What was this shit? The explosion had been at a chemical plant, but which chemical? She couldn't remember what they'd said on the news.

She noticed the silence. The slightly reverberating stillness of a place that has just been vacated.

There was nobody left on the forecourt. The battered white taxi was pulling out, everyone crammed inside. The sliding door was open, three men hanging out the side with their fingers hooked into the roof rim. Lynn ran after it on to the highway, but the only person who saw her was the blond toddler crushed against the back windscreen, one hand spread against the glass. He held her gaze as the taxi picked up speed.

The cloud was creeping higher behind her back, casting a murk, not solid enough to be shadow. She could see veils of dirty rain bleeding from its near edge. Earlier, in the city, she had heard sirens, helicopters in the sky; but there were none out here. It was silent.

Standing alone on the highway was unnerving. This was for cars. The road surface was not meant to be touched with hands or feet, to be examined too closely or in stillness. The four lanes were so wide. Even the white lines and the gaps between them were much longer than they appeared from the car: the length of her whole body, were she to lie down in the road. She had to stop herself looking over her shoulder, flinching from invisible cars coming up from behind.

She thought of the people she'd seen so many times on the side of the highway, walking, walking along verges not designed for human passage, covering incomprehensible distances, toiling from one obscure spot to another. Their bent heads dusty, cowed by the iron ring of the horizon. In all her years of driving at speed along highways, Cape Town, Jo'burg, Durban, she'd never once stopped at a random spot, walked into the veld. Why would she? The highways were tracks through an indecipherable terrain of dun and grey, a blur in which one only fleetingly glimpsed the sleepy eyes of people standing on its edge. To leave the car would be to disintegrate, to merge with that shifting world. How far could she walk, anyway, before weakness made her stumble? Before the air thickened into some alien gel, impossible to wade through, to breathe?

It was mid-afternoon but it felt much later. Towards the city, the sky was thick with blood-coloured light. It was possible to stare at the sun – a bleached disk, like the moon of a different planet. The cloud was growing. As she watched, a deep occlusion spread towards her, pulling darkness across the sky. She ducked reflexively and put her hands up against the strange rain. But the raindrops were too big, distinct – and she realised that they were in fact birds, thousands of birds, sprinting away from the mountain. They flew above her and around her ears: swift starlings, labouring geese. Small rapid birds tossed against the sky, smuts from a burning book.

As they passed overhead, for the first time Lynn was filled with fear.

Approximately fifty packets of potato chips, assorted flavours. Eighty or so chocolate bars, different kinds. Liquorice, wine-gums, Smarties. Maybe thirty bottles of Coke and Fanta in the fridges, different sizes. Water, fizzy and plain: fifteen big bottles, ten small. No alcohol of any kind. How much fluid did you need to drink per day? The women's magazines said two litres. To flush out the toxins. Would drinking Coke be enough? Surely. So: two weeks, maybe three. The survival arithmetic was easy. Two weeks was more than enough time; rescue would come long before then. She felt confident, prepared.

Boldly, she pushed through the wooden flap and went behind the counter. The till stood open. Beyond were two swing doors with head-high windows, and through them a sterile steel-fitted kitchen, gloomy without overhead lighting. Two hamburger patties, part-cooked, lay abandoned on the grill, and a basket of chips sat in a vat of opaque oil. To the right was a back door with a metal pushbar. She shoved it.

The door swung open on to a sudden patch of domesticity: three or four black bins, a skip, sunlight, some scruffy bluegums and an old two-wire fence with wooden posts holding back the veld. A shed with a tilted corrugated-iron roof leaned up against the back wall. The change in scale and atmosphere was startling. Lynn had not imagined that these big franchised petrol stations hid modest homesteads. She'd had the vague sense that they were modular, shipped out in sections, everything in company colours. Extraneous elements – employees – were presumably spirited away somewhere convenient and invisible at the end of their shifts. But this was clearly somebody's backyard. It smelt of smoke and sweat and dishwater, overlaying the burnt grease of the kitchen. Through the doorway of the shed she could see the end of an iron bed and mattress. On the ground was a red plastic tub of the kind used to wash dishes or babies. Two plastic garden chairs, one missing a leg. A rusted car on bricks.

Lynn laughed out loud. Her car! Her own car, twenty years on: the same model blue Toyota, but stripped to a shell. The remaining patches of crackled paint had faded to the colour of a long-ago summer sky. The roof had rusted clean through in places, and the bottom edges of the doors were rotten with corrosion. Old carpeting was piled on the back seat and all the doors were open. Seeing the smooth finish gone scabrous and raw gave Lynn a twinge at the back of her teeth.

She walked past the car. There was a stringy cow on the other side of the fence, its pelt like mud daubed over the muscles. A goat came avidly up to the wire, watching her with slotted eyes, and she put her arm through and scratched the coarse hair between its horns. The cow also mooched over in an interested way. Smelling its grassy breath, Lynn felt a tremor of adventure. She could be here for *days*. She felt no fear at the prospect: nobody else was here, nobody for miles around. (Although briefly she saw again: the hand sliding across the throat ...)

Out back here, the sky looked completely clear, as if the petrol station marked the limit of the zone of contamination. She shot her fingers at the goat and snapped them like the taxi-man, spun round in a circle, humming.

And breathed in sharply, stepping back hard against the wire. '*Jesus.*'

Someone was in the car. The pile of rugs had reconstituted itself into an old lady, sitting on the backseat as if waiting to be chauffeured away.

Lynn coughed out a laugh, slapping her chest. 'Oh god, sorry,' she said. 'You surprised me.'

The old lady worked her gums, staring straight ahead. She wore a faded green button-up dress, a hand-knitted cardigan, elasticised knee stockings and slippers. Grey hair caught in a meagre bun.

Lynn came closer. 'Hello?' she began. Afrikaans? Hers was embarrassingly weak. '*Hallo?*' she said again, giving the word a different inflection. Ridiculous.

No response. Poor thing, she thought, someone just left her here. Would the old lady even know about the explosion? 'Sorry... *tannie*?' she tried again. She'd never seriously called anyone '*tannie*' before. But it seemed to have some effect: the old lady looked at her with mild curiosity. Small, filmed black eyes, almost no whites visible. A creased face shrunken on to fine bones. An ancient mouse.

'Hi. I'm Lynn. Sorry to disturb you. Ah, I don't know if anyone's told you – about the accident? In Cape Town.'

The woman's mouth moved in a fumbling way. Lynn bent closer to hear.

'My grandson,' the old lady enunciated, softly but clearly, with a faint smile. Then she looked away, having concluded a piece of necessary small talk.

'He told you about it?'

No answer.

So. Now there was another person to consider, an old frail person, someone in need of her help. Lynn felt her heaviness return. '*Tannie*,' she said – having begun with it she might as well continue – 'There's been an accident, an explosion. There's chemicals in the air. Poison, *gif*. It might be coming this way. I think we should go out front. There might be people coming past who can help us. Cars. Ambulances.'

The old lady seemed not averse to the idea, and allowed Lynn to take her arm and raise her from her seat. Although very light, she leaned hard; Lynn felt she was lugging the woman's entire weight with one arm, like a suitcase. Rather than negotiate the series of doors back through the station, they took the longer route, clockwise around the building on a narrow track that squeezed between the back corner of the garage and the wire fence. Past the ladies, the gents, the café. As they walked, it started to rain, sudden and heavy. The rain shut down the horizon; its sound on the forecourt canopy was loud static. Lynn wondered how tainted the falling water was. She sat the old lady down on a sheltered bench outside the shop, and fetched some bottles of water and packets of chips from inside. Then she urgently needed to use the bathroom again.

The toilet was no longer flushing. Her empty guts felt liquid, but strained to force anything out. The headache was back.

Outside, she saw the rain had stopped, as abruptly as it started, leaving a rusty tang in the air. The old lady had vanished.

Then Lynn spotted movement out on the road: her car door was open. Coming closer, she saw that the woman was calmly eating tomato chips in the back seat. Having transferred herself from the wreck in the backyard to the superior vehicle out front, she was now waiting for the journey to recommence.

A neat old lady, Lynn noted: there were no crumbs down her front. She seemed restored by the chips. Her eyes gleamed as she whipped a plastic tortoiseshell comb out of a pocket and started snatching back wisps of hair, repinning the bun with black U-bend pins that Lynn hadn't seen since her own grandmother died.

In contrast, Lynn felt increasingly dishevelled, and embarrassed about her tip of a car: the empty Heineken bottles on the floor, the tissues in the cubbyhole. She should have kept things cleaner, looked after things better.

'My grandson,' the woman said to Lynn, with a nod of reassurance.

'Of course,' said Lynn.

Evening was coming. The clouds had retreated somewhat and were boiling grumpily over the mountain. The brief rain had activated an awful odour: like burnt plastic but with a metallic bite, and a whiff of sourness like rotten meat in it too. Lynn sat in the front seat, put the keys into the ignition and gripped the steering wheel. She had no plan. The sky ahead was darkening to a luminous blue. The silent little woman was an expectant presence in her rear-view mirror. Oppressed, Lynn got out of the car again and stood with her hands on her hips, staring east, west, willing sirens, flashing lights. She ducked back into the car. 'I'll be back in a sec. Okay? You're all right there?'

The old woman looked at her with polite incomprehension.

She just needed to walk around a bit. She headed off towards the sun, which was melting messily into smears of red and purple. The mountain was no longer visible. The road was discoloured, splattered with lumps of some tarry black precipitate. She counted five small bodies of birds, feathers damp and stuck together. Blades of grass at the side of the road were streaked with black, and the ground seemed to be smoking, a layer of foul steam around her ankles. It got worse the further she walked. She turned around.

There was someone stooped over her car. At once she recognised the moustache, the blue overalls.

Her first impulse was to hide. She stood completely still, watching. He hadn't seen her.

The clay-faced man was holding something ... a box. No, a can. He had a white jerry-can in his hands and he was filling her car with petrol. Suddenly her stomach roiled and she crouched down at the side of the road, vomiting a small quantity of cheese-and-onion mulch into the stinking grass. When she raised her chin, the man was standing looking back at the petrol station.

Deciding, she made herself stand, raising her hand to wave – but in that moment he opened the door and got in; the motor turned immediately and the car was rolling forward. She could see the back of the old woman's head, briefly silver as the car turned out into the lane, before the reflection of the sunset blanked the rear windscreen. The Toyota headed out into the clear evening.

Lynn sat in the back of the rusted car and watched the sky turn navy and the stars come out. She loved the way the spaces between the stars had no texture, softer than water; they were pure depth. She sat in the hollow the old lady had worn in the seat, ankles crossed in the space where the handbrake used to be. She sipped Coke; it helped with the nausea.

She'd been here three days and her head felt clear. While there'd been a few bursts of warm rain, the chemical storm had not progressed further down the highway. It seemed the pollution had created its own weather system over the mountain, a knot of ugly cloud. She felt washed up on the edge of it, resting her oil-clogged wings on a quiet shore.

Sooner or later, she was certain, rescue would come. The ambulances with flashing lights, the men in luminous vests with equipment and supplies. Or maybe just a stream of people driving back home. But if that took too long, then there was always the black bicycle that she'd found leaned up against the petrol pump. The woman's grandson must have ridden here, with the petrol can, from some place not too far down the road. It was an old postman's bike, heavy but hardy, and she felt sure that if he had cycled the distance, so could she. Maybe tomorrow, or the day after. And when this was all over, she was definitely going to go on a proper detox. Give up all junk food, alcohol. Some time soon.

Lynn snapped open a packet of salt 'n' vinegar chips. Behind her, the last of the sunset lingered, poison violet and puce, but she didn't turn to look. She wanted to face clear skies, sweet-smelling veld. If she closed her eyes, she might hear a frog, just one, starting its evening song beyond the fence.

Henrietta Rose-Innes was born in 1971 and lives in Cape Town. She is the author of two novels, *Shark's Egg* (2000) and *The Rock Alphabet* (2004), both published by Kwela Books, and was the compiler of an anthology of South African writing, *Nice Times! A Book of South African Pleasures and Delights* (Double Storey, 2006). Her short stories and essays have appeared in a variety of publications in South Africa and elsewhere. A translated anthology of short pieces will be published in Germany in 2008, and *The Rock Alphabet* has been published in Romanian translation. She was the winner of the 2007 Southern African PEN short story award, and was shortlisted for the Caine Prize in 2007.

The Day of the Surgical Colloquium Hosted by the Far East Rand Hospital

Gill Schierhout

THREE MONTHS AGO I lost my hand in a mining accident. Doctor sewed it on again. Now here I am at this Medical Conference, a marvel, picking up cotton reels, tying bits of string. Doctor is saying something, pointing to pictures of my X-rays that are projected up on a big white screen, like the Drive-In.

Strange seeing the stump of your wrist bloated up to 20 times its usual size, projected up there on the wall. I don't recall giving anyone permission to take that picture. There's no doubt it's my limb though. See, the same tattoo as on my forearm; the ink has sunk deep, its pinpricks of blue show up like the pores of a giant orange up there on the wall. I consider whether or not to roll up my sleeves so that at least in the tea-break the audience can see it's me – but then I'd have to take my jacket off and Doreen made me promise to keep it on. I just sit, waiting, like in church. Big holes of sweat are forming under my armpits.

Doctors are here from all over: Jo'burg General, Helen Joseph, Bloem, Chris Hani Baragwanath, everywhere, man. You can tell from the labels they've pinned to their coats.

Must be a good lens on that doctor's camera to take pictures like these. I wouldn't mind a better camera myself. One day I'd like to set up a dark room in the house, do the developing, play tricks with the light, put heads on bodies that do not match. I've seen this in the photographic magazines in the Hospital Waiting Room. I imagine Doreen as a twin. I could do with two wives – I'd let them grimace at one another, identical in blackened tooth, across the picture.

Every week Doreen does the crossword from the Sunday papers, and then she posts it off. They put all the entries into a hat and the first correct one to be drawn wins a lot of cash. She's never won the crosswords, to my knowledge, but she says it keeps her mind active. Recently she's taken to doing Sudoku too, but there's no cash prize there, it's just the challenge.

'If someone else can do it, so can I,' she says.

A severed hand is quite popular, it seems, but all the fuss over me is going to stop if I lose my head. No one wants to know you then. Like Geezer – he was an average sort of bloke, until the day he and his team were trapped underground for 26 days. He was the sole survivor. The pillars were mined too thin and the roof collapsed. Now he walks around with sticks in his hair, talking to himself. It depends on where you mine and how deep you go as to the size the pillars have to be. Under this hospital for example, it's all mined. There's more stress here; the vibrations, the tonnage of the trucks on the main road, the expansion and contraction. And the safety factor is higher – you can't take out too much of the pillars.

Perhaps one day Geezer'll come right, wake up and comb his hair. Doreen thinks so. She leaves him pots of food sometimes, out on the front step. He comes carefully, like an animal not yet tamed. I tell her not to waste. She just scowls, her face screwed tighter than the cloth she uses to wipe the washed floor dry. A colony lives off that man. The day he dies he'll decompose faster than a rotten cabbage. Every mine has its idiot.

From where I am sitting, I can see the sign stuck on the door of this room, hand-written, big easy letters.

'Conference Room. Surgical Colloquium.'

A big red arrow points inside.

The Doc is showing a picture of my hand – how it was before he sewed it on again. The hand is carefully laid out in its plastic bag on a wide strip of tissue paper; it looks as big as a corpse up there on the wall. It reminds me of a picture of Doreen that I have somewhere at home: she is in the garden, standing in front of last year's mielies. I had put her there to show the height of the crop that we planted beside the house. Man, they towered above her, and she's a tall woman, big-boned too, tallest maize plants you'll ever see. I remember picking up that picture not too long ago and noticing for the first time how her face was all creased up against the sun. She looked middle-aged, and quite worn out, standing there in a yellow Sunday dress and matching hat. A wife can seem so much part of a man. Thinking of that picture now, I have a curious feeling, like something is missing – a phantom pain. There is a sharp tick ticking sound. I look up. It is just the Colloquium sign flapping in a sudden gusty breeze.

Doctor has taken out a small torch now. He's using it to point to the pictures on the wall. The pin-prick torch beam hovers above the thin pale tendons – they hang from the severed wrist like roots off a turnip. One of the Doctors is blowing his nose on a large handkerchief, a frown across his brow. He turns his head briefly to face the window. Then he looks again at the slide show up on the wall. I remember what someone once told me, that a man tried to lip-print a thousand cows – each lip print was examined and found to be different from every other one. It is the same with humans; we are all made different, it is only our Culture and Education that makes us appear the same.

A new picture is flashed up now, a cross-ways view through my bones. Doctor drones on. That's such a clean cut through my hand. That 80-kg rock splintered from the face had an edge sharper than the blade of a knife. Doreen and I, we've got one child, a boy, there's another kid on the way and each day, she doesn't know if I'm going to come home again after the shift. I don't know how she does it. I don't know how she doesn't crack.

It's a gloomy afternoon here with most of the curtains closed.

I went underground the day I turned 16. Mining wasn't my first choice. I wanted to be a fitter and turner, but there were no positions. You can earn twice as much underground as on the surface, that's why I've stuck it out this long. Sometimes I stand at the main station and look up at the square of daylight, and, at night, sometimes see the stars. The square of light is 300 metres up; stars much higher. There is a longing I have, a longing built in for sunlight. Perhaps it is every miner's dream to own a farm.

When I met Doreen I was 19, just got my blasting certificate. She had passed her Matric and soon after she got a good job in bookbinding. I was working at Daunhauser, Natal. There we worked 11¾ hours a day, some regulation not allowing us to work 12 hours every day. Saturday was half-day, we worked only 9 hours, got drunk Saturday night, slept late on Sunday and back to work on Monday. Pay Day or nearest Friday we hired a car and went to Dundee where the shops stayed open until 9 at night. Used to go to Danhauser station to check on passengers or just to see the trains come in and out. After working underground for a few years I'd saved enough to buy a motorcycle. Doreen liked riding pillion, the faster the better. Until the day I lost my hand.

I didn't expect Doctor to sew my hand on again. But after he did, I taught the hand to do everything it used to: buttons and zips and folding papers, and building up the strength by squeezing rubber balls. By now I can do almost anything, even tie knots in pieces of string.

First thing I saw was the blood in fountains. I yelled out. Twin fountains gushing from inexhaustible veins, coursing from rivers that will never run dry. I tried to stop the fountain, pressing as close to the source as I could. My hand came right off; it was hanging by a bit of skin. And then it fell. I picked it up and called my mates; one led in front to stop me falling down the stope, one came behind to push a bit. I was holding the left hand with the right, using the hand to squash the blood, stop it shooting up to the roof, stop it shooting, but whatever I did, it flooded. I passed the First Aid station, swore, wouldn't let anyone touch me, passed the second medical depot at the top, swore, no one to touch me until I got to the hospital. Passed out, then came around the next day. I've been here before, 133 broken bones and counting. I am no stranger at the Far East Rand Hospital.

'Just keep breathing,' Doreen once told me.

At that time I was lying in hospital with a broken collar bone and four crushed ribs.

'Just keep breathing Frank. One day things will come right.'

And that's the longest speech I've ever heard her say. Doreen's not the sort to waste her words (only our food, on Geezer). But something else happened Underground that day – it took weeks before I realised it. They are always going on about safety at the mine. A miner tests each working place every day, and uses chalk to write the date on the hanging wall. Only then is the team allowed in that area to work. I've always been a Leftie. And after Doctor sewed my left hand on again, I taught the muscles to work as good as new. But something else changed for me, something I never would have expected. I can no longer write. Not left or right or toes or mouth. The muscles are here, the brain pumps out its thoughts, but whatever it is that takes the words from the brain to the hand to form the letters has gone.

I must have been sleeping or something when Doctor Morar walked in. I saw him first from the back. He was facing away from me, attending to the bloke in the bed opposite. Doctor is a big man, tall, bald as an egg, so that when he turned around and came towards me, I was surprised how young he looked, young, but tired.

'I want the dough, Doc,' I said, pointing with my good hand to the other one laid out on the plastic and crushed ice beside me. 'I won't beg for it, but I am telling you I want a way to get out. I'll try something new – anything on the surface.'

I had in mind to live a healthy sort of a life in the light with plenty of fresh air. Surely the loss of a hand is worth a living wage for a miner?

But when it finally came to do the paperwork required by the Compensation Board, Doc changed his mind. He was so pleased with his work in sewing my hand back on again, that he refused to sign. Back to work with me.

My name is down for the early shift, clocking in at 4am to water the stopes before the team comes in at 6. Then I'll be ahead of the boys, hitting the hanging for loose pieces of rock, sounding it for blisters or bad hanging – loose pieces must be barred down and every place made safe. Yet that day it happened there was no warning – we'd worked in that stope for two weeks already, it just cracked.

The storm is breaking now, the beautiful Jo'burg downpour of fresh angled rain sounding on the roof outside. The rain bounces on the tarmac, and the sky has broken open and the rain falls in torrents on the roof of the hall and already the gutters are overflowing, the rain spilling over their sides like sand.

I watch the back of Doctor's head from this strange angle. He'd talked me into it, how fine it would be to be on stage. The skull is made up of 29 different bones, the Occupational Therapist had once told me. Meanwhile, the hand only has 24. He's got a cheek this Doctor, showing me off like some prize bull. Sure, my hand works again, good as new. I can wield a hammer, flip a switch, pronate and supinate the wrist with the best of them, tie knots in pieces of string. Yes, it's true he sewed my hand back on again. My fingers close around the ball of string waiting here in my jacket pocket. With the rain, come sheets of lightening, and more and more rain and lightning, and it's suddenly fresh and cool. Doctor carries on with his lecture, as if nothing at all has happened.

It was the hardest thing I've ever done to get out of that stope. There was no oxygen, man, on top of the hand hanging by a bit of string, and the blood. You breathe, and there was nothing there, it's like breathing cotton wool, breathing nothing. Perhaps it was the shock that day I lost my hand, the loss of blood, something in my brain has gone.

I don't think I ever passed Standard Six. I'm not like Doreen, she's very clever. But it still feels peculiar to be unable to write. No doing. Do any of these Doctors have any idea what it's like? To have rising up inside you the things you need to get down: the shopping, the list of stuff you need to remember to do, the parts to buy, the date on the hanging wall, but no way to put it down? A bit of my brain must have died there in the shaft with no oxygen. It was horrible.

Some of them down in the audience are nodding and smiling now. I wasn't paying attention. Doctor must have been talking about me. I must get ready to do my demonstration. The sweat is cooling through my suit at the armpits. I didn't expect to sweat today, not out here on the surface where things are easy, not here in this place. Miners sweat a lot on account of the atmosphere; we pour the sweat from our boots after the shift. I have a little competition going between the left and right boot, to see which is holding more. It's a part of your brain that actually forms the letters, isn't it? I must focus on the string, not worry about the letters.

Doctor is tugging at my suit jacket. He takes my elbow as if to steer me like an old woman, towards the podium. I am supposed to walk now to the table and do my show. I pull myself together.

'I'm no invalid.' I say.

Still he walks with me to the table then pats me on the shoulder. Some of them nod and smile again. The water on the iron roof is making such a racket I can't hear my own thoughts in here. I'm supposed to show them how I can tie knots in pieces of string: a figure-of-eight; reef knot; granny knot; slippery hitch – any knot you like. And then I'm supposed to pick up cotton reels and do some knitting. The Occupational Therapist made me do it every afternoon in the hospital,

'To strengthen the 24 muscles you have in your hand. Doctor's orders,' she said.

I thought she was quite keen on me the way she carried on. And then I'm supposed to show them the splints they made me; each finger with its own sling and spring.

'How do you feel about your hand, Frank?' Doctor beams from his teeth.

'Talk to the audience,' he instructs.

When my voice comes through the microphone, it's full of breath like fuzz.

'Do you think you can work again?' Doctor asks.

He takes his hand from my shoulder and leaves me there in the centre of the stage. He is sitting down now, arms folded across his stomach. This is piss-easy, man. I see it clear as anything. It's peaceful really now, with the rain on the roof, and all these clever men smiling and listening to me, the world is almost sweet.

When I speak, it is only to try to make the tremble in my voice shut up, it is only to try to make the breath steady up, that I begin to talk. I hold the microphone just as I saw the Doctor hold it, just right, and I blow into it, and I smile.

'What is happening today is not about the compensation, fair is fair, I got my hand back, I can't have the cash.'

I look across the audience, sitting there, some with pens poised to take notes.

'Some other time,' I say, just to keep talking, just to keep my voice from losing itself to the shudder of the ground beneath us. 'Some other time I will tell you what happened the day I lost my hand, what it was like. It's nothing really, accidents happen all the time below the surface. I know you've come here to see me tie bits of string.'

I want to tell them that I can no longer write. I want to tell them how I have tried, sitting up at night with Doreen and the crossword and a pen, crying in rage, night after night, I want to tell them what it's like. But I am afraid that if I start to blubber, the weeping will never stop.

I take a breath. I put my hand in my pocket to pull out the string for the show. There is a pen here too. Just a piece of paraphernalia that the mine gives out for free, along with a handful of condoms in your pay packet. It has a slogan printed on the side:

'*AIDS is Real. Time to Change.*'

I carefully place the pen and the string on the podium beside the mike. I take the ball of string and cut the first length. The Doctor's camera zooms in on my hand. Up behind me, a live video of the hand has commenced, projected up there on the wall so that everyone can see exactly how my muscles move. I tie the first knot and the audience applauds. I nod. Nice and slow, I cut myself a second length of string. I am doing just fine. Then the storm breaks – lightning sheets across the faces in front of me and the picture of my hand behind me dissolves altogether into a grey-black wall. The remaining breath is squeezed out of the projector and its lights in a final hum. The audience begin to murmur and scrape their chairs. In a few minutes the storm will be over – what will be left is the sound of the rain on the roof, and the drip, drip, drip of those inadequate gutters on the paving.

No point in carrying on with this if they can't see what I'm doing. If I ever have a chance to build myself a house I'll give generous gutters, proper generous gutters that hold the water and that flow into a rainwater tank. And I'll build the house so it faces North with a good sunroom too, for Doreen to warm up on those late winter afternoons when we get old. She's always had poor circulation, such cold hands and feet.

I look up and see that the Doctor is waving the hand-function spring-thing in front of my face – the contraption they made, just for me, to get my hand to work again. Okay, I have forgotten to do that part of the demonstration.

'Sorry about the power,' he says to the audience. Without the help of the microphone, the Doctor's voice is a little lone cry at the edge of the world.

'Before we wrap up, I would like to demonstrate how the resistance experienced both in flexion and extension at the metacarpal joints…'

I watch him as if through a gauze, a safety net. I shake my head. Instead of taking the hand-function contraption he is trying to put on me, I pull my hand away. I pick up the AIDS pen and hold it out to him.

'You keep this Doc, you may as well have it,' I say. 'You've done a good job here, on my hand Doc. Congratulations.'

The Doctor reaches out as if to take the pen, to shut me up, and send me on my way so that everyone can applaud him.

'Give the brave man a hand.'

But I have something to say. My voice comes out much louder than I expect it to, a flood of anger shooting the words out of my body.

'I can't write with this hand he's put on me. I cannot even sign my name. What do you think of that? Is there anything more that medical science can do for me now?'

I push over the stupid little podium. And in the clatter, I give the table a kick for good measure. I brace myself to step down and lay a fist across a face or two. I look at the short fat one from Helen Joseph, and the one next to him with his stethoscope tucked in his pocket. No, I must back down. I must give them a chance. I must stay calm. I return shaking to my small seat on the stage. Every mine has its idiot.

I count three slow drips from the gutters and then the twittering from the audience begins.

'He's a miner,' someone shouts. 'Why does a miner need to write?'

'Hear, hear...'

'And anyway, use the other hand,' another voice calls from the back of the hall. 'He has another hand.'

'Come to my clinic on Tuesday, I'll sort you out.'

A gust of laughter sweeps through the room.

Outside, Doctor finds me. He gives me a bit of cash, as a 'thank you' and offers me a lift. He says it has to be quick because he needs to get back to the Conference Dinner.

'I like some fresh air,' I say. 'I've never seen such a lot of jerks in one place in all my life.'

I step carefully across the world all heavy with damp, the rain all stopped now. The leaves on the trees are so laden that a breeze or bump sends another shower beneath. I take off my jacket as I walk and sling it over the back of my shoulder. The Doc's Thank You is burning a hole in my pocket. The Queen's Hotel is on my way home. A broken bottle is lying near the gutter at the hotel entrance. I could kill someone with that bottle. I think of those Doctors' faces in front of me, and Doctor Morar droning on and on. He reminds me of a bulldog I used to have. Her name was Sally. I had to shoot her because she wouldn't let go of a black kid in the street, I felt bad about that, really bad – about shooting the dog, and about the kid – police made me do it. I turn into the Bar to wash the taste of the mine from my mouth.

Sometimes because of the brandy, Doreen and I have our differences of opinion, but I've never hit her. Well, since losing my hand, to be honest I've come pretty close. I'm sorry about it though, she knows I'm sorry. I know I haven't really been myself since this business.

Our house comes into view. A figure is swinging back and forth on the gate. It's our boy, nine years old, way past his bedtime. His bare feet are hooked in through the chicken wire. He calls from down the street.

'Where's my mother?'

As I come closer I see his eyes are swollen. He is trying to hide his tears through anger and grumbling. And his clothes are drenched through as if he's stood here through several storms. Water drips from his chin, his nose.

'What took you so long? I'm hungry, dad, I'm starved. Mom's gone.'

'Where is your mother?'

Ray follows me indoors like a dog. The golden liquid slides me through the house. (They say that skin is waterproof, but the scalp, so thickly imbued with oil, must be the most watertight of all, to stop the falling rain).

There is her absence – a bottle of shampoo missing from the bathroom shelf, her yellow Sunday dress gone from its hanger, a space on the shelf where a picture used to stand – Ray, last Christmas holding the pellet gun we gave him. The crossword puzzle sits unfinished in Doreen's top drawer. Beside it, her small folded umbrella. There is no note.

A little later I hear a scraping at the door, like an animal wanting to come in. I tell Geezer to bugger off. He scatters like seed into the dark wet night.

After Ray is in bed, hugging his pellet gun, I check again. I turn the house upside down but there is no note. A wife is supposed to leave a note, that's how they do it in the movies.

Gill Schierhout, born in Zimbabwe, has worked as an academic and public health consultant in Cape Town, London and Johannesburg. She began to write whilst working in London. She participated in writing workshops run by the late Lionel Abrahams in Johannesburg between 2001 and 2004. She has had stories selected as finalists in HSBC/SA PEN Literary competitions and published in the anthologies *African Compass* and *African Pens* in 2005 and 2007 respectively. She has recently completed a first novel. She lives in Johannesburg and works as a Director of a health consulting company.

Cemetery of Life

Uzor Maxim Uzoatu

I AM MY OWN ancestor. Nobody left me a heritage. I am here on my own. I make my own mistakes and I wallow in my own failures, and the point is that I do not know the difference. I simply carry on without looking back.

Some demon lives inside my head. I am utterly powerless against this demon and its dangerous noises about ancestor and heritage and failure. In the sixteenth year of my life of loss, the demon put me on the road to the great labyrinth of Nwogbaka. Unshod, Nwogbaka bestrode a naked womb and a red tomb.

'A tidy dream is no dream,' Nwogbaka said, patting me softly on the elbow. 'You are the child to tell our story.'

Suddenly he was no longer there, together with womb and tomb. It was more like he sank into the earth, into a sprawling cemetery. Rows of gravestones receded into the shadows. A figure just as suddenly rose from one of the graves, towering beanpole as white as good teeth. It grew as I watched. I beat a retreat, running as fast as the bizarre circumstances would allow. A hoary old man was coming toward me, appearing as though from nowhere.

'What are you fleeing from, young one?' asked the old one.

'I saw this growing tall thing in the cemetery,' I said in spite of myself.

The old man nodded. 'I made that mistake when I was alive.'

'What?' I was cracking up.

'Like all Nigerians you are a child who died old.'

Before I could gather my thoughts the old ghost had melted away, giving place to a smiling boy with red boxing gloves slung on his neck. He was at once brisk and assured.

'I am Boy Joe,' said the boy. 'With you by my side, I can come back.'

I could not utter a word.

'I have come to meet the spirits. And here you are my doppelgänger!'

I looked to my left where some grasses were making some noises in the Nwogbaka way.

'Nwogbaka speaks and we obey,' the boy continued, adjusting his boxing gloves. 'Let's go.'

I could not but follow him. He talked of Nwogbaka's uncanny presence in the abrupt transition from tradition to modernity until we got to an aged bungalow enveloped by creeping bougainvillea. The house was built into an extended compound with elaborate pathways bordered by whistling pine and red periwinkle. On one of the branches of an overgrown hibiscus in the compound sat a parrot in his cage. Inside the house, we met a dark and stout man presiding over a huge mahogany table festooned with files and papers and folders.

'What can I do for you?' asked the man, standing up to shake hands.

'I am Boy Joe and I have come to register for the boxing tourney...'

'Sorry, but the closing date...'

'Sir, I came here yesterday but I couldn't see you...'

The man looked into the boy's eyes and grinned. 'Where is your licence?'

'Lost.'

'Look, I can't register an unlicensed fighter,' the man said. 'I don't want an under-aged boy's blood on my head.'

'What has age got to do with correct hooks and jabs?' Boy Joe said, shadowboxing and going through the motions of some fancy footwork. 'I have the power and the speed and the deadly combinations.'

The man was unimpressed. 'Then produce your licence.'

Boy Joe raised his right fist. 'This here is my only licence.'

Before the man could say another word, Nwogbaka appeared and said, 'show him what you can do in the square!'

Boy Joe landed some blows at the iron-gate and started shouting.

'I am here to fight,' he boasted. 'I am dying to beat people up!'

The demon loosened my tongue and I joined in the shouting: 'This fighter has beaten the best all over the world. He in fact knocked out an evil spirit yesterday!'

Boy Joe threw a hook that missed the man's jaw by a couple of inches. 'It does not matter whether I miss a punch; the whirlwind that accompanies the blow equally brings my opponent down!'

'I see it everyday,' I said.

Boy Joe was still shadowboxing. 'Who says stroke is the shortest route to coma? Well, that was until the advent of my uppercut!'

Scores of people had come rushing from the street. Some patrons came from inside the club. I could see that Boy Joe felt good.

'Ask me why coffin-makers are always happy when I have a fight!' Boy Joe thundered.

'I'll bring the police to disperse these rascals,' one of the top guns of the club was saying.

'Nobody can send us away!' Boy Joe shouted. 'Why not come out punching?' The big man was aghast. 'Get me the police! The police!'

'The police don't stand a chance even with bullets!' Boy Joe retorted, jabbing the air repeatedly. 'You can't shoot what you don't see. I'm so fast the bullets can't keep pace.'

The demon in me took over. 'Who's heard of the new disease in the medical dictionary? Brokenitis: the breaking of every tissue and bone in the human anatomy. The disease has only two causes. And the two causes are Boy Joe's two fists!'

'You don win! You don win!' the crowd cheered.

The arrival of the chairman of the club, a portly fellow chewing on a Cuban cigar, saved the day. He asked Boy Joe what he wanted and he said he wanted to fight. The chairman ordered a free boxing exhibition.

Boy Joe knocked out his first opponent in under a minute. Boy Joe's next opponent vomited some balls of *foofoo* after some seconds of furious body punching. The next man took all Boy Joe had to offer and suddenly unleashed a roundhouse that exploded on Boy Joe's solar plexus. Seeing Boy Joe hurt, the man rushed in for the kill with about twenty unanswered punches. Boy Joe's mouth hung open as he was hit from rope to corner, a faraway look in his eyes. Blood dripped from his cut lower lip.

I gasped in relief when my sister Amara appeared suddenly from behind the crowd and jumped into the ring to stop the mayhem. She let Boy Joe sag over her shoulders. The crowd booed in the background while Amara shouted mad at the destroyer of Boy Joe, asking him if he did not know that God had a commandment: Thou shall not kill!

* * *

The boxing tourney was on. The roped square sat on a platform in the centre of the stadium that was now a vast jungle of man and spirit. An announcer climbed into the ring and went over the general rules: each fight lasts three rounds of three minutes, no butting, obey the referee, be on your guard always etc.

In the first fight of the afternoon, the man who destroyed Boy Joe climbed into the ring and ruined his opponent with just one punch.

'Mad Torito!' His name reverberated across the stadium.

Boy Joe won three straight victories via the knockout route. It was all easy, like eating sugar cane.

'The first semi-final,' the announcer intoned, sweeping the stands with his cat-like eyes, 'is between Boy Joe and Mad Torito!'

A thunderous cheer rose in the stadium. Mad Torito instantly jumped into the ring, shuffling and jabbing to the deafening applause of the crowd. Amara made to hold Boy Joe back but he was inside the ring in a jiffy, and before the referee could say a word blows were exploding like thunderclaps. Mad Torito was a matador in his elements while Boy Joe was a bull beyond control. A pile-driver of a hook sent Boy Joe crashing to the canvas but he bounced up, back, and was firing away at his foe. Mad Torito was obviously ahead on points, and the referee was moving in until he was stopped short in his tracks when Boy Joe loaded up on his right from as low as the canvas and detonated this evil uppercut on Mad Torito's jaw. Poor Torito was thrown off the canvas onto the rope and he fell outside the ring on the apron near the ringside seats. The referee could have counted until kingdom come. I can still hear the cheering. I can still see the dancing.

I cannot now say how we managed to get home, except that there was this disappearing act by Boy Joe that we did not understand. At home, Boy Joe made some smart moves trying to confess love to Amara.

'Your mouth reeks of beer,' Amara protested when Boy Joe audaciously made to kiss her. 'Who gave you beer?'

'I'm through with boxing,' Boy Joe said.

'Not when we still have the final match to fight tomorrow,' I said.

'No more boxing!' Boy Joe sounded more serious than a bishop.

I saw the bulge on Boy Joe's back pocket. I put a hand inside the pocket and wads of new banknotes fell on the floor.

'Who has this money?' I asked, wide-eyed.

Boy Joe suddenly started stammering. 'It was given to me.'

'Who gave it to you?' Amara cried.

'Baba Dudu,' Boy Joe said, looking at the floor.

'Baba Dudu!' Amara screamed. 'Why, but the man is supposed to be in prison?'

Long silence.

Amara shook her head. 'The likes of Baba Dudu do not just go about throwing money away. They ask for some little favours. What does Baba Dudu want from you?'

He scratched at the perspiration on his brow. 'He promised me a million naira if I could lose the final match tomorrow. This is the first instalment.'

'And you accepted?' I was aghast.

Tears welled up in Amara's eyes. Boy Joe was obviously struggling to fight back tears.

'I have never really wanted to fight,' Boy Joe said, tears percolating in his eyes and rolling down his cheeks. 'But I lost my master Zingo's money and I had to fight. In a sense, I was not actually fighting. I was only looking for money with which to pay back Zingo. Moreover, Baba Dudu has promised me the money. I have lost before. I can take the defeat tomorrow.'

'Where is your honour, our honour?' Amara was bitter.

'I take the blows,' Boy Joe said.

'Boy Joe, we are going to return the crook's money,' I said, holding Boy Joe's hand. 'We may even lose tomorrow, but let it be with our honour. The celebrated former Middleweight champion of the world, Jake La Motta, The Raging Bull, is still tainted because of a fixed fight he lost to the mob-backed Billy Fox. Do you want such justice for yourself, Boy Joe?'

'Return that money now or walk away from this house forever!' Amara screamed, walking into the bedroom and locking herself in.

Boy Joe followed into the car. It was a moonlit night. We were silent, Boy Joe, and me as we cruised along.

'Stop!' Boy Joe hollered within shouting distance of the Baba Crescent home of Baba Dudu.

I ground the car to a halt. 'What goes?'

'Let's go back home,' Boy Joe said. 'We can lie to Amara that we did send back the money.'

'Wretch!' I cursed. 'You double-crossing orphan! You have rammed our help right down our throats. For everything we did for you, you want to bring us into your criminal arrangements...'

I shot the car off with a screech.

'Well, we are in this together,' Boy Joe meekly said, clinging to the car. 'You have been through this path before me.'

'So you know...' I sighed with relief.

The crooked man and two quarter-naked girls were watching a blue movie on video when we entered Baba Dudu's lair. Boy Joe instantly wiped out the smile on Baba Dudu's face when he tossed the man's money at him.

'What?' Baba Dudu cried, sitting up.

'I'm returning your money, that's what,' Boy Joe said. 'I trained to fight and win, not to lose. Sorry, Boy Joe cannot lose.'

Baba Dudu was mad. 'I'll make sure you don't win any money tomorrow. Even if you win the fight, you cannot get a dime. And I can arrange your death for this bad insult...'

'Nwogbaka will soon come for you,' Boy Joe said, smiling.

'You can't kill a spirit,' I said, walking away with Boy Joe. 'Go back to prison where you belong.'

* * *

A super-heavyweight was presented as the fighter to face Boy Joe for the final match even though he entered for the lightweight category. We instantly knew it was Baba Dudu's arrangement. Amara was hopping mad and protested to the organisers. One of the organisers, a huge fellow with some ugly scars on the face, tried to placate Amara by holding her. Amara pushed him so hard that he promptly kissed the floor with his heavy buttocks.

While Amara protested, Boy Joe jumped into the ring asking to be turned loose on the overweight opponent. The name of the man was in the mouth of every spectator: Gorilla. Boy Joe danced as the man unleashed roundhouses that fetched no points. As the first round was ending Boy Joe dropped his guard, did a waltz and looked out of the ring to where Amara and I were enjoying how he was making Gorilla look very foolish. Bang! And Boy Joe was flat on his back. Gorilla threw punches on the felled boy, stamping his feet on Boy Joe before the bell for the end of the round mercifully rang.

'I am seeing three Gorillas,' Boy Joe said as he was revived with smelling salts.

'Punch the Gorilla in the middle,' said a voice from nowhere.

Nwogbaka's unbidden appearance threw the spectators into a tumult; he ran to Gorilla's corner and smoked out Nkapi, the fabled spirit child unborn but already living. Nwogbaka gave Nkapi a punch that sounded like thunder, and both spirits flashed past like lightning. Order took many minutes to return.

Boy Joe was all over Gorilla at the start of the next round. A patented right cross put away Gorilla for good.

'We want Boy Joe! We want Boy Joe!' the crowd sang.

Hoisted shoulder-high by the crowd Boy Joe did not know when the organisers sank into the earth like Nkapi. In the end, no prizes could be awarded but we sang songs of honour all the way home.

* * *

'Money is made on the move,' Nwogbaka spoke through darkness. 'After honour, comes destiny.'

'Here is your destiny,' said the strange man who visited after the other spectators had left. 'Go to the market and make clean money selling my drugs.'

The consignment of drugs he left behind was heavy. Boy Joe helped me to hurl the drugs into the car. It was a bright day, a clean afternoon. We parked the car by the edge of the market, near Upperclass Hotel. Boy Joe plugged on a cassette and started dancing extravagantly. A large crowd gathered around us in about fifteen minutes. Some in the crowd recognised Boy Joe as the boxer who was denied his diadem.

'This is the latest malaria tablet from the US of A,' Boy Joe shouted, holding aloft a greenish pack while sweat dripped in myriad rivulets down his body. 'When malaria comes you start dreaming. Malaria is the disease that builds Buckingham Palace for a pauper. When you are asleep in your face-me-I-face you shack and you find yourself in the midst of a dozen princesses, boy, that is malaria! Take one of these tablets and malaria will run faster than Ben Johnson together with his performance-enhancing drug!'

A melee of customers swooped on him. He sold feverishly, handing the money over to me.

Boy Joe picked up a red packet. 'There are diseases and there are diseases. Some diseases do not know big men. Take diarrhoea for example. It can catch up with you in a church or on the highway. In addition, your anus will suddenly start singing and dancing faster than Michael Jackson. Take this tablet and your stomach will never run faster than you!'

The customers fell over each other, buying.

'Before AIDS there was VD,' Boy Joe announced, holding up a pack of condoms. 'Buy your raincoat before the rainy day!'

More business.

The police jeep charged in with a jerk. About a dozen armed policemen surged into the crowd.

'If they move, shoot!' cried the police chief. 'Contraband! Smugglers! Get them!'

Boy Joe pushed me into the car, settling in swiftly by my side. I quickly engaged the gear and shot the car off with a screech. The police jeep came after us. We cut through traffic hold-ups, tearing through all the major streets and drawing spectators from their homes. Brakes jammed and tyres sang on the asphalt as I had only seen in trashy American movies. Just off Nnagboro Lane, I was stuck in this gully and the police jeep came at us full-speed; I somehow managed to take the car off before the jeep sped into the gully, somersaulted and went up in flames.

We ended our race of life deep in Urashi Forest, the home of Nwogbaka. We parked the car in the grove, covering it with green leaves, grass, and twigs. It was well after midnight that we sneaked to the house to try to get Amara to know the trouble afoot. We were at the window calling Amara when the police swooped. Boy Joe was promptly arrested. I ran into the night.

Curiously, the police officers did not come for me. Even when I accompanied Amara to the police station, the police people did not say anything to me. It was as though I did not exist.

'Do not enter into a plea until mother comes back from Denmark to take up your defence!' Amara told Boy Joe.

* * *

'Christ, but a sixteen-year-old orphan deserves better justice!' It was the holy cry of mother when she returned from Denmark.

She took Amara and me to visit Boy Joe in prison. Boy Joe narrated his many experiences, telling how he had been mysteriously attacked with an axe while in solitary confinement inside a dark and narrow room only large enough for one to stretch out the legs.

Mama's original line rang out. 'Would you want to be brother to Amara...'

'But...' Boy Joe looked at me and we nodded at a shared destiny.

'Well, let's set you free first.'

A tried and tested Amazon of the law, Mama was more than determined to set Boy Joe free. She knew that Boy Joe's case was bad: killing twelve officers of the law, committing contempt of court by making jest of entering into a plea and attempting to escape from prison...

The crowd in and around Umuchu High Court had come with an almost unanimous decision: the court would sentence Boy Joe to death. Mama was putting her unblemished career on the line. Moreover, Justice Anthony Ezeoke of Umuchu High Court was no respecter of reputations. Then Umuchu High Court had its own reputation as the graveyard of giants to guard jealously.

A booming voice broke the spell. 'Umuchu High Court is now in session. Mr Justice Anthony Ezeoke is presiding. Please be seated.'

The first witness Mama brought to the box was Nwogbaka. Great minds commune with spirits. Nwogbaka waved a hand and the court turned into a sprawling cemetery with rows of gravestones receding into the shadows. From the graves rose the twelve police officers and they took their place in the witness box.

'Here we are,' they intoned. 'A tidy dream is no dream.'

'What dream?' Justice Ezeoke asked, aghast.

'Reality is death,' Nwogbaka said.

'The spirit has spoken,' the police officers sang. 'And being dead we shall live forever.'

Justice Ezeoke scanned the court for the prosecution team led by Nkapi but they had massed together behind Boy Joe in a shield of weird solidarity. Justice Ezeoke was quite alone, deserted by reality.

And the chant rose: 'We are best friends with spirits!'

'No more! No more!' Justice Ezeoke cried, hitting his gavel on the table. 'I give up!'

As a roar rose in court Amara ran into Boy Joe's hands and promptly fell asleep while I dreamed with Nwogbaka past the receding rows of gravestones in the sprawling cemetery of this life.

Uzor Maxim Uzoatu was born in 1960. He took his first degree at the University of Ife and a Masters at the University of Lagos. He directed his first play, *Doctor of Football*, in 1979. He was the 1989 Distinguished Visitor at The Graduate School of Journalism, University of Western Ontario, Canada. He is the author of *Satan's Story, The Missing Link* and the poetry collection, *God of Poetry*. He is married with four children. He lives in Lagos, Nigeria.

Rules

The prize is awarded annually to a short story by an African writer published in English, whether in Africa or elsewhere. (Indicative length is between 3,000 and 10,000 words).

'An African writer' is normally taken to mean someone who was born in Africa, or who is a national of an African country, or whose parents are African, and whose work has reflected African sensibilities.

There is a cash prize of £10,000 for the winning author and a travel award for each of the short-listed candidates (up to five in all).

For practical reasons unpublished work and work in other languages is not eligible. Works translated into English from other languages are not excluded, provided they have been published in translation, and should such a work win, a proportion of the prize would be awarded to the translator.

The award is made in July each year, the deadline for submissions being 31 January. The short-list is selected from work published in the five years preceding the submissions deadline and not previously considered for a Caine Prize. Submissions should be made by publishers and will need to be accompanied by twelve original published copies of the work for consideration, sent to the address below. There is no application form.

Every effort is made to publicise the work of the short-listed authors through the broadcast as well as the printed media.

Winning and short-listed authors will be invited to participate in writers' workshops in Africa and elsewhere as resources permit.

The above rules were designed essentially to launch the Caine Prize and may be modified in the light of experience. Their objective is to establish the Caine Prize as a benchmark for excellence in African writing.

The Caine Prize
The Menier Gallery
Menier Chocolate Factory
51 Southwark Street
London, SE1 1RU
UK
Telephone: +44 (0)20 7378 6234
Fax: +44 (0)20 7378 6235
Website: www.caineprize.com

About the *New Internationalist*

The *New Internationalist* is an independent not-for-profit publishing co-operative. Our mission is to report on issues of world poverty and inequality; to focus attention on the unjust relationship between the powerful and the powerless worldwide; to debate and campaign for the radical changes necessary if the needs of all are to be met.

We publish informative current affairs titles and popular reference, like the *No-Nonsense Guides* series, complemented by world food, fiction, photography and alternative gift books, as well as calendars and diaries, maps and posters – all with a global justice world view.

We also publish the monthly *New Internationalist* magazine. Each month tackles a different subject such as State of the World's Ocean, Ethical Travel or Indigenous Peoples, exploring each issue in a concise way which is easy to understand. The main articles are packed full of photos, charts and graphs and each magazine also contains music, film and book reviews, country profiles, interviews and news.

To find out more about the *New Internationalist*, subscribe to the magazine or buy any of our books take a look at: **www.newint.org**